# THE FIRST LABOUR PARTY 1906-1914

# The First
# LABOUR PARTY
## 1906~1914

### Edited by K.D. Brown

CROOM HELM
London • Sydney • Dover, New Hampshire

©1985 K.D. Brown and Contributors
Croom Helm Ltd, Provident House, Burrell Row,
Beckenham, Kent BR3 1AT

Croom Helm Australia Pty Ltd, First Floor,
139 King Street, Sydney, NSW 2001, Australia

British Library Cataloguing in Publication Data

The First Labour Party 1906-1914.
   1. Labour Party ( Great Britain ) – History
   I. Brown, Kenneth D.
   324.24107'09   JN1129.L32

   ISBN 0-7099-3209-X

Croom Helm, 51 Washington Street, Dover,
New Hampshire 03820, USA

Library of Congress Cataloging in Publication Data
applied for.

Printed and bound in Great Britain by
Biddles Ltd, Guildford and King's Lynn

CONTENTS

Introduction

# THE EDWARDIAN LABOUR PARTY

On the eve of the first world war Philip Snowden, Labour MP for Blackburn since 1906, was feeling somewhat disenchanted with political life and with the prospects of his own party in particular. 'The present labour representation in parliament', he wrote, 'is there mainly by the goodwill of the Liberals, and it will disappear when that goodwill is turned into active resentment.'[1] His colleague, Keir Hardie, was equally gloomy, suggesting a little later that 'the Labour Party has ceased to count.'[2] While owing something to the unabated radical vigour being displayed by the Liberal government, such pessimism was also based on the delusion, shared by many in the British labour movement at this time, that the Labour Party ever <u>had</u> counted and that its somewhat dramatic entry into parliamentary life in 1906 had made it into a genuine political force. This misapprehension had been fuelled partly by the hysteria which Labour's electoral success had provoked on the extreme right of the Conservative Party.[3] Even a normally imperturbable Tory like Arthur Balfour was moved to suggest that the new Liberal Prime Minister, Campbell-Bannerman, was like 'a mere cork, dancing on a current which he cannot control, and what is going on here is the faint echo of the same movement which has produced massacres in St Petersburg, riots in Vienna and Socialist processions in Berlin.'[4] But the winning of some thirty seats had generated an equally distorted response in some labour circles, too. Snowden's mood in 1913 was a marked contrast to his buoyant claim of 1906 that at the next election 'we shall see the Labour Party strengthened to the extent of dominating if not directing the Government of the country.'[5] For a

1

while, the illusion was sustained. The government's decision to accept Labour's Trades Disputes Bill, the passage of a new Workmen's Compensation Act, an Exchequer grant for unemployment relief, and the provision of meals for needy school children, all seemed to confirm that Labour had acquired real influence and power in government. Yet for all that it had greatly increased its parliamentary representation since 1900, the party still held only thirty seats in a House of Commons of 670 members. By 1910 Beatrice Webb was lamenting the fact that the political running was being made by Lloyd George, Churchill, and the advanced wing of the Liberal Party.[6] General disappointment at Labour's failure to exert a continued pressure on government surfaced among party activists at annual conferences after 1908, appeared in print in manifestos such as Is the Parliamentary Party a Failure? (1908) and Let Us Reform the Labour Party (1910), and resulted ultimately in the defection of several branches of the ILP to the newly established British Socialist Party (1911).

It seems worthwhile, therefore, to examine the state of the Labour Party on the eve of war to see how justified were its leaders' apprehensions about the future. This will also throw further light on the still unresolved question of the extent to which the party had begun effectively to oust the Liberals in the years before war so fundamentally altered the nation's social and political climate. Such analyses have often been undertaken in terms of Labour's electoral performances before 1914 but the essays in the first half of this book set out to follow a different line, concentrating on aspects of the party's physical and regional organisation.[7] In this sense, perhaps, they build on the work of Dr McKibbin who has already shown how MacDonald, as chief party tactician, had directed much of his prewar energies into building an effective party structure.[8] In May 1912 a scheme was adopted for the regular appointment of local agents controlled by head office, and a system to channel financial aid to local party organisations was also established. But such organisational initiatives were not universally successful. As Dr Fraser shows below, London's intervention was not always welcome in Scotland where local initiative seems to have played a more significant role in such expansion as did occur before 1914. This is perhaps not surprising, given the independent line usually adopted by the Scots, but local activists were similarly important elsewhere, though several of the essays provide salutary reminders that effort and enthusiasm are not always the same as achievement. Elsewhere, there were areas where the party barely existed as a distinctive political entity at all. This was true of rural areas, which were long to remain a source of Labour weakness, and also of London. Such was the hold exerted on the capital's fragmented trade unions by the Social Democratic Federation via the London Trades Council that it was not until 1914 tnat a London Labour Party appeared.

The importance of dedicated local party support was enhanced by the fact that Labour apparently could not rely on the support of a specific political constituency, even among trade unionists. It has long been recognised that while the party was essentially the creation of the unions, rank and file support for it was frequently lukewarm - if that. When in September 1899 the TUC conference discussed the establishment of a Labour Party, most of the support came from delegates representing more recently organised workers, although several of the older unions had by then come under the influence, if not the control, of officers who were also members of the ILP, the body most vociferous in support of an independent line. Among the rest, however, there was considerable suspicion of the likely socialist influence within the new party. Consequently, the resolution calling for a special meeting of the unions, co-operative societies, and socialist organisations to make plans for labour representation in Parliament was only passed by 546,000 votes to 434,000. A substantial number of delegates apparently abstained from voting at all. When the inaugural meeting of the Labour Representation Committee assembled at the Memorial Hall in Faringdon Street the following year, union representation was thus relatively small. By 1902 only 455,450 out of a total of some two million trade unionists were affiliated to the party. This was changed dramatically by the impact of the verdict in the Taff Vale case. Since it was the House of Lords which was ultimately responsible for this decision to treat unions as corporate entities, thereby rendering their funds liable to claims for damages, it followed that the judgement could only be changed by altering the law itself. This gave an impetus to the idea of independent parliamentary representation and by 1904 trade union affiliations had soared to 956,000. As L.T. Hobhouse neatly put it: 'That which no Socialist writer or platform orator could achieve was effected by the judges.'[9] Trade union membership continued to creep upwards even after the effects of the Taff Vale ruling had been nullified by the Trades Disputes Act of 1906. Yet this should not be allowed to obscure the mistrust exhibited by many trade unionists, a theme which appears in several of the essays below. If socialists were growing restless at what they regarded as the overcautious outlook imposed on Labour by the trade union alliance, it was equally true that many trade unionists were unhappy at the direction in which they believed the socialists were trying to take the party. This is confirmed by the responses to the Osborne judgement of 1909, which is here examined in some detail by Dr Wrigley. The outcome of this case was to render illegal the political levy by which the affiliated unions financed the party. The enforced necessity of relying upon voluntary contributions showed just how indifferent many unionists were and plunged Labour's finances into a precarious state. The Osborne decision, MacDonald noted in his diary, is 'paralysing us especially in our local organisations, which are suffering for want of money.'[10] Even when an act of 1913 permitted the levy to be restored after a ballot among union members some of the unions returned sizeable minorities against it.

In some areas it is possible, as Dr Stead argues was the case in Wales, that rising industrial tension in the years after 1910 resulted in some shift of support towards Labour among trade unionists. Certainly the number affiliated to the party climbed to one and a half million by 1914, while the Lib-Lab element in Parliament had been pretty well squeezed out. On the other hand, the first of these developments might simply have been the natural corollary of rising trade union membership. Nationally, the proportion of trade unionists affiliated to Labour levelled off at rather more than fifty per cent between 1910 and 1912, but by 1914 it had fallen back to thirty-eight per cent, lower than it had been in 1903. This seems to reflect - in part at least - the inability of the fledgling political organisation to capitalise very fully on what some regarded as its natural locus of support. It is perhaps significant, therefore, that it was in this period of industrial unrest and union expansion that the party made a further bid for organisational expression by establishing its own newspaper. The Daily Citizen appeared in 1913 as the official organ of party policy. As such, it was dull and cautious. It was indicative of the tensions within the labour alliance that the militants persevered with the more provocative Daily Herald, which attracted an able team of writers and a first rate cartoonist in Will Dyson. Neither paper, however, was commercially successful. The Citizen became an early casualty of the war and the Herald only survived as a weekly. Deain Hopkin's survey of the labour press reveals clearly the enormous difficulty Labour experienced in raising finance for large scale publishing ventures. Such enterprises seem to have been less significant in this period than the plethora of small, local papers which did much to weld together local supporters, giving them a sense of purpose and identity.

Nor does the possession of a daily paper appear to have conferred any electoral benefit on the Edwardian Labour Party. Given its difficulty in winning the loyalty of trade unionists it is hardly surprising that the party appears to have been making little impact on the population at large. The highest vote it secured in any pre-war general election was 506,000 or 7.6 per cent of the electorate, though of course it was much higher in individual constituencies.[11] Whereas Labour had been able to win by-elections at Woolwich and Barnard Castle in 1903, Jarrow in 1907, and Attercliffe in 1909, it appeared to have run out of steam after 1910. Indeed, one recent study suggests that in the north east at least, it lost ground after 1906, the Jarrow victory being made possible only by a split anti-Labour vote.[12] Certainly, in fourteen by-elections contested between 1910 and 1914 Labour never finished higher than third and lost four seats in the process. It is possible of course that the criterion of electoral performance is a misleading guide to the extent of Labour support because only about fifty-nine per cent of adult males were on the electoral registers in this period. It has been argued that the bulk of those who did not have a vote - paupers, living in servants, most members of the armed forces, lodgers in unfurnished rooms worth less than £10 a year, and adult sons living with parents but without exclusive use of their own rooms - were working class and thus, by implication, potential Labour supporters.[13] Yet this does not necessarily follow. First of all, it is possible that rather more of the disenfranchised than is usually assumed were members of the middle class, such as nonconformist ministers or commercial travellers, who would perhaps not have been 'natural' Labour voters.[14] More significantly, there is no reason to assume that if given the vote, disenfranchised workers would have favoured Labour any more than did those who already enjoyed the right to vote. Indeed, deferential groups such as servants and servicemen might well have been more inclined to vote Conservative. Furthermore, many of those disqualified through failure to meet the residential requirement represented the poorest elements of society. They were thus peculiarly vulnerable to the patronage associated with Conservatism and were, by the same token, isolated from the main institutional pillars of radical politics, trade unionism and nonconformity.[15]

This is perhaps confirmed in Dr Cahill's study of municipal politics, an area in which Labour had high hopes. Yet despite the rather more favourable structure of the local government franchise the party still made only limited progress. Certainly Labour's total local vote increased from 170,000 in 1906 to 233,000 in 1913 and in the last three years of peace over a hundred Labour candidates were elected annually onto local councils.[16] In fourteen major cities Labour had ninety municipal representatives after the elections of 1913. Yet they were completely overshadowed by 427 Conservatives and 297 Liberals. Furthermore, it seems that many Labour victories were being won in conjunction with Liberals.[17]

Both locally and nationally, therefore, it is evident that many working class voters continued to vote Liberal. In areas such as Lancashire or in constituencies heavily dependent for employment upon shipbuilding and munitions the tradition of working class Conservatism was strong, though Dr Wrigley rightly points out that Conservative attempts to channel this support into 'Tory Labour parties' were totally unsuccessful. There is also evidence of considerable apathy and even positive hostility among those who might have been expected to view the party favourably. Thus Robert Tressell had his decorators condemning Labour MPs as 'a lot of b . . . rs what's too bloody lazy to work for their livin'. What the bloody 'ell was they before they got there? Only workin' men, the same as you and me. But they've got the gift of the gab . . .'18 Hannah Mitchell, the suffragette, recalled that her next door neighbour in a Derbyshire village did not scruple 'to inform me that in her opinion I might employ myself better than in running after Socialist speakers. All of these she regarded as either 'windbags' or mistaken fools who would do better to dig their gardens and help their overworked wives.'19 Many were the contemporaries who, like J.A. Hobson, deplored the fact that the typical British worker was more interested in sport than in political activity, prompting the comment from one recent writer that 'Marx might have been nearer the mark had he referred to sport rather than religion as the opium of the masses.'20

It is hardly surprising that by 1914 the Labour Party bore all the signs of its relatively recent birth. Even if slowly beginning to fill out, its physical organisation was still patchy, depending heavily on the enthusiasm and commitment of local activists. While some of the writers below argue that there were signs of growing trade union support this had not been very comprehensively translated into votes at either local or national level. This was due partly to the party's failure to produce much in the way of a distinctive political programme, a matter analysed more fully in the second half of the book. It was all very well for Snowden to claim that Labour was unique in that it intended to apply the single principle of collectivism to every parliamentary issue, but some very real practical problems stood in the way.21 Not least of these was the fact that Labour was in no position to determine what the major political issues should be: hence, for example, the parliamentary party's inability to accede to Victor Grayson's demand in 1908 that unemployment should be given precedence over the Licensing Bill. Other parties and forces decided what the central concerns of Edwardian politics should be. Thus deprived of any initiative Labour could only make responses, and it was not always possible to apply collectivist principles to some leading contemporary issues. Secondly, there were some matters on which the party spoke with more than one voice. With their religious connotations debates about Irish Home Rule or state education were always likely to expose internal disagreements, as Mr McDermott and Dr Griggs respectively indicate. Similarly, Dr Pugh's essay reveals that on occasion local enthusiasm for women's suffrage could lead to conflict with more cautious elements at party headquarters. In most cases, however, these internal differences were matters of emphasis rather than principle. In this, Labour was no different to any other party, except perhaps that it was new and trying to establish a distinctive political identity for itself. Finally, there was often little difference between Labour and Liberal responses to particular aspects of current political debate. Here again, the main difference between the two parties was usually one of priority. Labour might be keener to discuss measures relevant to trade unionists, but its reaction, for example, to the constitutional crisis of 1909 differed very little to that on the Liberal benches, as Dr Douglas shows. Similarly, Professor Morris brings out clearly the overlap between Labour's approach to foreign affairs and that adopted by broad sections of the Liberal Party, confirming the observation of an earlier writer that Labour's 'ideals in the realm of colonial and foreign policy have been the ideals of the Victorian Little-Englanders.'[22] Time and time again this lack of distinctiveness in Labour policy surfaces in the Edwardian period - hardly surprising in view of the common commitment of both Labour and Liberal parties to basic Victorian economic assumptions such as free trade. Thus local socialists complained that the LRC candidate at Darlington in 1906, Isaac Mitchell, had views virtually indistinguishable from those of the Liberal. The Speaker suggested that MacDonald's election address at Leicester could just as well have been written by a Liberal.[23] It was this similarity of outlook which made it relatively easy for discontented Liberals to slip into the Labour Party at the end of the first world war. Furthermore, it also hampered Labour's electoral prospects. In the context of Home Rule, for instance, few were going to vote for a Labour Party whose policy was identical with that of a Liberal Party which alone of the two had any prospect of implementing it.

The main exception to this overlap was perhaps in the realm of welfare. In education, Labour MPs were most clearly set apart from the Liberals by their greater interest in the welfare aspects. In other fields, however, as Dr Fraser mentions, Labour was able to develop a unique approach on particular local problems such as housing. At national level, the party's main claim to originality lay in the area of unemployment. Dr Thane argues convincingly that to Labour job security and fair wages were greater priorities than ameliorative welfare legislation. But while some of the arguments deployed on behalf of the Right to Work Bill did anticipate elements of later Keynesian economics, the measure was based more on an instinctive feel for the working of the labour market rather than upon any coherent analysis of it. In any case, unemployment was only briefly prominent over the winter of 1908-09. Thereafter it declined and the Liberals produced their own legislative remedies which did much to undermine the effectiveness of the continuing right to work campaign, pushing Labour back into its more customary role of commentator on other parties' initiatives. [24]

Unemployment, however, was the exception which proved the rule. Generally, Labour was unable to produce policies identifiably its own, and this was the direct consequence of the circumstances in which the party was founded. It was devised primarily as a vehicle for working class representation, not as a machine for the implementation of a particular political creed or a specific set of policies. This was precisely why the miners initially decided not to affiliate. Alone of all working class groups, they were sufficiently well organised and geographically concentrated to secure their own parliamentary representation. It is significant that most of the discussion at the inaugural meeting of the LRC centred not around policy, which was to be left to the parliamentary party, but around strategy. Three alternatives were canvassed. One demanded total independence from all other parties and commitment to the principle of class struggle. It was mooted mainly by the SDF and fell largely on deaf ears in an assembly, most of whose members would have agreed with Robert Blatchford's claim that the average British working girl was not concerned with 'the downtrodden proletariat or the theory behind International Socialism, but (with) what she was going to put in her stomach ...' [25] Nor was this essentially pragmatic approach to politics foisted upon reluctant provincial activists, as has sometimes been alleged, by a small clique of London-based leaders. It was the natural outcome of local leaders' everyday experiences.[26] As Dr Martin reminds us, Stead's investigation into the books that had influenced the first generation of Labour MPs produced many more references to 'the university of life' or 'the school of experience' than to abstract thinkers, least of all Karl Marx, who figured hardly at all.[27] British workers were notoriously uninterested in theoretical politics, as MacDonald admitted with some embarrassment. 'Every time I go abroad and see on the bookstalls evidence of intellectual and imaginative activity among foreign socialists, I am ashamed of our English movement.'[28] Certainly in Edwardian society it was Liberal thinkers like Hobhouse and Hobson who predominated, and it is also revealing that a New Society survey in 1962 revealed that one of the two most influential figures on the modern Labour Party had been the Liberal, Lloyd George.[29]

The second strategy advanced at the Memorial Hall conference was associated mainly with John Burns, the member for Battersea and also a member of the London County Council since its inception in 1889. Burns had achieved a fair degree of practical success within the Council by co-operating with all shades of progressive opinion and had followed a similar line in Parliament since his election in 1892.[30] He was the de facto leader of a small group of working class MPs who worked in close harmony with progressive Liberals and he could see no reason to change this approach by establishing a new, independent party. That it was a matter of strategy rather than policy which divided Burns from the supporters of the new party can be seen from the way in which both the TUC and the LRC continued to use him as the spearhead of their parliamentary campaign to reverse the Taff Vale decision. As late as 1903 Hardie was still urging Burns to 'come out and openly take your place as one of the active leaders in this work for the emancipation of the class to which we both belong.'[31] Labour's attacks on Burns' policies came later.

Burns' approach, however, was not likely to recommend itself to a conference whose very raison d'être sprang from working class frustration at the way in which Liberals were ignoring their aspirations. Some have suggested that this was a matter of ignoring working class wishes for particular reforms, especially in the sphere of welfare. There may well be something in this, although Dr Pelling has suggested that most working class people were in fact highly suspicious of Liberal interventionist politics.[32] Alternatively, it has been argued that late nineteenth century Liberal administrations were more responsive to labour pressure than is usually appreciated.[33] But the main Liberal offence as far as organised workers were concerned was the constant rejection of their wish to be represented in Parliament by men of their own social class. A number of local studies are now available which trace an identical process of labour pressure, Liberal resistance, and the consequent emergence of independent labour candidatures. In Attercliffe, for example, the boss of the local Liberal caucus, Sir Fred Mappin, resolutely opposed the notion of selecting a working man to fight in the Liberal interest in the 1894 by-election. This provoked the comment from MacDonald that 'local Liberal Associations have definitely declared against Labour.'[34]

Thus the establishment of the Labour Party owed little to any basic policy differences with the Liberals. Arthur Henderson's transition from Liberal election agent to LRC candidate at Barnard Castle in 1903 involved no fundamental shift of political outlook, and David Martin's essay confirms that there was little to choose in terms of occupation, social origins or political stance between the Labour members and those working men who continued to sit on the Liberal benches. This in turn made it very difficult for Labour to develop any distinctive policies of its own. As Brougham Villiers noted in 1912, the basic difference between Labour and Liberal 'is upon the independence of Labour, not upon any economic or political doctrine in àny ordinary sense at all.'[35]

It was only to be expected that a party born as recently as 1900 should, by 1914, be exhibiting all the signs of adolescence. As the essays below indicate, there had certainly been physical growth, though there were still frailties and black spots. By 1914 it had acquired a national press, was making inroads in some areas among trade unionists, had doubled the number of affiliated constituency bodies since 1906, and had seen off the Lib-Lab element within the Liberal Party. It had also acquired a group of recognised leaders who were developing considerable parliamentary and organisational skills. One important theme of the essays in this collection is the significant contribution to party progress made by local stalwarts whose role was vital in a party which was unique in being conceived outside the immediate confines of Westminster. These were the individuals who did so much to impress the party's claims on popular political consciousness, a process encouraged by continued Liberal intransigence in some constituencies. The electoral pact between MacDonald and Gladstone worked well during the campaign of 1906 but signs of Liberal unrest were soon evident. By 1909, the Midland Liberal Federation was complaining that in electoral negotiation Labour was willing to grasp much and concede little. In 1912 there was a major row in Hanley when both Liberal and Labour organisations claimed the right to nominate the successor to the Lib-Lab, Enoch Edwards. The Times was moved to observe with some acuity that 'there may be a loose coalition in the House of Commons: there is none at all in the country.'36

These organisational advances certainly seem to have outpaced the party's capacity for independent political thought, which remained immature. Policy, like social composition, tended to reflect Labour's Liberal-radical parentage, while parliamentary weakness generally restricted the party's function to that of commentator. More disappointing still to party leaders was the apparent inability to build on this structural expansion in order to make sustained electoral progress. Some of the contributors to this volume are of the opinion that the battle for working class hearts was already won by 1914. On this view, the main obstacle to electoral success apppears to be the limited nature of the working class franchise. As we have suggested, however, there are weaknesses in this argument and other historians, therefore, prefer to stress the barriers to further Labour success posed by the persistence of ingrained attitudes among British workers - deference, popular political apathy, suspicion of socialism, and a reluctance to change established voting patterns.37 In either case, it would appear that the war acted as the main solvent. Some suggest that the franchise extension of 1918 enabled Labour to tap its hitherto excluded 'natural' support. Others stress the way in which war undermined the social structures which buttressed traditional attitudes and values.[38] Certainly it exposed more workers to trade unionism, helped break up the Liberal Party and gave Labour leaders experience of office, albeit of a fairly limited kind. In the longer term war also brought to the forefront of British politics issues such as unemployment and industrial relations in which Labour was particularly interested and on which it could legitimately claim to possess some particular expertise.

Finally, it is perhaps worth putting the issues raised by these essays into the context of the broader debate which has raged for some years about the nature of the British Labour Party. The sense of disillusionment and disappointment which Edwardian activists expressed quite soon after the election of 1906 have lingered to the present day among elements of the British left. There has been a persistent strain of criticism to the effect that the modern party and the five Labour governments in office since 1923 have somehow betrayed the party's origins and the intentions of its founders.[39] It may well be that, given the opportunities afforded by the changed political climate after 1918, the maturing Labour party should have followed a different path. This, however, is an entirely different thing from suggesting that the intentions of the original founders were betrayed. Of that there is no evidence, if only because those intentions were so very modest.

NOTES

1. Labour Leader, 26 June 1913.
2. Quoted in R.E. Dowse, Left in the Centre. The Independent Labour Party, 1893-1940 (Longman, London, 1966), p.15.
3. For this euphoria see my essay, 'The Anti-Socialist Union, 1908-1949', in my Essays in Anti-Labour History (Macmillan, London, 1974).
4. B E.C. Dugdale, Arthur James Balfour (2 vols., Hutchinson, London, 1936), vol. 1, p.438.
5. Quoted in A.K. Russell, Liberal Landslide. The General Election of 1906 (David and Charles, Newton Abbot, 1973), p.209.
6. B. Webb Diaries, 30 Nov. 1910. British Library of Political and Economic Science. Passfield Papers, I, vol. 27, p.98. 'The big thing that has happened in the last two years is that Lloyd George and Churchill have practically

taken the limelight, not merely from their own colleagues but from the Labour Party.'

7. See the essays in the first half of Brown, Essays.

8. See R. McKibbin, 'James Ramsay MacDonald and the Problem of the Independence of the Labour Party, 1910-1914', Journal of Modern History, vol. 42 (1970) and the same author's, The Evolution of the Labour Party, 1910-1924 (Oxford, University Press, 1974).

9. Quoted in P. Clarke, Liberals and Social Democrats (Cambridge, University Press, 1978), p.139.

10. Quoted in H. Pelling, 'The Politics of the Osborne Judgement', Historical Journal, vol. 25 (1982), p.897.

11. C. Chamberlain, 'The Growth of Support for the Labour Party in Britain', British Journal of Sociology, vol. 24 (1973).

12. A.W. Purdue, 'Jarrow Politics, 1885-1914: the Challenge to Liberal Hegemony', Northern History, vol. XVIII (1982).

13. H.G.C. Matthew, R.I. McKibbin, and J.A. Kay, 'The Franchise Factor in the Rise of the Labour Party', English Historical Review, vol. 91 (1976).

14. D. Tanner, 'The Parliamentary Electoral System, the 'Fourth' Reform Act and the Rise of Labour in England and Wales', Bulletin of the Institute of Historical Research, vol. LVI (1983).

15. This is argued strongly in M. Pugh, The Making of Modern British Politics, 1867-1939 (Blackwell, Oxford, 1982), pp.141-144.

16. M.G. Sheppard and J.L. Halstead, 'Labour's Municipal Election Performance in England and Wales, 1901-1913', Bulletin of the Society for the Study of Labour History, vol. 39 (1979).

17. C. Cook, 'Labour and the Downfall of the Liberal Party, 1906-1914', in A. Sked and C. Cook (eds.), Crisis and Controversy (Macmillan, London, 1976), pp.38-65. See also R. Hills, 'The City Council and Electoral Politics, 1901-1971', in C. Feinstein (ed.), York, 1831-1981 (Ebor Press, York, 1981).

18. R. Tressell, The Ragged Trousered Philanthropists (Lawrence and Wishart, London, 1955), p.281.

19. H. Mitchell, The Hard Way Up (Faber and Faber, London, 1968), pp.109-110.

20. R.F. Wheeler, 'Organised Sport and

Organised Labour', _Journal of Contemporary History_, vol. 13 (1978), p.193. Hobson's comment is quoted in S. Collini, _Liberalism and Sociology_ (Cambridge, University Press, 1979), p.89, n. 53.

21. P. Snowden, 'The Labour Party and the General Election', _Independent Review_, vol. VII (1905), p.143.

22. T.F. Tsiang, _Labor and Empire_ (Columbia University Press, New York, 1923), p.215.

23. Quoted in Russell, _Liberal Landslide_, p.81.

24. On this see my _Labour and Unemployment, 1900-1914_ (David and Charles, Newton Abbot, 1971), chs. 4 and 5.

25. Quoted in S. Desmond, _Labour: The Giant with the Feet of Clay_ (Collins, London, 1921), p. 38.

26. B. Barker, 'The Anatomy of Reformism: the Social and Political Ideas of the Labour Leadership in Yorkshire', _International Review of Social History_, vol. XVIII (1973). Barker's interpretation is broadly substantiated in D. Howell, _British Workers and the Independent Labour Party, 1888-1906_ (Manchester, University Press, 1983). See also J. Hill, 'Manchester and Salford Politics and the Early Development of the Independent Labour Party', _International Review of Social History_, vol. XXVI (1981), p.188. 'There is, therefore, considerable value in the notion of two traditions, a "socialist" and a "labourist" in Manchester working class politics at this time ...' He goes on to argue, however, that the local Labour Party only made substantial progress when it subordinated the former to the latter.

27. W.T. Stead, 'The Labour Party and the Books that Helped to Make It', _Review of Reviews_, vol. 33 (1906).

28. Quoted in D. Marquand, _Ramsay MacDonald_ (Cape, London, 1977), p.88. There is a certain irony, therefore, in the fact that MacDonald, who was regarded as British socialism's leading intellectual in this period, was ultimately to be derided as a 'woolly utopian cliché-monger'. Kenneth O. Morgan, 'Edwardian Socialism' in D. Read (ed.), _Edwardian England_ (Croom Helm, London, 1982), p.101.

29. A point made in F. Bealey, _The Social and Political Thought of the British Labour Party_ (Weidenfeld and Nicolson, London, 1970), p.3. The other figure was Keir Hardie.

30. Kenneth D. Brown, 'London and the

Historical Reputation of John Burns', London Journal, vol. 2 (1976).

31. Labour Leader, 28 Mar. 1903. For Burns' later relations with the Labour Party see Kenneth D. Brown, John Burns (Royal Historical Society, London, 1977), chs. 6-8.

32. For Dr Pelling's contribution see his 'The Working Class and the Origins of the Welfare State', in his own Popular Politics and Society in Late Victorian Britain (Macmillan, London, 1978), pp.1-18.

33. D. Powell, 'The Liberal Ministries and Labour, 1892-1895', History, vol. 68 (1983).

34. J. Brown, 'Attercliffe 1894: How One Local Liberal Party Failed to Meet the Challenge of Labour', Journal of British Studies, vol. XIV (1975), p.75. For similar reactions in other areas see A.W. Purdue, 'The Liberal and Labour Parties in North East Politics, 1900-1914: the Struggle for Supremacy', International Review of Social History, vol. XXVI (1981): A.W. Roberts, 'Leeds Liberalism and Late Victorian Politics', Northern History, vol. V (1970).

35. Quoted in M. Petter, 'The Progressive Alliance', History, vol. 58 (1973), p.53.

37. F. Parkin, 'Working-Class Conservatives: a Theory of Political Deviance', British Journal of Sociology, vol. 18 (1967), pp.278-290.

38. For differing interpretations, see Matthews, McKibbin and Kay, 'The Franchise factor': B.A. Waites, 'The Effect of the First World War on Class and Status in England, 1910-1920', Journal of Contemporary History, vol. 11 (1976): J.M. Winter, 'A Note on the Reconstruction of the Labour Party in 1918', Bulletin of the Scottish Society for the Study of Labour History, vol. 12 (1978): Kenneth D. Brown, The English Labour Movement, 1700-1951 (Gill and Macmillan, Dublin, 1982), pp.233-238.

39. This debate can be followed in various issues of The Socialist Register. See also T. Nairn, 'The Nature of the Labour Party', New Left Review, vol. 27 and 28 (1964).

Chapter One

IDEOLOGY AND COMPOSITION[1]

Of the fifteen candidates endorsed by the Labour Representation Committee, only Keir Hardie and Richard Bell were returned at the general election of 1900. Yet between them they represented the two main strands that were to make up the Labour Party down to 1914, and beyond. Hardie, chairman of the Independent Labour Party, was the country's leading socialist politician, known through both his oratory and journalism as an unsparing critic of the exploitation and ugliness of capitalism. Bell was not a socialist. As general secretary of the Amalgamated Society of Railway Servants, he was mainly concerned to represent the case for trade unionism. Whereas Hardie had defeated a Liberal opponent, Bell had been elected with Liberal Party co-operation and by the general election of 1906 he had virtually entered the Liberal fold. However, Bell's defection had been offset by three LRC successes in by-elections at which two pragmatic trade union leaders, David Shackleton and Arthur Henderson, and a veteran of London Progressivism, Will Crooks, were returned. Of the three only Henderson had faced a Liberal opponent.

In January 1906 Hardie, Shackleton, Henderson and Crooks were re-elected, and with twenty-six other newly-elected MPs formed the parliamentary Labour Party. Of this thirty, twenty-two had been supported by their trade unions and eight were sponsored by the ILP. All the ILPers regarded themselves as socialists; of the trade unionists about half did not (eleven of the trade-union sponsored MPs were also members of the ILP). The members of the PLP were mostly middle-aged - in 1906 the average age was forty-six - and this meant that they had tended to form their views when

17

socialism in Britain was almost unknown. Consequently many had first entered politics via the radical wing of the Liberal Party. In some cases the connection with Liberalism had been intimate. Among the Labour Party's more prominent members, David Shackleton had been elected as a Liberal town councillor and Arthur Henderson had worked as an agent of the Liberal Party and was closely associated with the party in the north-east until the early 1900s. Hardie, the chairman of the PLP from 1906 to 1908, had earlier broken away from the Liberal Party, but the process had been a protracted one.[2] Moreover, in twenty-four constituencies Labour MPs had been returned in tandem with Liberals, as a result of the Gladstone-MacDonald pact. Nevertheless the Labour Party sat on the opposition benches (those on the government side were in any case crowded with four hundred Liberal MPs) and in other ways tried to emphasise the distinct nature of the party. Invariably, its members stressed their 'specialist knowledge' of the issues 'which affect the great mass of the workers'. 'When workers' questions come up for discussion', wrote Shackleton, Labour MPs 'have to do little more than open the book of their own lives' and 'consider what they have themselves in most instances gone through'.[3] Labour propagandists also stressed the vested interests bound up with Liberalism and the ways in which society was evolving towards a socialistic state.[4]

However, some of the flavour of the older party always stuck with Labour. In particular Labour politicians had the same attitude towards accepting piecemeal reforms and working within the existing framework.[5] Many had experience of trade union negotiations which conditioned them to think in terms of compromise and limited improvement. Some of the moral reform rhetoric of Liberalism was also found in Labour pronouncements. Collectivist solutions to society's ills were not regarded as putting an end to individual responsibility. There was held to be a need also for thrift and temperance, and about a dozen Labour MPs were known as supporters of teetotalism.[6] Such attitudes, however, were not invariably drawn from middle-class Liberalism. There was a long tradition of working-class radicalism in which emphasis was placed on self-improvement and individual effort, often coupled with a suspicion of local or central

authority. Dislike of the poor law was one aspect
of such an attitude. Another was opposition to the
established church, and inevitably matters of
religion were major influences on the ideology of
the early Labour leaders. No-one raised in
Victorian Britain could escape entirely the
pervasive influence of religion. Some reacted
against orthodox beliefs and not only rejected the
state church but also adopted a secularist
position. Many Social Democratic Federation
members had begun as followers of Charles
Bradlaugh, while Robert Blatchford and other
contributors to the Clarion were hostile to
conventional religion.[7] The Labour Churches
catered for the less dogmatic who accepted 'the
moral and economic laws that may be adduced from
the Fatherhood of God or the Brotherhood of Man',
and in a sense, too, the Socialist Sunday School
movement, with its 'Ten Commandments' and so forth,
acknowledged the role of religion even while trying
to rechannel it.[8] In this period 'the religion
of Socialism' made converts from Christianity. The
vocabularies of advanced politics and evangelical
Christianity contained similar phrases, and often
similar energies and aspirations were redirected
from religion to Labour propaganda.[9]

On the other hand, few Labour leaders ranged
very far from convention. In electoral terms,
there was more to be lost than gained from a
reputation for freethinking. MacDonald, for
example, had a complex and unconventional attitude
to religion, although he gave his denomination
simply as Free Church of Scotland.[10] In the
general election of 1906 the role of the
non-conformist churches was particularly
significant. In many constituencies Labour was in
unofficial alliance with the Liberal Party which in
turn was closely allied to non-conformity, probably
at this time more so than ever before.[11] Of the
Labour candidates elected, eighteen had described
themselves as non-conformists, and some of this
number were lay preachers. However, not all seem
to have had a firm adherence; of the eighteen only
eight - Crooks, Hardie, Henderson, A.H. Gill,
John Hodge, Walter Hudson, J.H. Jenkins and
J.W. Taylor - were claimed by the denominational
press.[12] For many, non-conformity probably
helped to provide an ethical underpinning to their
political creed. The remarks made by J.A. Seddon
while LRC candidate were not untypical of a section
of the Labour leadership. Addressing the men's

Bible class at a local Congregational chapel, Seddon, who had been raised as a non-conformist, referred to his own beliefs as 'a sacred personal matter between himself and his maker'. Even so, he believed that a man's religion should consist of 'his duty to his fellow man and his Creator' and that the churches had neglected some of their duties. 'While humanity was bleeding at every pore, and crying out for brotherliness, it was not for the churches to quarrel about "isms", but to see what they could do for their fellowmen, and so hasten the Kingdom of God upon earth'.[13]

Many Labour activists invoked the 'New Jerusalem' of the socialist millennium that was to arise. The similarity between the language of politics and that of religion was particularly marked in the northern areas where Labour had most support. Undoubtedly other factors, notably occupational structure, help to explain the regional variations in Labour-voting.[14] But it is probable that by using the phraseology of the non-conformist pulpit, speakers helped to secure the allegiance of workers inculcated with the values of the chapel. The final passage in one of Philip Snowden's most popular lectures offers a striking example of religiosity in the service of socialism.

> But the only way to regain the earthly paradise is by the old, hard road to Calvary - through persecution, through poverty, through temptation, by the agony and bloody sweat, by the crown of thorns, by the agonising death. And then the resurrection to the New Humanity - purified by suffering, triumphant through sacrifice.[15]

II

'What culture they have', wrote W.T. Stead rather patronisingly of the first generation of Labour MPs, 'they obtained from the chapel, from that popular university the public library, or still more frequently from the small collection of books found in the homes of the poor'. These remarks prefaced the perennially-fascinating replies that Stead received from twenty-five Labour and twenty Lib-Lab MPs to a question about which books they found 'most useful' in their early days when the 'battle was beginning'.[16] Perhaps not surprisingly, many wrote respectfully of the bible, The Pilgrim's Progress and Shakespeare, while Dickens was the most popular novelist.[17] Only James O'Grady, a Roman Catholic, and Will Thorne, who had retained his SDF membership, mentioned Marx. Five Labour Party MPs referred to Henry George - Hardie, O'Grady, George Barnes, John Hodge and Thomas Summerbell - and all were of an age to have been influenced in the first half of the 1880s when George lectured in Britain and when Progress and Poverty circulated widely.

Perhaps most significantly, many of Stead's respondents mentioned the works of those two pillars of Victorian social criticism, John Ruskin and Thomas Carlyle. Ruskin seems to have been regarded by many who were active in the movement as a fellow socialist. Blatchford, for instance, wrote 'I know many Socialists, and many Socialistic leaders. I know none who can make profit of it. Most of the leaders, such as Ruskin, Morris, Hyndman, Carpenter, Shaw, De Mattos, Annie Besant, and Bland, would lose in money and position were Socialism adopted now'.[18] Such views were held notwithstanding the opening sentence of Ruskin's autobiography: 'I am, and my father was before me, a violent Tory of the old school; Walter Scott's school that is to say, and Homer's'.[19] Ten of the Labour MPs included in Stead's survey acknowledged Ruskin, and the work most often referred to was Unto this Last. Fred Jowett, for example, said it was the book that made him a socialist.[20]

Carlyle was about equally well regarded. Hardie wrote that though he had 'learned much of the human failings and weaknesses of Carlyle', he remained 'a worshipper at his shrine'. O'Grady stated that 'above and beyond all Carlyle is my solace and inspiration', while James Parker thought he perhaps owed more to Carlyle than to any other writer.[21] Both Sartor Resartus and Past and Present were admired, presumably because of their critique of vanity and materialism - in spite of the fact that Carlyle favoured a society that was hierarchical and ordered by what he regarded as true aristocrats. Similarly, the authoritarian and paternalistic aspects of Ruskin were discounted. He was no democrat and it was probably in the ethical case against injustice that his appeal lay. Quentin Bell in his biography of Ruskin records that he had questioned a veteran of the Labour Party who doubted that its early members had

in fact read <u>Unto this Last</u>. As an explanation
Bell suggests that 'Ruskin, before his death, had
been canonised. Ruskin was culture and British
socialism in its youth was respectful of educated
opinion'.[22] This might be part of the
explanation, though on balance it seems probable
that the writings of both Carlyle and Ruskin, which
were then extensively circulated, had been sampled
by the Labour members. One contemporary,
W.H. Mallock, accepted their influence and pointed
out the apparent contradiction of workers'
representatives basing their ideas on bourgeois
authors.[23] However, it might well be that
criticisms from within of the prevailing system of
values were regarded as more telling than those of
proletarian authors, who were in any case few in
number.

There can be neither precision nor certainty
in discussing something as nebulous as men's ideas
and the ways in which they seek to apply them.
Perhaps more than from religious faith and reading,
views are formed by more immediate, day-to-day
experiences. Even though details about books had
been sought, some of Stead's respondents made this
point. 'All life is a book' replied the 'Lib-Lab'
Henry Broadhurst ,'in street, bus, railway carriage
and railway platforms'. In terms befitting a
Wesleyan lay preacher, Arthur Henderson made a
similar point: 'My best book has been my close
contact with, and deep interest in the spiritual,
moral, and social and industrial affairs of life'.
Another 'Lib-Lab' and secretary of the TUC
parliamentary committee, W.C. Steadman, stated 'I
gained most of my experience in the hard school of
adversity from my boyhood days upwards'. Richard
Bell's reply mentioned only Ruskin and ended with
the remark that 'the greatest book from which I
have gained most is the book of experience'. The
coalminers' leader, Thomas Glover, echoed this, but
put his views more bluntly and at greater length:

> I am sorry to say that I have not gained my
> experiences out of books, but from the
> everyday experiences of how the workers have
> been treated by the employers and the class
> which do not work, and whose main object has
> always been to keep the working man as much in
> the dark as they can. I had to work in the
> mines from a very early age - nine years old
> when I started and very long hours - and the
> little I learned was at the night schools, and

then by seeking to get into company always above myself and learning from them, which was most valuable to me.

Shackleton gave as his 'chief guide' the practical experience gained from trade union work and Snowden believed that men and 'a close observation of the minds and manners of the people' among whom he had lived had taught him more than his library of 2000 volumes.[24]

Propagandist work in the ILP or posts as trade union officials meant that most Labour MPs had not for some years worked in their original occupations. Nevertheless, the great majority had spent lengthy periods as workers in factories and mines and could reasonably claim an intimate familiarity with the working conditions of the majority of the population. They had also directly encountered experiences of other aspects of working-class life. Some had suffered poverty, including the ministrations of the poor law, at first hand; others, though the sons of skilled workers earning better wages, were familiar with the hardships of less fortunate neighbours. It would be remarkable if experiences such as these had not shaped the attitudes of Labour politicians.

Moreover, other forces were also exerting an influence around the turn of the century. Increasing world competition was causing British employers to put more pressure on their work-forces. Some consequences of this were mentioned at the 1902 conference of the LRC by W.J. Davis, an old-fashioned and non-socialist leader of Birmingham trade unionism. Davis referred to the 'displacement of labour by machinery' and the way a 'mechanic or a labourer if on the wrong side of 45 years of age, when applying for work, is often told that he is too old'. Moreover, manufacturers were compelling their workers 'to take out the finish, smoothness, and beauty, in order that they can get into the market cheap.'[25] Trade unionists also felt they were being unfairly blamed for the country's failure to resist newer competitors. In particular, the series of articles on 'The Crisis in British Industry' published during 1901-2 by The Times caused much resentment. In its report to the LRC conference in February 1902 the executive committee referred to the paper carrying on 'the traditions of the Pigott forgeries and lies'.[26]

The economic and social changes that were taking place in the twenty or thirty years before

1914 have been seen as helping to create a more distinct and homogeneous working class. This was 'the era of . . . the fish-and-chip shop, the football team and its supporters, the working class seaside holiday, the public elementary school, the working class pattern of betting . . . and not least, the Labour Councillor and the "new" union'.[27] The forces that were shaping communities of the urban working-class were also affecting the lower middle class and it is generally accepted that the gap between these classes was widening.[28] Many Edwardians felt that they were experiencing a growth in class consciousness. The advent of the Labour Party and the upsurge in trade unionism, especially in the years of the 'labour unrest', were among the developments that led politicians and others to look more closely at the changes that were taking place within society. However, few members of the older, upper-class parties were able to understand the everyday life of the majority of the population. As the Liberal Chancellor of the Exchequer, Lloyd George undoubtedly had an appeal to many of the working class. He could on occasion speak movingly of the hardships of the poor and condemn the 'idle rich' - though he confessed that he did not fully realise the nature of poverty until he came to administer the old age pensions act.[29] Another exponent of the 'new Liberalism', C.F.G. Masterman, also tried to penetrate the way of life of what he referred to as 'the multitude', but his tone was often similar to the strictures of the 'national efficiency' school of social reformers.[30] While some progressive Liberals had social consciences their knowledge of working-class life was limited. As for the average politician the philanthropic George Cadbury was near the truth when he told a party of LRC delegates to Bournville that 'few of the present members [of Parliament] knew or cared to know much about the condition of the working men of the country'.[31]

On the other hand, working-class propagandists emphasised their immediate contact with society's less fortunate members. They could voice the sort of appeal for fairer treatment of their class that would seem false if made by a bourgeois politician. For instance, at an open-air meeting during his by-election campaign of 1903, Will Crooks produced 'thunderous volleys of applause' when, after describing the trials of the unemployed, [he] cried 'Give 'em a chance'.[32] It was the same simple, even simplistic philosophy that Tressell gave his character Joe Philpot: 'If you see a poor b----r wot's down on 'is luck, give 'im a 'elpin' 'and'.[33]


### III

Most Labour MPs would have had first-hand knowledge of unemployment, either from being out of work themselves or through the experiences of friends and relations. The 'right to work' was a demand never far from the centre of Labour politics, and it was an issue that distanced the party from Liberalism.[34] In his election address at Jarrow, in July 1907, Pete Curran emphasised the 'grave national evil' of unemployment and blamed the Liberal government for creating obstacles rather than assisting the out-of-work.[35] Later in the month, at Colne Valley, Victor Grayson made the 'right to work' the first heading of an election address. It was a 'stinging disgrace', he wrote, 'that men and women were unemployed in a community professing to be civilized and Christian', but the Tories and Liberals refused to tackle the problem because 'the continuance of unemployment is necessary to their rents and profits'.[36] Both Curran, who was sponsored by the gasworkers and general labourers' union and had the endorsement of the LRC, and Grayson, who stood as an independent socialist, were elected. Curran's success seemed to be based on an appeal to trade union solidarity, particularly that of the Durham miners and the shipwrights who worked in Palmers yard at Jarrow.[37] He had topped the poll against Liberal, Conservative and Irish Nationalist candidates, and this strengthened Labour's belief in its effectiveness as a party. His election helped to raise morale at the following annual conference. W.A. Appleton, for instance, the General Federation of Trade Unions' fraternal delegate, optimistically spoke of most differences between the trade union and socialist wings as 'terminological and not fundamental'.[38] On the other hand, in the Colne Valley Grayson had preached a type of evangelical socialism that found an enthusiastic response in an area where trade unionism was relatively weak but where the ethical basis of politics was unusually strong.[39] His election - against both Liberal and Conservative candidate - led some Labour supporters to press for a stronger attack on the Liberal Party, more in line with Grayson's own controversial tactics in the Commons.

The Labour leadership, however, remained characteristically cautious. Though the activities of the PLP might have seemed lacklustre to the left-wing critics, some achievements could be claimed by the leadership. While on the floor of the Commons the party had been overshadowed by the government, behind the scenes it had made gains. In particular there was the virtual eclipse of the Lib-Labs. After the election of 1906 some twenty MPs had formed themselves, rather loosely, into the 'Trade Union Labour Party'. The majority of this group were miners' leaders, representing districts unaffiliated to the Labour Party (in Lancashire, where the hold of Liberalism was weaker, the Lancashire and Cheshire Miners' Federation had affiliated to the LRC in 1903). In 1906 the MFGB balloted its members on the question of joining the Labour Party. So small was the majority that the pro-affiliation element was encouraged to call for another ballot, held in May 1908. This reversed the decision by 213,000 votes to 168,000 – an indication of the shift of opinion at grass-roots level towards independent labour representation.[40] Although for a few more years a handful of 'Lib-Lab' MPs survived, the majority were absorbed into the Labour Party while one or two others were designated simply as Liberals.[41]

At the time of the MFGB ballot there were fifteen 'Lib-Lab' miners' MPs in Parliament and it was afterwards decided that they would 'be not called upon to sign the constitution of the Labour Party except in the event of a by-election or at the next General Election'.[42] However, at a by-election in July 1909 J.G. Hancock of the Derbyshire Miners was elected under Liberal auspices – an early indication of the problem that was to last for three or four years, the severing of the links between some miners' leaders and Liberalism. Even so, the Labour leaders could tolerate difficulties such as this, given the financial and other advantages that the affiliation of the MFGB brought. There had also been a by-election success in May 1909 when Joseph Pointer, a patternmaker and ILP member, won Sheffield Attercliffe. Labour had been fortunate in that an Independent Conservative intervened to make the contest a four-sided one and Pointer took the seat with only 27.5 per cent of the votes cast. In a dozen other by-elections fought by Labour candidates between 1906 and 1909 the party had been unsuccessful. Three had been straight fights against Conservatives, but in the other nine Liberal candidates had also been present and Labour had ended up in third place.

The problem of having to share the 'progressive' vote was less acute at the general elections of 1910 when the spirit of the understanding reached in 1903 between MacDonald and Gladstone was revived. In January 1910 all forty of the Labour MPs elected benefited from Liberal co-operation; a similar number of Labour candidates were defeated, the majority ending up at the bottom of the poll in three-cornered fights. Of the two earlier by-election successes, Pete Curran lost but Pointer held his Sheffield constituency where an agreement to allow a straight fight had been reached with the Liberals. Five other sitting MPs were defeated (Macpherson, Summerbell, T.F. Richards, Crooks and Jenkins) while Kelley retired on medical grounds. Thus of the thirty Labour MPs of 1906, twenty-four continued their parliamentary careers. With the retirement of Richard Bell, the railwaymen secured the election in Derby of J.H. Thomas, who was regarded as firmly committed to independent Labour politics. The other fourteen members represented what were classed as mining constituencies (the proportion of miners in the electorate ranged from over half down to about ten per cent). In all, sixteen Labour MPs were sponsored by the MFGB.[43]

Most of the new intake had graduated from trade union officialdom. Characteristically they started work at an early age and had by dint of self-improvement achieved some standing in their locality. Some had links with non-conformity, several had been elected to positions in local government and had been appointed as magistrates. Middle-aged by the time they reached the House of Commons, they were similar in outlook and temperament to the majority of Labour MPs elected in 1906.

Nor did the composition of the party change greatly as a result of the second general election of 1910 held in December. Will Crooks regained his Woolwich seat, on this occasion sponsored by the Fabian Society instead of the small coopers' union. Another London constituency, Bow and Bromley, was won by George Lansbury, a dedicated socialist. Tom Richardson, a Durham miner who was also an active ILP member, was successful at Whitehaven (an understanding with local Liberals meant that they put up no candidate in return for a free run at Cockermouth). William Adamson, a miners' official, defeated a Liberal candidate at West Fife (the agreement between MacDonald and Gladstone had not applied to Scotland). The seat at Sunderland, lost in January, was regained for Labour by F.W. Goldstone, a schoolteacher and campaigner for reform of the educational system. Against these five gains, there were defeats in Lancashire for Thomas Glover, James Seddon and Harry Twist. Shackleton did not contest Clitheroe, having accepted a post as a Home Office labour adviser, but the seat was retained by Albert Smith, a trade union leader in the local textile industry. Thus Labour emerged with forty-two MPs. Sixteen other Labour Party candidates had gone unsuccessfully to the polls, where in all but two cases they had faced both Liberal and Conservative opposition.

IV

Labour's reliance on the Liberals at the hustings was paralleled at Westminster. The Osborne judgement had made the party dependent on the willingness of the government to bring in amending legislation at a time when sections of the broader labour movement were becoming increasingly militant. The sharp rise in trade union membership was associated with a wave of strikes which brought to the fore younger leaders who were critical of the way the working class was being represented by the Labour Party. Some critics regarded Parliament as, in Tom Mann's words, 'brought into existence by the ruling class' to provide a ' more effective means of dominating and subjugating the working class'. Should a socialist get into Parliament, declared A.G. Tufton of the Carpenters and Joiners, 'he simply gets swamped by his new environment'.[44] To James Gribble - 'General' Gribble of the Raunds Strike of 1905 - the Labour Party had become 'a piece of potter's clay in the hands of the Liberal Cabinet'.[45] Though Gribble was an SDF activist his view was similar to that of Beatrice Webb. Though a hostile observer of 'the new left - the Syndicalists', she was equally contemptuous of the way 'Lloyd George and the Radicals have out-trumped the Labour Party'.[46]

Even allowing that Labour had always been subject
to attacks from the left and that Beatrice Webb was
given to olympian judgments on the party, there
appeared to be some cause for pessimism. There was
too a renewed challenge from the SDF (since 1907
known as the Social-Democratic Party), which merged
with some Clarion groups and about forty defecting
branches of the ILP to form the British Socialist
Party in 1911. For a time the proselytizing of
Grayson, who had lost his seat in January 1910, and
others revived the slogan about the need to 'make
socialists'.

In the Commons the Labour Party could still be
regarded as the tail of the Liberals, as 'a tick
carried along on the Asquithean sheep' as one
historian has expressed it.[47] The party was
divided over the National Insurance Bill and seemed
to lack purpose and direction. By July 1912
MacDonald privately reflected that the party was
acting in a way that made him think it was
'hopeless to go on' in trying to prevent it
becoming 'a disorganised mob'. Hardie, who was
also given to periods of melancholy, was similarly
pessimistic.[48]

Yet in the shorter term MacDonald and the
other leading figures in the party had limited room
in which to manoeuvre. The state of national
politics and Labour's finances was such that there
could be no question of trying to force another
general election. Within the party there was a
need to strengthen its organisation and personnel.
In particular, the miners' affiliation - though in
the longer term of inestimable benefit - brought
problems. As W.V. Osborne, a critic of the unions'
involvement with the Labour Party, wrote of the
MFGB members, 'instead of joining in the headstrong
pursuit of impossible ideals, they acted rather as
a drag'.[49] The older leaders were so set in
'Lib-Labism' that they were loathe to sign the
Labour Party constitution or to establish separate
Labour organisations in their constituencies. Nor
was the MFGB in a position to bring these men into
line. It was recognised that many miners were
Liberal voters who would not wish the federation to
appear subservient to the Labour Party. There was
also a feeling of loyalty to the elderly
parliamentary leaders. Three veterans of mining
trade unionism, Burt, Fenwick and Wilson, continued
as before, though most of the others, as Gregory
notes, 'were less scrupulous: they disagreed with
the constitution, signed it, and then ignored

it'.[50]  Unfortunately for the Labour Party, the deaths of three miners' MPs - Enoch Edwards in June 1912, James Haslam in July 1913 and W.E. Harvey in April 1914 - led to by-elections which resulted in the return of two Liberals and a Conservative.  The complicated details of these elections need not be given here, but the defeats did strengthen the impression that Labour was failing to make progess.[51]  In addition George Lansbury resigned his seat at Bow and Bromley in order to contest the resulting by-election, held in November 1912, on the women's suffrage issue.  Having, in the words of Augustine Birrell, 'let his bleeding heart run away with his bloody head', he lost the seat.[52]

These by-election defeats have been regarded as evidence that Labour was in decline in the years prior to 1914.  This view and the related question of the fortunes of the Liberal Party cannot be examined in detail here, although some general points might be made.[53]  In the first place, though hostile towards syndicalist doctrines and remote from the labour unrest, the Labour leadership was able to criticise the Liberal government's handling of the contemporary industrial unrest.  Some disputes involved Liberal MPs who also had business interests, although such men were aware of the political difficulties that could arise and had tried to avoid them.[54] Nevertheless, a combination of growing trade union membership, a series of major strikes and the emergence of a younger more militant leadership was bound to emphasise the gap between the political parties.  Thus in MacDonald's constituency of Leicester in 1913, local socialists intent on contesting a by-election - against the wishes of the parliamentary party - 'deeply and strongly resented' several government actions, including those in the railway and mining strikes and the prosecution of Tom Mann and others.[55]  At the same time, and despite all its limitations, it was becoming more accepted that the Labour Party had a role to play in representing the working class.  An acknowledgment of this was the way in which a majority of members of almost all trade unions voted to pay the political levy.  It is true that a substantial minority of trade unionists who took part in the voting, which was required under the terms of the Trade Union Act of 1913, opposed the setting up of political funds but the decision, once made, was to tie the fortunes of the growing trade union movement more closely to Labour.  At the local level trade union officials often took on the task of organising the activities of the Labour Party while the number of full-time agents was also increasing.[56] This improved organisation at the grass roots also contributed to Labour's efforts in municipal elections. Another indication of the way the Labour Party was consolidationg its position came in June 1914 when the British Socialist Party formally applied for affiliation. On balance, then, it seems that Labour had consolidated its position rather than lost ground in the years between 1910 and 1914.

V

Writing up her diary for 12 February 1914 Beatrice Webb accepted the view of a fellow Fabian that apart from MacDonald, Hardie, Snowden and Henderson the Labour MPs were 'a lot of ordinary workmen who neither know nor care about anything but the interests of their respective Trade Unions and a comfortable life for themselves'.[57] Such a judgment contains an element of truth. Yet the ordinariness of the MPs gave them a unique understanding of the class that elected them, a class that was becoming more cohesive and aware of its political and economic strength. Moreover, without its association with trade unionism the party would not have had the backing of a vested interest that was growing in size and influence.

In other respects, Beatrice Webb over-simplified the character of the party which, at times, she both despised and cultivated. There was more involved in Labour's make-up than narrow sectionalism and complacency. Sometimes the elements seemed too diffuse, and doctrinally its ideas were eclectic even for a body that was fairly indifferent to intellectual consistency. It combined the rhetoric of Victorian moral reform with newer slogans urging social and economic revolution. There were libertarian elements that drew on Shelley and Carpenter, and Fabian programmes based on bureaucratic control. To some members socialism was the equivalent within a society of biological evolution, to others it was neither scientific nor desirable. Secularists dedicated to an earthly paradise in the form of 'Merrie England' and the precept that 'fellowship is life' were part of the same movement as those who believed that the Labour Party incorporated the

teachings of the Sermon on the Mount. Little
regarding any intellectual contradictions, many
individuals combined several strands of thought.
Politicians are seldom troubled by questions of
logical consistency, which enabled differing
beliefs to be apparently reconciled. That
differences were tolerated - or if not, that the
party survived anyway - is explicable in terms of a
deeper force. By 1914 the idea of independent
political representation was well established in
trade union and other working-class bodies. The
belief that workers should have their own spokesmen
in Parliament was the Labour Party's main source of
strength and unity. Thus the ideology of the early
Labour Party can be understood as more than a
series of political and legislative proposals; it
also incorporates, to use the phrase of a modern
political scientist, 'values which spring from the
experience of the British working class'.[58] It
was this ethos that gave the party its reason for
being and which helps to make intelligible its
subsequent history in both government and
opposition.

NOTES

1. I am grateful to David Rubinstein and the
editor of this volume for their helpful comments on
an earlier draft of this essay.
2. A.W. Purdue, 'Arthur Henderson and
Liberal, Liberal-Labour and Labour Politics in the
North-East of England, 1892-1903', Northern
History, vol.11 (1976), pp.198-205. Kenneth O.
Morgan, Keir Hardie: Radical and Socialist
(Weidenfeld and Nicolson, London, 1975), pp.17 ff.
3. J.K. Hardie, Philip Snowden, and
D. Shackleton, Labour Politics: A Symposium (ILP,
London, 1903), p.16.
4. The evolutionary argument is contained in
J. Ramsay MacDonald, Socialism and Society (ILP,
London, 1905). Hardie's criticisms of the
reactionary and aristocratic elements in the
Liberal programme are quoted in W. Stewart, J. Keir
Hardie: A Biography (ILP, London, 1921), pp.221-3.
5. The SDF's withdrawal from the LRC in 1901
removed the main group of socialists that advocated
more revolutionary methods. Individual Social
Democrats continued to attend party conferences as
delegates of other organizations. In 1908, for
instance, Harry Quelch, representing the London
Trades Council, unsuccessfully supported a

resolution calling for the 'overthrow of the present competitive system of capitalism'. Labour Party, Annual Report, 1908, p.58.

6. Thus provoking Ben Tillett to write in Is the Parliamentary Labour Party a Failure? (Twentieth Century Press, London, 1908), p.13: 'Messrs. Henderson, Shackleton, Snowden and others have "out-Heroded" the worst ranters in denouncing their own class (the workers) for supposed drunkenness and thriftlessness'.

7. For a recent discussion of Blatchford's views in the context of 'plebeian autodidactic culture', see Logie Barrow, 'Determinism and Environmentalism in Socialist Thought', in R. Samuel and G. Stedman Jones (eds.), Culture, Ideology and Politics (Routledge and Kegan Paul, London, 1982), pp.194-214.

8. Labour Church Record, Jul. 1900, quoted in R.B. Rose, 'Protestant Nonconformity', in W.B. Stephens (ed.), A History of the County of Warwickshire, (Oxford, University Press, 1964), vol. 7, p.459. For the 'Socialist Ten Commandments' see F. Reid, 'Socialist Sunday Schools in Britain 1892-1939', International Review of Social History, vol. 11 (1966).

9. For example, see H. Pelling, The Origins of the Labour Party 1880-1900 (Clarendon Press, Oxford, 1965), ch.VII; Kenneth O. Morgan, 'New Liberalism and the Challenge of Labour: The Welsh Experience, 1885-1929', Welsh History Review, vol. 6 (1973), p.297; and S. Yeo, 'A New Life: The Religion of Socialism in Britain, 1883-1896', History Workshop, no.4 (1977), pp.11-12.

10. MacDonald stated his membership of the Free Church of Scotland in W.T. Stead, 'The Labour Party and the Books that Helped to Make It', Review of Reviews, vol.33 (1906), p.577. But he attended the Free Church only when on holiday in Lossiemouth; see D. Marquand, Ramsay MacDonald (Cape, London, 1977), p.53, where there is also a discussion of MacDonald's attitude to religion.

11. There was soon to be a reaction against the closeness of the link; see D. W. Bebbington, The Nonconformist Conscience: Chapel and Politics, 1879-1914 (Allen and Unwin, London, 1982), pp.157-8.

12. Kenneth D. Brown, 'Non-conformity and the British Labour Movement: A Case Study', Journal of Social History, vol.8 (1975), pp.116 and 119.

13. Earlstown Guardian, 12 Jan. 1906.

14. P. Joyce, Work, Society and Politics: the Culture of the Factory in Later Victorian England

(Harvester Press, Brighton, 1980), pp.331-44: David Howell, British Workers and the Independent Labour Party 1888-1906 (Manchester, University Press, 1983), chs. 7-11,

15. P. Snowden, The Christ that is to be (ILP, London, 1904 [?]), p.13.

16. Stead, 'The Labour Party and the Books that Helped to Make It', p.568.

17. Crooks declared 'Bunyan is the ideal of our working people'. G.H. Roberts found a powerful appeal in the struggles of Christian which were like those 'in which mankind is involved when striving to right the wrong, to remove injustice, and to create a new heaven and a new earth'. Ibid., pp.573, 578.

18. R. Blatchford, Merrie England (Walter Scott, London, 1894), p.197.

19. Ruskin made the statement in Letter X of Fors Clavigera (1871) and began the first volume of Praeterita (1885) with it. Several Labour MPs also admired Scott, including MacDonald who stated 'the "Waverley Novels" in conjunction with Scottish History, opened out the great world of national life for me and led me on to politics'. Will Crooks was rhapsodic about Homer. Stead, 'The Labour Party and the Books that Helped to Make It', pp.577,573.

20. Stead, 'The Labour Party and the Books that Helped to Make It', p.575. The others who cited Ruskin were Crooks, J.R. Clynes, Charles Duncan, Walter Hudson, J.T. Macpherson, James Parker, T.F. Richards, J.W. Taylor and George Wardle.

21. Ibid., pp.570, 578. Carlyle was also mentioned by Clynes, Duncan, Jowett, Macpherson, Seddon, Wardle and Stephen Walsh. Both Carlyle and Ruskin were equally appreciated by the Lib-Lab group.

22. Quentin Bell, Ruskin (Hogarth Press, London, 1978), p.147.

23. W.H. Mallock, 'The Political Powers of Labour: Their Extent and their Limitations', Nineteenth Century, vol.60 (1906), p.211.

24. Stead, 'The Labour Party and the Books that Helped to Make It', pp.572, 574, 580.

25. LRC, Annual Report, 1902, pp.17, 19.

26. Ibid., p.12. To discredit Parnell The Times in 1887 printed a facsimile letter, allegedly written by the Irish leader but in fact forged by Richard Piggott.

27. E.J. Hobsbawm, 'The Aristocracy of Labour

Reconsidered', in Michael Flinn (ed.), Proceedings of the Seventh International Economic History Congress (Edinburgh, University Press, 1978), vol.2, p.463.

28. Some of the evidence for this has been discussed by Geoffrey Crossick in ch.1 of a book he edited under the title The Lower Middle Class in Britain, 1870-1914 (Croom Helm, London, 1977).

29. D. Lloyd George, Better Times (Hodder and Stoughton, London 1910), p.331. His attack on the idle rich is on p.339.

30. For instance, in the account of 'the Peckham Crowd' during a by-election of 1908: 'the extraordinary latent forces, so concealed as to be unknown even to themselves, in these shabby, cheery, inefficient multitudes of bewildered and contented men and women, were the dominant impressions of this gigantic entertainment'. The Condition of England (Methuen, London, 1912 ed.), p.112. Cf. Edward David, 'The New Liberalism of C.F.G. Masterman, 1873-1927' in Kenneth D. Brown (ed.), Essays in Anti-Labour History: Responses to the Rise of Labour in Britain (Macmillan, London, 1974), pp.19-21.

31. Report of the Second Annual Conference of the Labour Representation Committee, 1902, p.27.

32. Masterman, Condition of England, p.126. See also Chesterton's comments on Crooks's ability to express 'the popular qualities of the populace' in G. Haw (ed.), From Workhouse to Westminster. The Life Story of Will Crooks MP (Cressett, London, 1897), p. xvii.

33. Robert Tressell, The Ragged Trousered Philanthropists (Panther Books ed., London, 1965), p.142.

34. K.D. Brown, Labour and Unemployment 1900-1914 (David & Charles, Newton Abbot, 1971), passim. An analysis of LRC election addresses shows that unemployment was, after increased working-class representation and the Taff Vale case, the issue most mentioned; among Liberal candidates it came fourteenth in importance. A.K. Russell, Liberal Landslide: The General Election of 1906 (David & Charles, Newton Abbot, 1973), pp.65, 79.

35. The Times, 10 June 1907.

36. D. Clark, Colne Valley: Radicalism to Socialism: The Portrait of a Northern Constituency in the Formative Years of the Labour Party 1890-1910 (Longman, London and New York, 1981), p.152. Grayson also emphasised the difference

between himself and would-be reformers from the middle class when he claimed 'One needs to be poor to study poverty'. Quoted in R. Groves, The Strange Case of Victor Grayson (Pluto Press, London, 1975), p.24.

37. H. Pelling, Popular Politics and Society in late Victorian Britain (Macmillan, London, 1979 ed.), p.135. When the Bill Quay branch of the Associated Society of Shipwrights declined to support Curran, Alex Wilkie MP, the union's general secretary, disowned the action in a telegram pledging 'hearty support' for Curran. The Times, 24 June 1907. Cf. A.W. Purdue, 'Jarrow Politics, 1885-1914: The Challenge to Liberal Hegemony', Northern History, vol. 18 (1982), pp.195-6.

38 Labour Party, Annual Report, 1908, p.53. As an example Appleton said he might speak of an agricultural implement, whereas Curran would term a spade a spade. For his part, Curran, in speaking against Quelch's motion for the overthrow of capitalism, emphasised how well socialists and trade unionists were working together.

39. Clark, Colne Valley, pp.145ff.

40. Details of the voting and subsequent agreement between the Labour Party and the MFGB are given in R. Gregory, The Miners and British Politics 1900-1914 (Oxford, University Press, 1968), ch.3. In Gregory's view, the major role in changing the voting was the propaganda work of ILP members in the coalfields. For the position in Lancashire, see J. Hill, 'The Lancashire Miners, Thomas Greenall and the Labour Party 1900-1906', Transactions of the Historical Society of Lancashire and Cheshire, vol.130 (1981), pp.115-30.

41. The Liberal Year Book for 1914 listed only five 'Liberal & Labour' MPs: the veteran miners' leaders Thomas Burt, Charles Fenwick and John Wilson, John Ward, the navvies' leader, and John Burns.

42. MFGB, Annual Report, 1908, quoted Gregory, Miners and British Politics, p.34.

43. They are listed in ibid., p.43. Glover and Walsh had previously sat as Labour MPs, by virtue of the Lancashire miners' early affiliation; two, Harry Twist and J.E. Sutton, (both officials of the LCMF) were newly elected in 1910; the remainder had been 'Lib-Labs'.

44. Industrial Syndicalist, Jan. 1911, p.15, Mar. 1911, p.21.

45. A History of the National Union of Boot and Shoe Operatives, 1874-1957 (Blackwell, Oxford,

1958), p.337, from a letter in the union's Monthly Report for Dec. 1911.

46. Margaret I. Cole (ed.), Beatrice Webb's Diaries 1912-1924 (Longmans, London, 1952), pp.5, 8. She was writing in 1912.

47. R. Barker, Education and Politics, 1900-1951: A Study of the Labour Party (Clarendon Press, Oxford, 1972), p.8.

48. Marquand, Ramsay MacDonald, p.150; Morgan, Keir Hardie, pp.238-40.

49. W.V. Osborne, Sane Trade Unionism (Collins, London & Glasgow, 1913), p.161.

50. Gregory, Miners and British Politics, p.75.

51. The details are given ibid., pp.156-67, 171-3. In discussing these by-elections, McKibbin concludes that MacDonald's policies were 'both firm and correct' and received less credit than they deserved: R.I. McKibbin, 'James Ramsay MacDonald and the Problem of the Independence of the Labour Party, 1910-1914', Journal of Modern History, vol.42 (1970), p.225.

52. P. Snowden, An Autobiography (2 vols., Nicholson and Watson, London, 1934), vol. 1, p.258.

53. Pelling, Popular Politics and Society, pp.ix-xi, summarises the recent contributions, including Roy Douglas, 'Labour in Decline 1910-14' in Brown, Essays in Anti-Labour History.

54. David Rubinstein, 'Trade Unions, Politicians and Public Opinion 1906-1914', in Ben Pimlott and Chris Cook (eds.), Trade Unions and British Politics (Longman, London, 1982), p.59.

55. R. McKibbin, The Evolution of the Labour Party, 1910-1914 (Oxford, University Press, 1974) p.65, quoting a report made in June 1913 by T.D. Benson.

56. Although by 1918 only eighty or so full-time agents had been appointed; in 1912 there were seventeen. - Ibid., pp.33, 89.

57. Cole, Beatrice Webb's Diaries, p.18.

58. H.M. Drucker, Doctrine and Ethos in the Labour Party (Allen and Unwin, London, 1979), p.9.

Chapter Two

THE LABOUR PARTY IN SCOTLAND

Seven weeks before the Memorial Hall Conference in 1900, 266 delegates met in the Free Gardeners' Hall in Edinburgh and formed the Scottish Workers' Parliamentary Elections Committee to work for 'Direct Independent Working-Class Representation in the House of Commons, and on Local Administrative Bodies'. Such representation was needed to press for 'these important measures of social and industrial reform which are absolutely necessary for the comfort and well-being of the working classes.[1] The conference was quite specific about the issues which it expected an independent party to take up:

> A legal Eight-Hour Day; Old Age Pensions; and ample provision for those Disabled; Accumulative Taxation of Land Values and all other forms of Unearned Income . . .; the organisation by Imperial and Local authorities of self-supporting industries by which the right to work would be secured to everyone, especially in times of trade depression; the fixing of a minimum wage by law, particularly in the sweated trades, as had been done in the colony of Victoria.

An amendment to add nationalisation of the means of production, distribution and exchange was rejected by a large majority.

The delegates came from trades councils, trade unions, the ILP and the SDF, summoned by a resolution of the 1899 Scottish Trades Union Congress. Unlike the London Conference, the Co-operative movement in Scotland was also represented, with delegates from four Co-operative conferences and from fourteen local societies.

This Co-operative representation was to remain a distinctive feature of the Scottish movement and, although Robert Smillie, the Lanarkshire miners' leader, presided over the first conference, the first chairman of the SWPEC was a Co-operator, Henry Murphy of Lanark (a member of the ILP). More than a decade of battling, legally and politically, against an organised boycott of Co-operative societies by private traders had politicised the Scottish movement.

It is not really surprising that the Scots should have pioneered this move to co-ordinate the activities of different groups working to get labour representation. Socialists of diverse views and factious nature had been active in most Scottish cities since the early 1880s. Keir Hardie had declared for independence in the aftermath of the Mid-Lanark by-election of 1888 and from his base in the Scottish Labour Party had campaigned among the trade unions for support for direct labour representation.[2] The beginnings of a trade-union-backed labour party had appeared in 1892 when the Scottish United Trades Councils Labour Party had endorsed seven candidates.[3] But intense personal jealousies and regional diversities caused problems and produced a plethora of, sometimes rival, organisations. Some success had been achieved in local politics and by the end of the 1890s twelve 'Labour' members sat on the Glasgow Town Council, but in national politics there had been little progress. Smillie, in the first of his many by-election defeats, doubled Hardie's 1888 vote in another Mid-Lanark by-election in 1894, but William Maxwell, a leading Co-operator, backed by the ILP into which the Scottish Labour Party had merged, could only manage 448 votes in the Glasgow Blackfriars and Hutchesontown Division in the same year. In the general election of 1895 eight, mainly ILP, candidates stood but showed little improvement on the 1892 results. The most spectacular result came the following year in Aberdeen, an area where an active group of radicals and socialists had for a decade gone their own way in defiance of any west of Scotland domination. They had retained a fierce loyalty to H. H. Champion, who stood in the constituency in 1892, and a deep-seated suspicion of Keir Hardie. At the North Aberdeen by-election in 1896 Tom Mann came within 500 votes of defeating the Liberal candidate in a straight fight.[4]

In the west of Scotland the ILP was by far the strongest influence among politically active trade unionists and the first Parliamentary Committee of the STUC, formed in 1897, had eight ILP supporters among its eleven members. Smillie, the chairman of the STUC, and George Carson, its secretary, both close associates of Hardie, were the moving forces behind the initial steps at the congress that led to the 1900 conference.[5] No doubt the experience of the Edinburgh conference stood Hardie and his ILP associates in good stead when it came to managing the meeting in the Memorial Hall. Significantly, it was the Glasgow-based ILPer Joseph Burgess, who attended both conferences, who kept the LRC at a manageable twelve members just like the Scottish Committee, with its four trade unionists, four Co-operative delegates, two ILPers and two from the SDF.[6]

There was little chance for the new organisation to make much progress before it was faced with the 1900 Khaki election. The committee endorsed only the anti-war journalist, A.E. Fletcher, the ILP candidate in Glasgow Camlachie, who stood as a Labour candidate though with no Liberal opposition. It declined to support William Maxwell in the Tradeston Division because he took the Liberal label, though individual members of the committee did speak in his support.[7] Also the STUC and the Glasgow Trades Council gave support to five Liberal candidates in Glasgow divisions.[8] Although there was strong anti-war sentiment in Scotland it was more than balanced by jingoism and imperialism and for the first time since 1832 Scotland returned a majority of Conservatives and Unionists. Even in that election, however, Liberals still managed to get more than fifty per cent of the votes. Old Liberal issues like religion, temperance and land reform, which south of the border had an increasingly dated look, still had an appeal in Scotland.

I

With the establishment of the LRC the issue of the two committees' areas of jurisdiction was quickly raised. MacDonald confirmed that all north of the Tweed was for the Scottish committee, but he was not willing to allow the Scots to approach unions whose membership spanned the border for contributions in proportion to their Scottish

membership.[9]   Indeed, MacDonald was soon pressing
one union, the Amalgamated Railway Servants, to pay
for its Scottish members.[10]  A yet further
complication arose when the Postmen's Federation,
which had its headquarters in Glasgow, sought
affiliation to the LRC.[11]  MacDonald, of course,
had his own financial worries and he was anxious
not to have appeals to unions coming from two
different directions.  The Scottish committee, on
the other hand, was dependent on voluntary payments
and needed to be able to appeal as widely as
possible, especially since the number of
specifically Scottish unions was in decline.  A
meeting of representatives of the Scottish
committee with Hardie and MacDonald did little to
resolve the differences.  The LRC delegates would
not negotiate on the issue and MacDonald caused
great offence by suggesting that the two commitees
be 'centralised in one', the Scottish conference
abolished, and a local committee appointed to look
after things in Scotland.[12]  It was clear that
those Scots who had taken the high road to London
and were well represented in the inner councils of
the LRC had little sympathy with the nationalist
sentiments of their fellow countrymen.
     The Scottish committee had other problems.
The SWPEC was not recognised as the sole body for
co-ordinating political action.  There were already
a number of active local municipal committees and
by encouraging the establishment of local LRCs the
SWPEC found that it was impinging upon existing
local bodies.  Important feathers were ruffled when
it was suggested that new local committees should
undertake local as well as parliamentary work.[13]
Again there were difficulties in too many appeals
for limited financial support and for many
political activists success in local politics
undoubtedly seemed a much more realistic and,
probably, more important prospect than the
hopelessness of most general elections.  The
Glasgow Trades Council, by far the largest of the
Scottish councils, and, as a result, generally a
law unto itself, directly challenged the authority
of the new body by organising its own conference of
labour and socialist representatives in September
1900 without any reference to the committee.[14]
     Not surprisingly, there were also considerable
differences over policy and tactics.  The SDF was
particularly vocal at the first annual conference,
getting nationalisation of land, railways and mines
made a plank in the committee's platform, but the

same conference reversed a previous decision that sponsored candidates should not appear on the platform of candidates from other parties.[15] As a result of this, the SDF, which in Glasgow contained a strong 'impossibilist' element that was soon to lead to a break with Hyndman, disaffiliated. Nevertheless, with delegates at the 1901 conference from 20 co-operatives, 80 trades councils and trade unions as well as from socialist groups, the committee could claim to be widely representative.

A new test came in September 1901 at a by-election in North-East Lanarkshire, the heart of the iron and steel industry and one of the largest mining constituencies. The Scottish Liberals had been anxious for some time to rally support among miners. In Fife and Midlothian they had been cultivating the miners' leaders and encouraging the view that they would not oppose a miners' candidate.[16] At least some Liberal MPs recommended that a miners' candidate be accepted in North-East Lanarkshire, but local Liberals strongly resented this.[17] The initiative in selecting a labour candidate came from a local committee, pulled together by Joseph Burgess.[18] The choice for candidate fell on Smillie and his campaign was financed largely by the miners, who, since 1900, had been committed to promoting labour representation. The miners' union put up some £400, while Hodge's steel smelters' union, on the other hand, gave a mere £18 and the SWPEC could manage only £25.[19] This was an area where about a third of the electorate were miners, though by no means all of them were unionised; perhaps more significantly, it was also an area which had about the largest Irish vote in Scotland.[20]

The issues were South Africa and Irish Home Rule and focused on the attitudes of the Liberal Imperialist candidate, Cecil Harmsworth. Because of Harmsworth's known luke-warmness to Home Rule, reflected in the Harmsworth-owned Glasgow newspapers, Smillie was the approved candidate of the United Irish League and William Redmond and other Irish Parliamentary Party members spoke for him in the constituency. But it is clear that for many of the Catholic population in an area where even the Co-operative society was split on religious lines it was too much to accept this Ulster Scot. The debates within the Irish community went on right up to polling day.[21] In addition, the miners' vote was further divided by

Chisholm Robertson, who campaigned against Smillie, in association with some miners who objected to the union's political involvement. Robertson's Central Miners' Union was strong among the Irish Catholic miners of the Bellshill district and was poaching in the area of the Lanarkshire County Union. Rivalry between Robertson and Smillie had existed for a number of years and Smillie had recently been largely instrumental in having Robertson ousted from the presidency of the Glasgow Trades Council, after a public denunciation for financial malpractice. The rivalry had deep roots, to a large extent in the ambition and tetchiness of Chisholm Robertson. He suggested that 'No Catholic should vote Socialist', and was eventually expelled from the United Irish League for his activities.[22] Unofficial strike action among steel workers at Mossend meant that John Hodge's endorsement was of doubtful utility to Smillie and, in the end, his respectable 2,900 votes had clearly made only limited inroads into traditional voting patterns.[23]

At the 1902 conference there were further pleas for consolidation of the various bodies 'into a working class party' and the committee's name was changed into the Scottish Workers' Representation Committee (not to the Scottish Workers' Party as Smillie wanted).[24] The financial problems of the committee would not go away, however, and at the beginning of 1902 it had only £8 in hand. A mere £19. 16s had been subscribed by 24 unions; the only British unions were three branches of the Amalgamated Railway Servants and a branch of the National Labourers' Union; the only trades council was Glasgow; the only miners' union was Lanarkshire, and it contributed a quarter of the total income from unions. With £3. 7s from the ILP and £44. 15s from the 15 Co-operative societies there was little margin. The committee decided again to approach the executives of British unions for the Scottish proportion of the fees paid to the LRC and this brought the wrath of MacDonald upon their heads.[25] There was another acrimonious exchange of letters and another conciliation meeting. The result was disastrous.

A working arrangement for a common fund and common constitution was devised, but, whereas MacDonald assumed that this meant a pooled fund, the Scottish committee insisted that 'Scottish societies contribute to the common fund through the Scottish committee' and that the Scots be

43

represented on a new committee to disburse the fund.[26] The Scottish committee, with all the sensitivity of the weak, seems to have assumed some kind of equality with the LRC, which MacDonald was never going to accept. Nonetheless, a joint parliamentary fund was established though MacDonald was soon complaining about the small sums coming from Scotland. A meeting at the Scots' request, this time with Arthur Henderson, to discuss affiliation to the LRC tried to find a compromise. Now, however, the LRC refused to allow two Scots on the financial sub-committee and instead offered them two places on the executive of the LRC. While that was acceptable, a demand from London for an affiliation fee of 15s per 1000 members was rejected on the grounds that it would absorb all the Scottish funds.[27] By 1904 MacDonald was convinced of 'the deadness of the Scottish Committee' and talked of 'the imminent necessity of taking over the whole country'.[28] Separation also presented many practical problems and candidates for Scottish seats who were backed by British unions, like Barnes in Glasgow, Wilkie in Dundee and Hill in Govan, were on the LRC list of candidates.

Meanwhile, most initiatives were being taken outside the SWRC. In line with the MFGB, the Scottish Miners' Federation had agreed after a ballot in 1901 to contest seats at the next general election and it was the federation which backed John Robertson in another North-East Lanarkshire by-election in 1904. The sitting LRC members issued a manifesto in his support.[29] The SWRC issued a pamphlet on Chinese Labour in South Africa to coincide with the campaign.[30] It also tried to get support from the Irish nationalists but without success and, although he had backing from all the labour organisations in Lanarkshire, Robertson still tended to be seen as 'the miners' candidate'.[31] Nonetheless, he succeeded in adding more than a thousand to Smillie's 1901 vote.

II

The MacDonald-Gladstone agreement did not cover Scotland and in the 1906 election all the Labour candidates had to face Liberal opposition. The lack of some agreement was not for want of trying on the part of the Liberals. They had been anxious about the emergence of independent labour since the 1890s and had a committee since 1894 that hoped for future negotiations with the leaders of the Independent Labour Party 'if opportunity should occur'.[32] In 1900 the West Fife Liberals would have been prepared to accept a miners' candidate, but John Weir, the much-respected but aged Fife miners' leader, declined to stand.[33] The issue surfaced again for the Liberals in 1902 when the miners announced plans to put up Smillie in South Ayrshire and when Barnes was adopted as Labour candidate for Blackfriars and Hutchesontown. There was considerable Liberal opposition to any suggestion that seats might be handed over to the ILP, but the Liberal leadership was keen for talks. Smillie was prepared to withdraw from South Ayrshire if the Liberals in North-East Lanarkshire would accept a Labour candidate.[34] When this proved impossible to arrange, a meeting between the committee of the Scottish Liberal Association and four representatives of the Scottish Miners' Federation resulted only in a refusal by the miners to consider any 'working arrangement or understanding . . . between the Miners' Federation and any Political Party'.[35] In his first speech after adoption for Blackfriars, Barnes emphasised that he would have no dealing with the Liberal Party and he spurned approaches from the local Liberals.[36] In spite of these rebuffs the Scottish Liberals set up a Conciliation Committee that 'should direct its attention, not merely to obviating electoral disputes between Liberal and Labour Candidates, but should also endeavour to unite all the progressive forces'.[37] In the end it was never asked to act and other approaches to Labour met only a reaffirmation of independence.[38]

There were only two successful candidates in the 1906 election, both of whom were backed by the LRC. George Barnes, the secretary of the ASE, defeated Bonar Law and a Liberal in Blackfriars. His success has generally been explained as the result of Labour getting the Irish vote due to the lack of Liberal commitment to Home Rule.[39] Certainly John Redmond, the UIL and the veteran Glasgow-Irish political organiser, John Ferguson, all recommended support for Barnes, as they did for two other Labour candidates, Burgess in Camlachie and Sullivan in Lanarkshire.[40] But with just over a thousand Irish voters and the Irish organisation split on the issue, Barnes must have attracted considerably wider support and the Liberal view was that he took votes equally from

45

Liberals and Conservatives.

The one other successful candidate was the shipwrights' secretary and member of the LRC executive, Alexander Wilkie in Dundee. Dundee had a Central Workers' Committee which had been active since before 1900. The SDF secretary of the London Trades Council, James Macdonald, had stood in 1892 and in 1895. Even earlier, in an 1889 by-election, when the Dundee Labour Electoral Association had threatened to put up John Burns against the Liberal newspaper proprietor, Sir John Leng, there seems to have been one of these not untypical half-promises of a future Lib-Lab candidate.[41] In 1900 the Dundee Workers' Committee had been keen to get Barnes as a candidate, but, at this stage, the ASE would not agree to his standing against a Liberal.[42] With rumours of Leng's resignation in 1901 an approach was made to Smillie, though he too refused.[43] In 1902 Barnes had actually got to the position of negotiating with Leng, but eventually opted for Blackfriars. The local committee then adopted W.F. Black of the Labour Leader, but he dropped out at the end of 1904 when the publication of the Leader was moved to Manchester. Wilkie was adopted in 1905 and seems to have expected Liberal backing in this two-member constituency. However, a group of Liberal worthies split over the selection and went ahead to choose their own candidate, a London barrister, giving great offence to working-class Liberals.[44]

Wilkie ran a lavish campaign with a proliferation of posters throughout the constituency, 'squandering money like water on torchlight processions, magic lantern entertainments, rosettes and other flummery of the Barnum and Bailey order', according to the hostile press.[45] He succeeded in splitting the two Liberals and coming second. There is no doubt that Wilkie attracted Liberal votes and, indeed, he went out of his way to present himself as a progressive, emphasising the help he had given to John Morley at Newcastle in 1892 and 1895 and managing to avoid altogether the use of the word 'Labour' in his election address. David Shackleton, speaking for him, stressed that the 'Labour Party was going to be the left wing of the Liberal Party, pushing them on to work'.[46] How much Irish support he got is not possible to assess. He was not endorsed by the UIL but he must have picked up some Irish backing in this large Irish constituency.

The miners' candidates, John Robertson in

North-East Lanarkshire, Joseph Sullivan in North-West Lanarkshire, Smillie in Paisley (an odd choice since there were few miners in the constituency), James Brown in North Ayrshire and David Gilmour in Falkirk Burghs all came bottom of the poll, as did the boilermakers-backed John Hill in Govan and the ILP's Burgess in Glasgow Camlachie. But the intervention of Hill and of Sullivan was enough to lose the Liberals the seats. In North Aberdeen, the SDF put up Thomas Kennedy, their organising secretary in Scotland. What made this a particularly interesting contest was that the Conservative candidate was the 'Tory Democrat', Maltman Barrie, who still retained credentials in this area from his days as an associate of H.H. Champion and who still had as his main platform support for a legislative eight-hour day.[47] Reputedly, there were letters from Champion giving backing to Barrie and claiming also the support of Tom Mann, who was in Australia at the time.[48] Kennedy got the support of the trades council only grudgingly and his candidature was unrelentingly opposed by Joseph Duncan, secretary of the Fishermen's Union and the ablest of the young ILPers. He objected to the way in which Kennedy's candidature had been imposed by the SDF without any consultation with other labour groups.[49] Nonetheless, Kennedy managed nearly 2,000 votes and pushed Barrie into third place.

The limited success of Labour in the 1906 election and the weakness of the SWRC sometimes seem at odds with the extraordinary amount of labour activity in Scotland in these years. Glasgow alone had the SDF and its purist breakaway, the Socialist Labour Party, a very active ILP, Clarion Scouts, Clarion Glee Clubs, ILP choirs and speakers' clubs, socialist Sunday schools, socialist rambling clubs, Fabians, Women's Labour League and the Labour Army. John Wheatley was launching the Catholic Socialist Society and there was a strong and politically active trades council. The Labour Leader was published in Glasgow until 1904, when it was moved to Manchester, but Tom Johnston, a young Fabian, started Forward in 1906 to publicise socialist views. On Sunday evenings the Clarion Scouts or the ILP could pack hundreds into the Albion Halls or into the Pavilion Theatre to hear samples of the whole range of British left-wing thought. Forward vans and Clarion vans toured the country with speakers. During the summer months open-air meetings were held in rural areas and in holiday resorts. Literature from the Reformers' Bookstall and the Civic Press was widely distributed and Liberal organisers enviously contrasted Labour literature sales with their own difficulties in getting supporters to buy, let alone read, the material which they produced. The strongest element was the ILP, which doubled its membership between 1906 and 1908, by which time there were 130 branches in Scotland, though the SDF also was actively recruiting in Fife as well as in its traditional Glasgow and Lanarkshire areas.[50]

Yet despite all this surface activity the movement was not really strong. A small number of activists hogged a disproportionate amount of attention. A great deal of effort was still concentrated in Lanarkshire and the west of Scotland, so much so that James Leatham in Aberdeenshire warned, 'You cannot carry the Social Revolution in Glasgow alone!'[51] Trade union involvement was very slight and it was difficult to get them to take part in what were often seen as essentially miners' political activities. Scottish unions were weak both numerically and financially, touching only a small proportion of the workforce. Even in the heartland it was hardly gaining ground. Gone were the days of the late 1890s when a dozen Labour 'stalwarts' had swept into the Glasgow Town Council on a wave of enthusiasm for municipalisation and in harmony with the Irish political machine. By 1907 the cosy arrangement with the Irish League had broken down and there was only one independent Labour member on the corporation. In 1908 seven Labour candidates went down to defeat. Even among the miners, whilst a majority was clearly in favour of affiliation to the Labour Party, a smaller proportion of the extended membership voted for it in 1908 than had done so in 1906. Elsewhere, there was often enthusiasm and little else. In the South Aberdeen by-election of January 1907 Fred Bramley, the candidate, was only selected ten days before the election and halfway into the campaign the local committee had succeeded in raising only £10.[52] It was also a bitterly divided movement. Its supporters saw themselves as in competition with the ILP, and when Joseph Duncan was organising in Fife for the ILP he, on more than one occasion, found John MacLean and the SDF people nipping in and setting up a branch a few days before he arrived.[53]

The emerging labour movement was also confronting a Liberal Party in which attitudes were hardening. With all efforts at compromise rebuffed and stung by defeats and near-defeats attributed to Labour intervention, many Scottish Liberals were demanding a counter-attack. In Dundee, local Liberals were threatening to discontinue their payments to party funds unless socialism was confronted.[54] After the particular bitterness of a by-election defeat at Cockermouth caused by Smillie's intervention, the Scottish Whip, the Master of Elibank, talked of the possible need for 'a crusade against socialism' and warned that 'unless the Liberal Party stood upon its own legs its very vitals would be consumed and it would fall between two stools, and disappear as an active force in British politics'.[55] There was at least some talk among Liberals and Unionists of ways of avoiding three-cornered fights. In local elections distinctions between liberalism and conservatism were increasingly being submerged in a crude anti-socialism united behind one candidate.[56]

III

The issue of relations between the Labour Party and the SWRC still hung fire and a new agreement was worked out with MacDonald, Henderson and Pete Curran in June 1906. By this an attempt was made to retain a distinctive existence for a Scottish committee whilst getting closer co-operation. In fact, the Scottish committee would be powerless since it could not place any candidates on the common parliamentary fund, and if Scottish unions wanted a man placed on the Labour Party's list of candidates they had to contribute to the parliamentary fund and also pay an affiliation fee to the SWRC. The committee now became the Labour Party (Scottish Section).[57] Once again the agreement broke down with the Scots failing to pay the affiliation fees and MacDonald complaining of the failure to levy the Scottish unions. During 1907 there were a number of requests to MacDonald from Scottish unions for affiliation to the Labour party. The Associated Blacksmiths were the most persistent, but the Aberdeen LRC also sought membership.[58] At the 1908 Labour Party conference in Hull it was recommended that in future, 'failing a satisfactory arrangement with the Scottish Labour Party', requests for affiliation from Scottish societies should be accepted. The Scottish section now again insisted on a fraction of funds from national societies and from the Scottish ILP branches.[59]

By now relations were clearly hopelessly embittered between the two organisations and made worse by the tensions aroused in the series of by-elections that followed the retirement of Campbell-Bannerman. Joseph Burgess stood as a socialist candidate against Robert Vernon-Harcourt in John Morley's old seat of Montrose Burghs, backed by a lively ILP and SDF group which had been talking about a labour candidate since 1902. Burgess was a well-known activist in Glasgow ILP circles, though he had recently returned to Bradford to edit the Yorkshire Factory Times. He went out of his way to emphasise his socialism and although the STUC and the Scottish Section supported him only Hardie and Snowden from the PLP spoke for him. Arthur Henderson refused a telegram of support, although Burgess was an endorsed candidate.[60] He was able, however, to push the Unionist into third place.

The candidacy of G.H. Stuart in Dundee was more divisive. Stuart was backed by the Postmen's Federation and in contrast to Burgess, played down any socialism, explicitly denying that he was a member of the ILP or the SDF or the SLP. Indeed, at least some of the Dundee labour movement objected to his lack of socialism. Nevertheless, in his speeches he favoured extensive nationalisation of land, railways and the means of production. The Scottish Section gave backing to Stuart as candidate for the second Dundee seat against Churchill, who was seeking a replacement for his lost Manchester seat. However, the NEC decided 'that both seats in double-barrelled constituencies should not be fought at present' and refused to sanction Stuart's candidature.[61] Wilkie conspicuously absented himself from the constituency and only Hardie and J.A. Seddon came to speak for Stuart. On the other hand, he did get a telegram of support from the Parliamentary Committee of the TUC and from George Barnes.[62] The Dundee Courier, embarking on a feud with Churchill that was to continue through to the Second World War, gave extensive coverage to Stuart's campaign, revelling in his descriptions of Churchill as 'a slippery gentleman', 'a fraudulent and dishonest politician' and 'no friend to the workers'.[63] However, the Labour cause itself was

split by the presence of the monomaniac pro-
hibitionist 'Labour' candidate, Edwin Scrymgeour,
though, even without that, Churchill was safely
returned.[64]

The Labour Party's actions in this by-election
left a disillusioned membership in Dundee and
members dropped away.[65] For the Scottish Section
the consequences were even more serious. The NEC
now decided to use this as an excuse to go ahead
and affiliate Scottish societies and to plan their
own candidates for Scottish seats. Further efforts
at compromise during the summer of 1908 came to
nothing and there was clearly a growing feeling in
Scotland that the position had to be
regularised.[66] When the miners and the one
remaining large union, the Scottish Ironmoulders,
affiliated to the Labour Party, it was all over.
At the ninth conference, in spite of complaints
about the English 'treating Scotland as a
province', it was accepted that the unsound
financial position ruled out independence. Smillie
condemned those unions that had failed to give the
committee adequate support, while John Robertson
blamed the divisiveness of the SDF in a speech
scorned by Shinwell as a 'multitudinous mass of
platitudinous nonsense'.[67] Amid such mutual
recrimination, that somehow summed up the problems
of the Scottish labour movement, the Scottish
committee voted itself out of existence and agreed
to 'approach the Labour Party with a proposal to
establish a Scottish Committee to be directly
financed and controlled by the Labour Party'.[68]

The Scottish Workers' Committee, under its
changing names, had never really succeeded in
establishing itself as the decisive focus of
independent labour activity. Hamstrung by
financial inadequacy right from the start it was
never able to give a clear directional lead to the
movement. It could not impose its authority or
even enforce payment of dues from affiliated
unions. After a formal system of affiliation fees
had been agreed in 1904 only thirteen unions
actually paid them.[69] At first it was identified
with Smillie and the miners, but they soon went
their own way as part of the miners' political
movement rather than of a wider Scottish labour
organization. The secretary, George Carson, while
no doubt a competent enough administrator and
well-liked within the movement, combined the job
with the secretaryship of the Glasgow Trades
Council and of the STUC and never gave any kind of

leadership. It attracted few leading unionists after about 1904 and was run by some worthy, but second-rank figures. Increasingly, it just ceased to matter and was ignored by local committees. At the same time, there seems little doubt that from a very early date MacDonald and most the NEC were out to kill the separate Scottish activities. The last thing they wanted was the continuation of the regional proliferation of groups that had bedevilled the movement for a decade or more. Central co-ordination and control was the essence of their policy and as long as the Scottish committee existed it was a potential obstacle to that.

IV

At the first of the 1910 elections, with three more candidates than in 1906, the Labour vote in Scotland more than doubled, though this was nothing when compared to the advances made in Wales. Wilkie, this time with no second Liberal opposing him, held Dundee. Barnes, also with no Liberal opposition, held Blackfriars. These were the only successes. Burgess, against the advice of the NAC of the ILP and unendorsed by the Labour Party, once again fought Montrose Burghs. He was left to raise his own funds and conduct his own struggles against incursions from neighbouring Dundee by Churchill, who described Burgess as 'a socialist jackal'. He had also to face denunciations (from the pulpit of the parish church) of socialism as 'the modern Anti-Christ'.[70] The SDF's Tom Kennedy in North Aberdeen, this time with rather wider backing from within the local labour movement though still refusing to sign the party constitution, did less well than he had done in 1906. In Leith, William Walker, backed by the Amalgamated Carpenters, came a poor third; O'Connor Kessack of the ILP went down in Camlachie as did J.T. Brownlie of the ASE in Govan. The miners' candidates were no more successful. Sullivan was bottom in North-East Lanarkshire, Robert Small was squeezed out in the North-West division in a bitter sectarian battle between a Liberal Home Ruler and a fanatical Orangeman Conservative candidate, and even miners' trade-union officials who were Irish worked for the Liberals.[71] Smillie in his home territory of Mid-Lanark and James Brown in North Ayrshire were no more successful. There was, in fact, no sign of

Labour building on earlier campaigns and, except in Dundee and Blackfriars, the only two constituencies in which the Irish were advised to vote Labour, Labour candidates did substantially worse in the seven seats contested in both 1906 and 1910.

The one spark of hope came in West Fife where William Adamson, secretary of the Fife miners, polled 4,736 votes in his first contest. Eleven months later, in spite of decisions in the Court of Session paralleling the Osborne judgement, he was successful. Adamson's success seems to have been due largely to the remarkable organising skills of his agent, J.C. Macbeth, and of the miners' political organiser, William Watson.[72] They succeeded in getting some 25 per cent of the electors who had not voted in January to turn out for Adamson and, in a straight fight with a sitting Liberal, Adamson became the first Scottish miners' member. Wilkie and Barnes were again safely returned with no Liberal opposition, though the latter had to contend with SDF posters advising electors to 'Vote against the candidate who supports the Liberal Government'. Smillie found his usual place at the bottom of the Mid-Lanark poll, while O'Connor Kessack, the only other candidate, lost ground in Camlachie to a Liberal who accepted most of the Labour programme.[73] Elsewhere lack of money and lack of adequate organisation prevented action, though in Aberdeen the SDF, in another piece of mischief-making, withdrew Kennedy just before the election and too late for an ILP candidate to be put up.[74]

The NEC showed considerable concern at the lack of success in Scotland and a series of conferences was held in 1911 and 1912 to look at organisation. There was a double problem, for both internal cohesion and popular support were lacking. Various reasons were pinpointed for the weakness: firstly, a lack of effective and continuing local organisations between elections; secondly, a concentration on Lanarkshire at the expense of other areas; thirdly, a division produced by religious sectarianism which weakened unions and political groupings and, according to some, was not helped by the party in Parliament taking up 'political' issues (sc. Irish Home Rule) at the expense of 'economic' ones; fourthly, fear of letting Unionists in as a result of three-cornered fights deterred many voters, though frequently the leading activists were violently anti-Liberal and critical of the PLP's collaborative activities in Parliament.[75]

Such issues and tensions were all too apparent in the Kilmarnock by-election of September 1911 when Labour intervened against the Liberal W.G.C. Gladstone. Labour's choice, Thomas McKerrell, was a strong candidate in this constituency, made up of the heavily industrial towns of Kilmarnock, Port Glasgow, Rutherglen, Dunbarton and Renfrew, where, it was claimed, five out of six of the voters were working class. He was a miners' agent for Hardie's Ayrshire Miners' Union and had served on Kilmarnock town council. The Liberals had wanted this by-election to be a straight fight with the Conservatives in order to focus exclusively on the issue of Irish Home Rule as some kind of test of public opinion, only to find themselves on the defensive and faced with unwelcome questions of women's suffrage and social policy.[76] Their parliamentary allies, the Irish Party and the Labour Party were publicly at odds. Irish parliamentarians worked to keep the two thousand Irish in the constituency on the Liberal side, so that Hardie angrily warned that the Irish Home Rule Bill was not yet through, and if the Irish Party continued to oppose Labour candidates 'the working men will have a word to say before Home Rule becomes law'.[77] In spite of considerable effort, McKerrell polled only 2,761 votes to the Liberal's 6,923 and the Conservative's 4,637. Labour had not been successful in winning trade-union support and attempts to do so had merely revealed deep divisions: trade unionists had shown themselves to be 'either good nationalists or good orangemen'.[78] All that had been gained was a further embittering of relations with the Liberals. As a result of what were perceived as 'Labour's unscrupulous tactics' at Kilmarnock, the Dundee Liberal Association agreed that at the next election, it would run two candidates to squeeze out Wilkie.[79]

There was an acceptance in London that Scottish issues were different and that some kind of Scottish committee was required. What was not so readily agreed was the structure of such a committee. Conferences were held in Aberdeen, Dundee, Edinburgh and Glasgow in August 1912 and the recommendations of these reflected the structure and tensions within the labour movements in these areas. In Aberdeen, where the struggle between SDF and ILP had been going on since the 1890s, the ILP committee wanted strong trade-union representation. The Dundee committee, now at odds with Wilkie, wanted no special trade-union representation and a Scottish council, with delegates from each constituency possessing organisations affiliated to the Labour Party. Edinburgh proposed a committee on a geographical basis selected by ballot of affiliated societies. Glasgow, caught up in its own internal reorganisation, failed to submit an opinion.[80]

While these meetings were being held yet another by-election opportunity arose, with the resignation of the Master of Elibank from Midlothian. The Scottish Miners' Federation annual conference was in session at the time and this fortuitous combination of circumstances allowed a quick nomination of Robert Brown as Labour candidate. Brown was the long-time secretary of the Lothian Miners and a provost of Dalkeith, the main town in the constituency. On the one hand, the miners' action was a determined assertion of independence from the Liberals in the immediate aftermath of the Hanley by-election; on the other hand, in selecting Brown they were clearly taking someone who might be acceptable to the Liberals. Brown, whom <u>Forward</u> described as 'an old Liberal henchman', had blocked a Labour candidate standing against Elibank in January 1910 and perhaps in return for this, Elibank recommended the avoidance of a three-cornered fight, giving approval to Brown as 'a thoroughly experienced politician of wide sympathies, sound commonsense and strong progressive views.[81]' But again the Gladstonian connection of this seat made it one of great symbolic importance and the local Liberals rejected Elibank's advice.

Two issues at the front of the campaign were land reform, with Brown campaigning for nationalisation of the mines and of land, and the National Insurance Act of which he was critical. The 600–700 Irish miners were advised by the United Irish League to vote Liberal, but, it was claimed that a majority supported Brown. In the event, a Liberal majority of over 3,000 in December 1910 was overturned and the Unionist candidate squeezed in with a majority of 32. Brown's 2,413 had been enough to shatter the Liberal heartland.[82]

At the end of 1912 the NEC decided to go ahead with a Scottish Advisory Council of delegates from the Scottish trade unions, the Scottish district councils of British unions, affiliated LRCs, trades councils, the Scottish ILP Council and the Women's

Labour League. Henderson's rather too blatant compromise of giving trade unions strong representation at the annual conference, but weak representation on the executive committee inevitably caused complaints. Smillie and the miners, in particular, objected to this, while the north of England, in the shape of Tom Shaw of the textile workers, protested at preferential treatment for Scotland. The scheme was thrown out by the 1913 conference and had to be revised to give more power to the unions. The proposals were adopted in the following year, though even then, there were northern complaints that Scotland was being given a special position.[83]

The penultimate pre-war by-election came in December 1913 when the miners put up Tom Gibb in South Lanark. Gibb generally stayed clear of the Irish issue, but with a large agricultural work force and only twenty per cent of the electorate miners it was not a promising area. Gibb was, however, a well-known protestant evangelical lay preacher and he blamed racial and religious prejudices for his defeat, though he also apparently failed to get the railwaymen's vote.[84] His 1674 votes, however, were enough to lose the Liberals the seat and hand it to the Unionists. A similar splitting of the Liberal vote came in February 1914 at Leith when J.N. Bell, general secretary of the National Amalgamated Union of Labour, stood. Bell campaigned largely on the need for more labour representation and little else. But Home Rule was the overshadowing issue, with the Scotsman warning of impending civil war. The estimated 1,800 Irish voters were again instructed to back the Liberal, but with Bell getting a quarter of the votes, the Unionists managed a majority of sixteen.[85]

In spite of a lack of success in national politics, there were a few signs that Labour was making inroads into the consciousness of Scottish workers. In unions like the important Associated Ironmoulders younger socialist officials were taking over from retiring Lib-Labs. Organisation was being worked at. The ILP appointed John Taylor as full-time organiser in the west in 1910. The local LRC in Dundee appointed a registration agent and organiser in 1909 and for a year had managed to publish a monthly magazine.[86] Some important advances were also taking place in municipal politics. After years in the doldrums labour representation on the Glasgow town council began to increase from 1910 onwards. Labour made three gains in 1910, another four in 1911 and, with extended city boundaries in 1912 yet another four, including the indefatigible John Wheatley. Just before the war some seventeen could be claimed as labour councillors, though not all were amenable to party discipline. Edinburgh elected its first labour councillors in 1909 and, on the eve of war, had six. Over Scotland as a whole the Labour Party had 69 town councillors and 13 county councillors by 1915.[87] The issue of housing was becoming particularly important and Labour, with a commitment to cheap housing, was offering a distinctive alternative to other parties. Also, in local politics the division was increasingly between Conservatism and Socialism.

Linked with these successes and, perhaps in the long term more important, were improvements in political organisation. Since at least 1910 attempts had been made to co-ordinate the activities of the various local electoral groups, socialist parties, trades councils and Co-operatives, all of whom liked to involve themselves in elections. It had proved difficult to overcome the barrier of inflated amour propre among the members, but eventually a Glasgow Labour Party was formed in March 1912 to organise both local and parliamentary activity, though at the price of losing Co-operative support. The Co-operators wanted a more broadly based 'Progressive Party' that would admit those who were not eligible for membership of the Labour Party.[88] Even after that, however, it required some fine diplomacy to persuade the trades council to surrender its Labour Party affiliation to the new body. In Aberdeen and Edinburgh also Labour Parties came into existence, though generally confining themselves to local politics, and, as in the case of Aberdeen, often not including some of the most dynamic elements in the labour movement. There were also considerable efforts made to persuade trade unions to take advantage of the 1913 Act and ballot in favour of political action.

Even more important organisational advances were made with registration. The fact that so many potential Labour voters never found their way on to the electoral role had long been recognised as a major weakness and admonitions to work for registration had been frequent in the labour press. Generally, however, the activists had preferred the thrill of the street corner meeting to the anonymity of door to door canvassing. From 1910 onwards, inspired by William Watson's success in organising the Fife vote, the miners in particular took up the problem of registration. A key area was that of the lodger franchise. The annual registration of lodgers before the sheriff had generally been carried out by mutual agreement between Liberal and Unionist agents to accept lodgers in houses above a certain rental. In Mid-Lanark this was as high as £18. The effect was, of course, to exclude working-class lodgers and Duncan Graham claimed that in 1910 there was not a single mining village in the whole of Mid- and North-East Lanarkshire that had a lodger vote. He found that only 45 out of 475 lodgers in Mid-Lanark and 145 out of 1138 lodgers in North-East were miners. Graham now proceeded to challenge the whole basis of lodger representation and insisted that discrimination on grounds of rental should be abolished. He proposed instead that agents agree to one lodger for a two apartment house, two from a three apartment and so on. When this was resisted he organised the flooding of the registration court with claims and insisted on the personal appearance of middle-class lodgers. As a result agreement was reached that two lodger claims be 'admitted from a room and kitchen house irrespective of rent . . . an additional lodger claim to be admitted from each additional room',[89] an agreement that speaks volumes about the state of Lanarkshire housing. By 1913 the number of miners' lodgers had increased thirteen fold. From Lanarkshire Graham moved into Ayrshire and was able to force a similar agreement. In the east William Watson continued his work on these lines in Fife and in Midlothian.

As the pinnacle of all this new organisational fervour, the inaugural meeting of the new Scottish Advisory Council was planned for August 1914. In the event, it had to be postponed and it was not until a year later that the new body was launched with Ben Shaw, secretary of the Glasgow Labour Party, as its secretary and treasurer. At its first meeting, Shaw, who had been in post since March 1914, was able to review the state of Scottish organisation: 15 divisional Labour Parties, 15 local LRCs, several miners' political associations, 14 trades councils, 40 British trade unions, 6 Scottish trade unions, the Scottish ILP Council, 12 Women's Labour League branches and 3 Fabian Societies. However, not affiliated were 25

Scottish trades councils, 39 purely Scottish trade unions, and 71 British unions with Scottish members. Nonetheless, the new body was recognised as the Labour Party in Scotland and in the most likely constituencies the selection of candidates was well advanced.[90] What was not solved was the problem of the new body's powers nor its relationship to head office. The issue of devolved authority in Scotland was for long to prove an intractable one.

V

The remarkable feature of pre-war Scottish politics was the ability of the Liberal Party to retain its support among the Scottish working class. The issues that Liberalism stood for still had an appeal. There were few signs that a belief in free trade was seriously questioned in a country whose leading industries were so dependent on exports. The issue of land reform, with both urban and rural problems blamed on the rapacity of Tory landowners, still won votes for Liberals at least until 1911 when the much watered down Scottish Smallholders' Act was eventually passed. It is significant that Tom Johnston's most successful book, Our Noble Families, serialised in the pages of Forward, was a vitriolic attack on landlordism and that he and other Labour people were behind the relaunching of the Highland League. As long as such issues remained at the forefront Liberals were going to retain support. Temperance too was seen as vital and there was hardly a Labour candidate who did not preface his election statements with assurances that he had been a staunch teetotaller since his early days in the Band of Hope. Religion also remained important and deep-seated sectarianism was readily brought to the surface by the threatened conflict in Ireland. Fear of letting in a Tory by splitting the radical vote seems often to have caused a last-minute swing back to the Liberal candidate, even when Labour felt it had been making advances.

Yet, it may be that blaming Orangemen for voting Tory or Irishmen for voting Liberal was a ready excuse for more fundamental failures. Clearly, most of the activists in the movement put an inordinate amount of faith in their own powers of oratory and believed that socialism could be won through propaganda rather than organisation. There was a determination not to compromise despite the fact that those candidates who were successful were those who were prepared either to modify their socialism or organise their electorate. The small shopkeepers, the petty businessmen, the teachers and the professional union organisers who made up the leadership of labour politics in Scotland had still much to do to make real contact with most of the Scottish working class. They moved in a rarefied atmosphere of the politically militant. It required the major changes of the war years to create the necessary links between leaders and masses. The war and its aftermath brought a heightened political awareness, but, of more importance, it brought greatly extended trade-union membership and the development of an improved and efficient political organisation. The fruits of this were to be harvested in 1922 when Labour won ten out of the fifteen Glasgow seats and with 29 members in all became by far the largest party in Scotland.

NOTES

1. SWPEC, Minutes, 6 Jan. 1900. National Library of Scotland, Microfilm Mss. 141.
2. J.G. Kellas, 'The Mid-Lanark By-Election (1888) and the Scottish Labour Party (1888-1894)', Parliamentary Affairs, vol. XVIII (1965), pp. 310-32.
3. K.D. Buckley, Trade Unionism in Aberdeen, (Oliver and Boyd, Edinburgh, 1955), pp. 136-154; W. Hamish Fraser, 'Trades Councils in the Scottish Labour Movement' in I. MacDougall, (ed.), Essays in Scottish Labour History (John Donald, Edinburgh, 1978), pp. 19-22.
4. Buckley, Trade Unionism, pp. 175-7.
5. Third Annual Report of the Scottish Trades Union Congress (Glasgow, 1899).
6. F. Bealey & H. Pelling, Labour and Politics 1900-1906, (Macmillan, London, 1958), p. 28.
7. SWPEC, Minutes, 4 Aug. 1900.
8. Glasgow Trades Council Minutes, 30 Oct. 1900. Mitchell Library, Glasgow.
9. SWPEC, Minutes, 28 Apr. 1900, 30 Mar. 1901.
10. Bealey & Pelling, Labour and Politics, p. 295.
11. LRC, EC Minutes, 13 June 1901.
12. SWPEC, Minutes, 30 Sept. 1901.
13. Ibid., 9 June 1900; SWPEC, Annual Report, 1901; Paisley Parliamentary Elections Committee,

Minutes, 14 Mar., 18 Apr., 25 May 1900. Paisley Central Library.

14. SWPEC, Minutes, 1 Sept. 1900.

15. Ibid., 5 Jan. 1901.

16. Scottish Liberal Association Minutes, 12, 26 Apr. 1900. Edinburgh University Library. See also Glasgow Herald, 19 Jan. 1910.

17. SLA, Minutes, 16 Oct. 1901; see also Master of Elibank's speech, Scotsman, 27 Aug. 1906.

18. SWPEC, Minutes, 31 Aug., 20 Sept., 26 Oct., 1 Nov. 1901.

19. SWPEC, Annual Report,1902.

20. For the size of the miners' vote in particular constituencies I have relied on the figures given in R. Gregory, The Miners and British Politics 1906-1914 (Oxford, University Press, 1968), p. 96; for the size of the Irish vote the figures used are mainly those published in the Scotsman, 18 Nov. 1909, reprinted in J. McCaffrey, 'Politics and the Catholic Community since 1878', in D. McRoberts (ed.), Modern Scottish Catholicism 1878-1978 (Burns, Glasgow, 1979), pp. 153-155.

21. Motherwell Times, 6, 13, 20 Sept. 1901; the co-operative split was in Wishaw. L. Campbell, 'Retail Co-operation in the Greater Glasgow Area c.1860-1914', unpublished PhD thesis, University of Strathclyde, 1983.

22. Glasgow Observer, 21, 28 Sept., 5, 12, 19 Oct. 1901.

23. Forward, 9 May 1908; Labour Leader, 5 Oct. 1901.

24. SWRC, Annual Report, 1902.

25. SWRC, Minutes, 21 June 1902.

26. Ibid., 20 June 1903.

27. Ibid., 30 Sept. 1905.

28. Quoted in M. Keating and D. Bleiman, Labour and Scottish Nationalism (Macmillan, London, 1979), p. 55.

29. LRC, Quarterly Circular, no. 9, Sept. 1904.

30. SWRC, Minutes, 16 July 1904.

31. Motherwell Times, 15, 29, July, 5 Aug. 1904; Labour Leader, 5 Aug. 1904.

32. Some negotiations in 1892 are referred to in Forward, 4 Sept. 1909; SLA Minutes, 11 May, 5 Oct. 1894.

33. SLA, Minutes, 12, 26 Apr., 12 July 1900.

34. Ibid., 30 Dec. 1902, 21 Jan., 1 Apr., 17 June 1903.

35. Ibid., 30 Dec. 1902, 21 Jan., 1 Apr., 17 June 1903.

36. Ibid., 1 Apr., 11 June 1903. The national

headquarters encouraged the Blackfriars' Liberals to give Barnes a clear run; Bealey and Pelling, Labour and Politics, pp. 145-6.

37. SLA, Minutes, 30 Mar. 1904.

38. 'Confidential Memorandum on the Socialist and Labour Movements in Scotland . . .' (February 1908). National Library of Scotland. Elibank Papers, Mss. 8801.

39. H. McShane and J. Smith, Harry McShane. No Mean Fighter (Pluto Press, London, 1978), p. 16.

40. Glasgow Observer, 13 Jan. 1906.

41. Dundee Courier, 2 Jan. 1906; J. Handy, The Rise of Labour in Dundee 1885-1910, (n.p., Dundee, n.d.).

42. SWPEC, Minutes, 27 Oct. 1900.

43. Ibid., 30 Mar. 1901.

44. Dundee Courier, 17 Jan. 1906.

45. People's Journal, 20 Jan. 1906.

46. Dundee Courier, 12 Jan. 1906.

47. J.T. Ward, 'Tory Socialist: A Preliminary Note on Michael Maltman Barry', Journal of the Scottish Labour History Society, no. 2 (Apr. 1970), pp. 38-40.

48. Aberdeen Free Press, 15 Dec. 1905.

49. Ibid., 21, 22 Dec. 1905; Aberdeen Trades Council, Minutes, 20 Dec. 1905. Aberdeen University Library.

50. Forward, 20 Feb. 1909.

51. Ibid., 21 Mar. 1908.

52. Ibid., 23 Feb., 2 Mar. 1907.

53. Joseph Duncan letters, 16 July 1906. National Library of Scotland. Mss. Acc. 5490.

54. Master of Elibank to Lord Knollys, 7 Nov. 1906. National Library of Scotland. Elibank papers, Mss 8801.

55. Scotsman, 27 Aug. 1906.

56. J.P. Croal to Master of Elibank, 9 July 1907. Elibank papers, Mss. 8801.

57. SWRC, Annual Report, 1907.

58. Labour Party, NEC minutes, 22 Jan. 1907, 16 Jan. 1908.

59. Labour Party (Scottish Section), Minutes, 7 Mar. 1908.

60. Dundee Courier, 27, 30 Apr., 1, 7 May 1908; Arbroath Herald, 17, 24 Apr., 1 May 1908.

61. Labour Party, NEC Minutes, 28 Apr. 1908.

62. Scotsman, 9 May 1908; Dundee Courier, 9 May 1908.

63. Dundee Courier, 5, 7 May 1908.

64. For Scrymgeour see W. Walker, Juteopolis. Dundee and Its Textile Workers 1885-1923 (Scottish

Academic Press, Edinburgh, 1979), ch. 8.
65. Forward, 12 Dec. 1908.
66. Ibid., 20 June 1908.
67. Ibid., 6 Feb. 1909.
68. Labour Party (Scottish Section), Annual Report, 1909.
69. SWRC, Fifth Annual Report, 1905.
70. Forward, 22 Jan. 1910, Dundee Advertiser, 17 Jan. 1910.
71. Forward, 22 Jan. 1910, 25 Mar. 1911.
72. Labour Party, NEC Minutes, 15 Feb. 1910; Forward, 24 Dec. 1910.
73. Forward, 17 Dec. 1910.
74. Ibid., 31 Dec. 1910.
75. Labour Party, NEC Minutes, 5 Aug. 1911.
76. Scotsman, 26 Sept. 1911.
77. Ibid., 21 Sept. 1911.
78. Forward, 7 Oct. 1911.
79. Scotsman, 26 Sept. 1911.
80. Labour Party, NEC, Special Scottish Report, 10 Aug. 1912.
81. Forward, 27 July 1907, 11 Sept. 1909.
82. Scotsman, 10 Aug. - 12 Sept. 1912.
83. R. McKibbin, The Evolution of the Labour Party, 1910-1924 (Oxford, University Press, 1974), p.41; Labour Party, Annual Report, 1913; Report of Special and Annual Conferences, 1914.
84. Scotsman, 5, 6, 8, 15 Dec. 1913.
85. Ibid., Feb. 1914.
86. Tocsin, nos. 1-7, Apr.-Oct. 1909.
87. Report of the Inaugural Conference of the Scottish Advisory Council of the Labour Party, Glasgow, 21 Aug. 1915.
88. Glasgow Labour Party Minutes, 18 May, 13 June 1911. Mitchell Library, Glasgow.
89. Report of the Inaugural Conference of the Scottish Advisory Council.

Chapter Three

ESTABLISHING A HEARTLAND - THE LABOUR PARTY IN WALES

'The handwriting is already upon the wall'.
So thought 'Cymro' who was writing in the <u>Labour</u>
<u>Leader</u> in the summer of 1906. He had just taken a
good look at Welsh miners and he could see that
'the spirit of Labour independence is working
mightily amongst them', and his feeling was that
these Welsh miners would soon begin to feel like
traitors if their support was not given to Labour.
Soon they would be demanding that their leaders,
who had so far shown so little enthusiasm for
independence, 'fall in line with Labour' for,
according to 'Cymro', it was 'useless offering the
Welsh miner Labour wrapped in the swaddling clothes
of Liberalism' as 'he knows it for make-believe and
his wrath will fall upon those who would work the
imposture upon him'.[1]
'Cymro' had read the handwriting correctly,
for just a few months later the miners balloted on
affiliation to the Labour Representation Committee
and in south Wales 41,843 voted in favour as
compared to 31,527 against. This result was a
personal triumph for Keir Hardie who in the last
two general elections had been returned for Labour
in the south Wales constituency of Merthyr and who
during the campaign leading up to the ballot had
often exchanged sharp words with some of the more
senior miners' leaders. The result was a triumph
too for the Independent Labour Party whose 49 south
Wales branches had helped ensure that every miner
in the coalfield knew precisely what was at stake
in the ballot. Above all, the result had been a
triumph for a group of south Wales miners' leaders
who had been frustrated at first when their
president, William Abraham or Mabon, had failed to
give the casting vote which would have meant the
South Wales Miners' Federation Executive

recommending affiliation to the Labour Party, but who had nevertheless been able to dominate the ensuing coalfield debate. The dominant figure amongst these Labour men on the SWMF Executive was Vernon Hartshorn, the miners' agent for the Maesteg area, whose argument had been that 'for twenty years the workers of this country had been simply hangers-on', whereas now 'the Labour movement was giving to the working classes a new conception of politics and a spirit of self-respect and independence which when fully developed would completely revolutionise our social life'.[2]

The result of the south Wales ballot was unambiguous but in the short term it seemed irrelevant as the Miners Federation of Great Britain had already decided to act as one and the national ballot went against affiliation. In fact Keir Hardie, Hartshorn and their friends in the South Wales District of the ILP had won a famous and decisive victory. In national terms the south Wales example no doubt encouraged the ILP in other coalfields and may well have helped to ensure the national vote for affiliation in 1909 when the south Wales miners themselves voted even more decisively for the Labour Party.[3] Meanwhile in south Wales itself the 1906 result was clearly a major landmark. The battle had in reality been won once and for all, there could be no going back, no reversing of this decision. By 1906 the majority of the members of the union that dominated the social and political life of south Wales had become supporters of independence in labour politics and they had clearly notified the Labour Party and the ILP that the future belonged with them.[4] From 1906 onwards every working-class leader in Wales who was not a supporter of independence was forced on to the defensive. There were still many details to be worked out and many minor battles and skirmishes that suggested complications but whatever the setbacks nobody involved in trade unionism and working-class politics really doubted that if history had not quite turned it had given a firm indication that it was in the process of turning. In the years after 1906 there were to be many angry debates and bitter contests but what those indicated were not options or possibilities but rather the distaste and disappointment of those who could see history moving away from them. To identify the significance of the 1906 south Wales ballot in this way suggests that hindsight has played a part, but it is offered as an interpretation which arises out of an appreciation of the ineluctable momentum of trade union opinion in those years before 1914. The grand argument had been won but the pay-off could only come when the rhetoric, conventions, institutions and images of the Labour Party had been more fully worked out. In the years after 1906 the Labour Party had to turn an argument and a logic into an ethos. In particular names and faces would have to be made familiar.

Vernon Hartshorn remained a key figure in this process, for he was the most able and best known of those south Wales miners' leaders who fully believed in the value and potential of the Labour Party. On the SWMF Executive he continuously argued Labour's case and in particular he urged his colleagues to sanction his adoption as a fully-fledged Labour candidate in the Mid-Glamorgan constituency. Hartshorn's struggle to make a Labour breakthrough in Mid-Glamorgan was to become quite a saga but it enabled him to develop a perceptive understanding of the norms of Welsh political behaviour. In 1908 he told a socialist demonstration at Porthcawl that 'there was more personality than principle in the politics of Glamorgan, and when the personalities were removed the miners to a man would be with the Labour and Socialist movement'.[5] This was to become a frequent complaint in the following years and in 1910 for example one local newspaper pointed to the way in which Labour candidates in local government elections found it difficult to succeed when elections were 'decided on personal issues not principle' and when councillors were 'chosen because of some outstanding personal trait'.[6] What Hartshorn and his fellow critics had in mind was the way in which Welsh politics had become the monopoly of a particular kind of personality. The Liberal Party had emerged in the Victorian period not only as the party which reflected the values and opinions of the Welsh electorate but as the most convenient vehicle and agency for the energies of ambitious young Welshmen. As far as Wales was concerned it was impossible to separate the hegemony of the Liberal Party from the individual careers of those businessmen and especially those lawyers who wished to go into public life. To be returned as a Liberal MP guaranteed status in Wales but furthermore it opened up all kinds of opportunities in London and of course the empire. The great bonus for this generation of rising

Welshmen was that individual fame and prosperity
were disguised as an expression of Welsh religious,
radical and national identity. For several cohorts
of Welsh leaders individual ambition had been
inspired and then sanctioned by the emergence into
democratic politics of a whole society. A social
process had quite specifically defined those
qualities needed by any man wanting to develop a
political persona.[7]

The 1906 ballot meant that the majority of
south Wales miners had voted against what was
traditionally thought of as 'personality' in
politics. A certain residual respect lingered on;
Lloyd George carried all before him in north Wales
but he still had his supporters in the coalfield
and he enjoyed his occasional visits. That other
ambitious young man, Winston Churchill, was the
chief guest at a Rhondda miners' gala in July 1908
where he shared the platform with several Welsh
Liberal MPs. But in general the miners and other
organised trade unionists were already distancing
themselves from professional politicians, and this
process was already well underway before it was
clinched by the industrial unrest after 1910. Even
in north Wales disputes in the quarries had led to
a distancing of the quarrymen from Liberal
politicians and the first tentative discussion of
labour representation. With a Liberal government
in power and with mounting pressures on the miners'
standard of living there was no disguising the
increasingly ambiguous position of Liberal MPs and
the hollowness of their radical pose. In 1910
Llais Llafur pointed at the Welsh members and asked
what they had done for Wales: the answer was
'Nothing - except for securing appointments for the
lawyer-members and honours for themselves'. The
paper looked in detail at the south Wales Liberal
members and identified seven major industrialists,
five members of the government, a whole host of
county court judges and recorders, and an
impressive list of knighthoods. The list would
have been more spectacular if Lloyd George's north
Wales had been included. It was clear to Llais
Llafur 'that the party which flaunts its nationalism consists entirely of lawyers "on the make"
and financial magnates with huge interests to
safeguard'. The paper went on to explain that it
was using nationalism in the Mazzini sense of representing the full aspirations of a people and by
that standard Liberalism was 'a mere sham - the
hollow simulacrum of Nationalism' and its conclusion

was that 'the Labour Party can if it cares become the real national party'.[8]

It is not difficult to see that this is precisely what happened in Wales but, of course, there were many stages to be gone through. In the years after 1906 working-class issues became the day-to-day stuff of politics and it became easy to identify the anomalous position of middle-class politicians, but it did not become easier to determine who should take their place. One alternative had already become well established by 1906 and that was the idea of Lib-Labism, the notion that labour, in the sense of working-men, deserved special representation and that this was best done by professional trade unionist leaders standing with the general support of the Liberal Party. Inevitably, hindsight has made Lib-Labism look an anomalous and makeshift position but for many years in areas like Wales it was sanctioned by a range of social forces and it appeared as the legitimate philosophy of a whole community. The whole political and strategic validity of the Lib-Lab position was made far more powerful by the moral and emotional qualities of Welsh nationalist and religious feeling of which it seemed an expression. The Welsh miners' leader, Mabon, had won the Rhondda in 1885 and then after twenty years he was joined in the House of Commons by three of his colleagues, William Brace, Tom Richards and John Williams. This long delay was a reflection of how reluctant the Welsh Liberals were to accept trade-union candidates, of how slow were the Welsh miners in organising (their Federation was only established in 1898 and their Parliamentary Scheme in 1902) and how difficult it was for a trade unionist to establish himself as a public figure well enough known to consider standing for Parliament. In Wales the irony was that the Lib-Lab breakthrough came perhaps twenty but certainly ten years too late. Similarly in north Wales the argument for Lib-Lab representation was just becoming accepted at the very moment when the more advanced logic of Labour was about to strike. The society that had made Lib-Labism an obvious creed was already moving away from it. It is evidence and not hindsight which suggests that even as they enjoyed the support of the majority of their electors the Welsh Lib-Labs had been forced on to the defensive. At their every public appearance the four Lib-Labs elected in 1906 were compelled to combat the logic of the ILP and the

result of the ballot in October 1906 meant that
their political position, however intelligible in
social terms, was in political terms absurd.[9]
   The Lib-Labs developed a whole battery of
arguments and their deployment of them became
increasingly frenetic. What tended to happen was
that an argument that had initially appeared to be
common sense and legitimate would be pounced on by
the ILP and made to appear in the ensuing
controversy as a line of expediency and
special-pleading. The Lib-Labs were distinguished
and able men who had been created by and who sought
to represent a clear constituency of opinion but
the logic and tenacity of the ILP on the one hand
and the general remoteness of the Liberal
government on the other made them look like
dissemblers. The argument that isolation was
dangerous and that Liberal government legislation
was the only hope meant that they were pinning
their hopes on a party of industrialists and
lawyers, and of course any reference to the nature
of the electorate looked like the naked opportunism
that was increasingly thought to characterise the
Liberals themselves. During the 1906 ballot debate
Vernon Hartshorn challenged William Brace, the
newly elected member for South Glamorgan and
perhaps the most important miners' leader in south
Wales, to explain why he was not taking part in the
public debates on the LRC issue. Brace's reply was
that 'people seemed to talk as if it was easy for
the Labour Party to work like a machine always
voting together without difficulty' but 'as a
matter of fact it should never be forgotten that
the claims of constituencies were factors that must
be reckoned with and no member of Parliament who
knew his business would fail to realise that in the
arrangement of his Parliamentary work the needs and
wishes of those he directly represented in the
House must be given every consideration'.[10] This
was a reasonable argument but the ILP had no
difficulty in making it look as if William Brace
saw his membership of Parliament as a personal
distinction rather than as an adjunct of his being
an elected miners' leader. South Glamorgan was not
an obvious seat for a miners' MP but that fact just
seemed to confirm Brace's individualism.
   One of the Lib-Labs' strongest arguments was
that they were professional and full-time
trade-union leaders and that their greatest loyalty
was to the South Wales Miners Federation. They had
been elected to Parliament under the MFGB

Parliamentary Scheme and their general hope was that in time at least another eight miners' leaders could be returned by the application of this scheme to other south Wales constituencies. The sudden breakthrough of the ILP threatened to overtake this purely SWMF master-plan. A bold and fully autonomous strategy was being eclipsed by a national and doctrinaire movement whose inspiration lay outside the day-to-day considerations of mining trades unionism. A strategy determined by the needs of professional union leaders was going to be handed over to men, most of them outsiders, for whom socialism was the main consideration. The Lib-Labs were fighting to hold on to a politics that they could comprehend and control. In 1906 one south Wales journalist suggested that 'those who object to the LRC do so on the ground principally of the rigidity of its constitution which all candidates must sign', and Mabon warned that 'if they joined the LRC they would be bound by the rules of that organisation, one of which was that they would have to stand aloof from giving assistance at election times to anyone who did not belong to the LRC' and that condition he thought 'unwise and unfair'.[11] There were many complaints about the autocratic nature of the LRC and in particular of its disdain for the older trade union MPs. It was depicted as a party of 'Johnny-Come-Latelys' who did not really understand the nuances of political lobbying and who by their arrogance were threatening the whole principle of working-class representation. Mabon instanced the LRC opposition to the candidatures of Havelock-Wilson and Enoch Edwards and argued that this 'throwing away of two seats' showed that the LRC was not really interested in labour representation. To Mabon it seemed that 'the ILP did not go in for direct labour representation whereas the Miners Federation did'. The Lib-Lab establishment was threatened by a new kind of parvenu of whom Keir Hardie had been the forerunner. The miners would be handing over their hard-won parliamentary representation to rootless men, for in Mabon's eyes 'the LRC was like a party roaming in the wilderness without a place to put down its tent'.[12]

The arguments went on throughout the whole period from 1906 to 1910. They were intensified by the decision of the MFGB to affiliate to the Labour Party in 1909 and in south Wales they were given sharper definition by Vernon Hartshorn's determination to mount what would be an unambiguous Labour Party candidature in Mid-Glamorgan. It was always relatively easy for the ILP to win debating points but in a way these quibbles over precise political definitions and logic were quite irrelevant, for the senior Lib-Labs in Parliament and the more junior Lib-Labs at local level knew that their authority and prestige did not rest on labels nor indeed on argument. The Lib-Labs were their own argument; they were, as Hartshorn had rightly suggested, personalities, and in some cases as with Mabon they were really institutions. They had become men of stature in part by aping the general conventions of Victorian public leadership but also in part by fighting with great determination to widen the notions of public consensus. As outsiders they had fought their way to the inside and now all the benefits accrued as they were granted the status of statesmen. In every case initial Liberal opposition or at least suspicion had been overcome, but then nothing succeeded like success and soon there were suggestions of indispensability. The Liberal establishment needed these men and so every effort was made to build them up, a task made easy by a raw material that lent itself to praise. The Lib-Labs were senior, patriarchal, professional and very much part of a wider social round. They were veterans of all the activities that went into the making of community. They were prima donnas but somehow their massive personal vanity was thought of as being part of their very professionalism and quiddity as working-class leaders. They were formidable men and so well-entrenched that they became great survivors. In north Wales their equivalents were the quarrymens' leaders like W.J. Parry and D.R. Daniel, men appointed from outside the union but who developed a tremendous expertise as professional trade unionists and whose status and personality made them essentially political personalities within the community.[13] In south Wales the Lib-Labs survived the coming of the Labour Party and, with the exception of the ageing Mabon, they were to survive the "Great Unrest" of 1910 to 1913. In the middle of the turmoil of 1911 one collier wrote to the press contrasting what he called 'the new idealists - the book students and ex-student preachers, those who are all things to all men to suit themselves' with 'the tried ones in many battles, the school of weight'. Looking at Mabon, Brace and Tom Richards he concluded, as did so many voters and trade unionists, that in normal times 'old friends are best'.[14]

The Lib-Labs had a 'gravitas' which no Labour man could rival and in fact mere membership of the ILP seemed to work against any person seeking to achieve a public reputation. This was partly a matter of doctrine because it was very easy to suggest that socialism was an alien, atheistic and dangerous creed. The last years of the nineteenth century had seen an indigenous socialism developing in Wales but sudden political and industrial developments had shifted the grounds of the argument and it was a different socialism that now loomed. The debate was far more about basic loyalties. To be an ILP or even an LRC man was to belong to a section, and a rigidly defined section, rather than to belong to more open groups which fed into a wider consensus. Labour men were substituting a part for the whole and therefore they could never be generally accepted as natural leaders of the community. In a democratic age they were closing doors and restricting politics rather than opening up new opportunities. After the 1906 ballot the political logic of the ILPers on the SWMF Executive, men like Vernon Hartshorn and James Winstone, was quite impeccable and yet in social terms they seemed to lack authority. The one exception to this pattern was Keir Hardie who remained throughout these years the area's one example of a straight-forward Labour MP. Hardie's initial election had rested on the determination of an ILP branch operating in a two-member constituency in an unusual election, but it had also owed much to Hardie's own charisma. The novelist Jack Jones talked of how Hardie 'had spoken a different language' but perhaps his appearance, his accent, his style and his flair for publicity were as important as the details of his socialism.[15] In subsequent years Hardie retained that image of being a prophet and of being his own man, of being independent in the fullest sense, but what he could not be, of course, was a direct inspiration to other would-be MPs. In south Wales Hardie could only be a one-off success for the ILP. His formula had been just right, his name was well-known and yet he was essentially an exotic. Local leaders found it more difficult to disguise themselves as prophets in their native land. Charles Stanton developed a tremendous charisma in the Aberdare Valley but found that demagoguery and populism were not enough at election times, and another exotic, Ben Tillett, came on far too fiercely for the electors of Swansea. Even Hardie's position had its difficulties for there were times in these years when his position outside the day-to-day affairs of the SWMF made him look extremely light-weight as compared to the miners' leaders and it was very easy for them to suggest that he was just a professional politician with no real responsibilities. At election times his magic could work but at other times Hardie seemed to be on the periphery of Welsh industrial politics. The Lib-Labs always enjoyed emphasising the careerism of Labour politicians in contrast to their great experience as professional representatives of labour.

The three or four years following the 1906 ballot formed a strange period in Welsh political history and perhaps we may best conclude that occasionally political situations can be multi-faceted and unresolved. The south Wales miners had voted in favour of affiliation to the LRC and that encouraged the ILP to step up the pace of its activities in the area. We can identify a veritable crescendo of ILP organisation and propaganda and yet all this seemed to go on within the shadow cast by the Lib-Lab giants. Personality eclipsed frenetic activity; but activity there certainly was. When the sixteenth annual conference of the ILP was held at Huddersfield in April 1908 some 34 Welsh delegates were in attendance and they were given reports which indicated that there were some 84 branches in south Wales and a further 8 in north Wales. The directory of elected members estimated that in south Wales the ILP could claim 4 county councillors, 27 urban district councillors, 18 town councillors, 3 rural district councillors, 18 parish councillors and some 29 poor law guardians. Of the ILP's 29 full-time propagandists it appeared that 5 were employed in south Wales, and certainly the names of Messrs Trainer, Bibbings, Eastwood, Black and T.I. Jones dominated the press reports of ILP activity in the area. In November 1908 the ILP held its own south Wales conference and it was now claimed that there were 130 branches in Wales and that during the first 9 months of that year the south Wales secretary, Mr Field, had arranged some 2,000 meetings.[16] There were still occasional press reports of scuffles in the street and of difficulties with the police but in general the picture that emerges is of propaganda reaping a rich organisational harvest. At Aberdare in Hardie's Merthyr constituency there was a district ILP group of four or five councillors who were in close touch with their active ILP branch and with the local trades council, and this was a clear model for the rest of Wales to follow. A Swansea Valley Socialist League had mushroomed into existence north of the town and it seemed as if the affiliated ILP branches were using virtually every school on almost every evening for lectures and debates. In Cardiff too there was non-stop activity and in December 1907 the local secretary reported that the previous year had seen membership increase by 200, over 18,000 penny pamphlets and over £100's worth of literature had been sold, and in all some 340 meetings had been held. From all over south Wales the message was the same: the ILP was carrying the day. William Field, who represented the region on the executive of the ILP, spoke of how a south Wales that had once 'lagged behind the rest of the country - would soon be in the forefront of the Socialist movement' and one leading south Wales reformer contrasted the shallow emotionalism of the recent religious revival with the more profound political revival that was under way. This observer was sure that 'Socialism was likely to be co-ordinated with the religious instincts of the people in a way which has never been done with Liberalism' and that the 'time would soon come when the religious Welshman will regard Socialism as the component of his religious belief'.[17]

These were heady days for ILPers and the press reports suggest that south Wales in particular had become theirs. The reality was perhaps somewhat different. It only took a few people to start an ILP branch but branches could come and branches could go. The five full-time organisers had plenty of time to file press reports, and there is no doubt that in this period these propagandists were trying to talk themselves and their followers into a revivalist atmosphere and trying to create a bandwagon effect. There were well-organised ILP branches and there was a slow but steady increase in the number of ILP councillors, but there were very few areas in Wales where the Aberdare model of a local labour movement focusing itself clearly on local government matters can be detected. Not every ILP branch was viable and even those that were did not mesh fully into the local trade union structure let alone in keep in touch with a wider public opinion. What the hectic propaganda campaign of these years had done was to create an ILP structure and presence but what it had failed to do was to establish a political organisation capable of eclipsing the existing day-to-day calendar of trade-union activities. In many areas the local ILP branch was seen as a useful source of propaganda and an alternative to the chapel as far as the organisation of concerts, picnics and debates was concerned but not as a powerhouse from which the take-over of either the local authority or the parliamentary constituency could be planned. Even where there was a group of local councillors it was difficult to sustain a full round of ILP activity and even more difficult to distract unions from their industrial business.

Whatever the euphoria in the press reports, the ILP was up against tremendous difficulties. In the first place there was anonymity of its leadership. Keir Hardie was a must for any mass demonstration and Philip Snowden or Bruce Glasier could be brought in to address any special meeting. In north Wales the Rev Silyn Roberts was perhaps the first leader with anything like charisma and the first to suggest that the ILP could become an indigenous force. In general though activities were in the hands of local officers or full-time organisers and many south Walians must have wondered precisely who were these Messrs Trainer and Bibbings of whom they read so often. Mr G.H. Bibbings was a splendid publicist and there were constant reports of his organisational efforts and of how the whole area was responding to them. As he whipped the people of Neath into action he warned them that 'there must be no hob-nobbing with the rack-renter or sweater' and that 'tea-parties or whisky parties have nothing to do with Labour man'.[18] The organisers obviously behaved like school-teachers and the branches were clearly their unruly pupils, but as one reads the press reports one begins to wonder about the real nature of this relationship. There was certainly resentment that these outsiders, men with no real stature in the community, should loom so large in ILP circles. Already in 1908 there were complaints from many branches about the new salary scales for the organisers and these grumblings were attributed to a general lack of understanding with regard to the expenses that had to be met. Things came to a head

75

in the autumn of 1909 with the demise of the South Wales ILP Federation and the dismissal of Bibbings and the other organisers. The fact that the South Wales Federation was some £30 in the red occasioned a major debate on the whole situation in south Wales. According to William Field the branches had wasted the organisers' abilities by making them do propaganda work on platforms and street corners rather than by allowing them to organise. The feelings amongst the organisers themselves was that 98 branches and 4,000 members should have been able to support full-time officials (it was pointed out that 50 nonconformists could usually support a minister) but that branches were preferring to look after themselves and were loath to come together in wider schemes.

The most interesting aspect of this debate was the general admission that four years of organisational activity had not really been successful. W.H. Stevenson of the ILP admitted that throughout the whole area there was a disposition to regard the officers of the South Wales Federation 'as Machiavellian conspirators, whose object is to gain control over the branches and dictate to all and sundry their sovereign will'. He conceded that the branches had not been fully informed and consulted but was also forced to admit that much more might have been achieved for 'outside Briton Ferry and a few others there is not a properly organised branch in the whole of South Wales'.[19] As people were asking why the South Wales Federation had failed, Llais Llafur published a letter from Nun Nicholas, a prominent Swansea Valley socialist and adult educationalist. Nicholas was impatient with the whole debate and he argued that 'the only remedy is to appeal to the class interests of the people' and this could only be done by 'ceasing to prattle about the co-ordination of all the forces and tendencies that lead to Socialism' and by working 'for the only force which makes for the Social Revolution, a force which must necessarily be a proletarian party conscious of its own strength'. For him failure had been caused not by a lack of organisation or funds but rather because the ILP had not 'touched local matters'. He told of how the organiser Mr Black had come to a village meeting that had been poorly attended; he had returned two months later and talked about a local colliery dispute from which he had drawn a socialist moral. At the second meeting there had been an enthusiastic response and a significantly higher collection. The federation had failed said Nicholas, because it had 'not understood the working class'.[20]

The problem for the ILP, of course, was that of necessity it was operating one step away from reality as understood by miners, quarrymen and other trade unionists. Organising lectures and concerts for clerks, teachers and even nonconformist ministers could only be subsidiary to the infiltration of trade union branches. Everyone knew that this was going on and the 1906 and 1909 ballot figures were evidence of the ILP's success. Writing in 1909 one correspondent asked how long the infiltration was to go on and complained that 'the ILP and other Socialist societies are at it every week . . . they seize every opportunity'.[21] Since its inception the ILP had realised that the trade unions were the essence of the labour movement and that the socialist bid for power had to be built on a trade union foundation. In south Wales the miners were the dominant group and in their case, more perhaps than with other trades, the union was rapidly becoming the all-powerful expression of collective identity. For the south Wales miner the pride and hope that came from union membership were relatively new sensations and every industrial and political argument seemed to be sanctioning the logic and the power of the new South Wales Miners Federation and of its local manifestation, the lodge. The ILP had to run pretty hard to keep up with this run-away enthusiasm and had to clamber over several hurdles to stay in the race at all. To convince an individual miner that independent representation made more sense than to support Liberalism or even Lib-Labism was one thing, but to convince him that attendance at ILP meetings was as important as attending lodge meetings was another, and then to go on to persuade him that the most important thing of all was to make this lodge contact other trade union branches in order to set up and sustain a local LRC, was perhaps to make an unreasonable demand. To start with there was no tradition of political organisation, for the Liberal Party had never attempted to recruit working men and their unions into any formal political movement, and now it was difficult for the ILP to create the kind of enthusiasm for political structures that was being generated for trade unionism. The miners in any case were jealous of anything that challenged their autonomy at any level: even trades councils were initially regarded with suspicion but at least there was some industrial justification for them and they did tend to operate within recognisable communities. There was a reluctance to commit union lodges and branches and certainly their funds to any purely political organisation, especially as most parliamentary constituencies were fairly artificial creations and not meaningful enough to transcend village or valley loyalties.

These years did see the emergence of some local LRCs in south Wales but in general there was an 'ad hocery' about them that prevented them from moving into the centre of political life. The model for south Wales was provided by the town of Swansea where there was no problem caused by the dominance of miners and where a well-organised trade union movement, taking its inspiration mainly from the docks and already organised in a trades council, set up a Labour Association in 1906.[22] The Swansea Party was to be somewhat chastened by the defeat of its candidate, Ben Tillett, in the first general election of 1910 but slowly and surely it was building up the political side of the movement and mounting an effective challenge in local government terms. Things happened more slowly in the mining valleys where ILP branches, miners' lodges, union branches and trades councils found it more difficult to come together in any permanent fashion. Sometimes there were LRCs in particular villages but not at constituency level, and in other constituencies there would be occasional conferences representing 'all the labour forces in the area'. Whatever inertia there was tended to be encouraged by the Lib-Labs and those who wanted to defend the autonomy of the miners' own scheme of representation. The run-in to the general elections of 1910 highlighted the whole problem as far as south Wales was concerned. There was a major row in the East Carmarthenshire constituency where the local miners chose their own candidate only to find that other organisations would not approve their choice, claiming that they had played no part in the selection procedure. In time and after several complications the ILP came up with its own nomination and there were all kinds of appeals to the national Labour Party. One local observer praised the miners for their pioneering Parliamentary Scheme but reminded them that 'it is now full time that other methods should be adopted in the selection of candidates and all the other trades interested brought into consideration'.[23]

Eventually Dr.J.H. Williams of the ILP was chosen to fight the seat in December 1910. A recently formed LRC played a part in his selection but in the election he was very reliant on his own resources and the need for an effective organisation which included the miners was made very apparent. The situation was somewhat different in Mid-Glamorgan where a constituency LRC had been formed based on the work of one or two good ILP branches but even more on the work of Vernon Hartshorn. Local Labour people were raring to contest Mid-Glamorgan but the Lib-Labs on the Miners' Executive were very loath to put a miners' candidate in the field against Samuel Evans, a prominent Liberal and a solicitor who acted for the SWMF. Hartshorn was prevented from fighting two by-elections and the first general election of 1910 and only allowed into the fray in a March 1910 by-election after Sir Samuel Evans had vacated the seat. By that time every voter knew of the marked difference between Hartshorn and the widely respected Lib-Labs on the Miners Executive and, realising the significance of this contest between the Liberals and a fully-fledged Labour Party miner, the local press and the churches unleashed their full venom.[24]

Hartshorn was the miners' leader who should have become Wales's first home-grown Labour MP in the years before 1914. His position was the one classically defined by the LRC ballots in 1906 and 1909, for he was a miners' leader, an ILP member, and a supporter of the Labour Party. He was an able and prominent man but he had failed to create a parliamentary bridge-head because of the fight of the Lib-Labs to retain control of electoral tactics and because the local Liberal, nonconformist, and business interests could see in 1910 that he, far more than the exotic Keir Hardie or the wild men like C.B. Stanton or Ben Tillett, was pointing to the future and had to be destroyed. The Liberal victories over Hartshorn in the by-election of March and the general election of December 1910 were very largely victories for propaganda but they were not entirely so. The re-invigorated and perhaps even desperate Liberals still had one really powerful argument and that was that they stood for the community whilst Labour stood for a section and perhaps even more, a clique. There was undoubtedly a general prejudice in the popular mind against the guild-like or exclusive nature of Labour's organisation and it was thought to be something new in Wales and something quite different from the traditional openness of politics. There were always to be accusations that Labour nominations and decisions had been determined behind closed doors. In December 1905 a press article suggested that James Winstone's candidature in the Monmouth constituency had 'been engineered by the ILP' and so a respected miners' leader was relegated to the status of a sectional candidate. In 1907 a local paper commented on the decline in quality of councillors at Neath for 'the apotheosis of Labour has given birth to workmens' representatives who neither possess the brains or the dignity which obtained a few years ago'. It continued: 'all it has done is to produce puppets with platitudes connected by wire with the Trade Council', for 'every fortnight these "free and independent representatives of the electors" have to give an account of their stewardship to a coterie who meet in a public house and who certainly have no just claim to be representatives of the general public'.[25] At the annual meeting of the Pontardawe Board of Guardians in 1908 there were protests against the 'hole-and-corner meetings' of the ILP and the 'action of the Labour sections in making appointments to the chairs and committees in accordance with a plan prearranged at a caucus meeting'. One member suggested that 'they might as well carry in bloc the resolution of the preliminary meeting held that morning by one section of the guardians at the Dynevor Arms'. Another speaker told the Labour section that he considered himself 'as much a Labour representative as any of you', for 'you have a grocer, a draper, and a cycle agent in your party' but that he would 'never attend your meetings for the sake of personal honour'.[26] There must have been some electors who believed that ILP men were revolutionary atheists as suggested by the press and by preachers but there were many more who resented Labour's style and modus operandi, for in many important respects Labour was working against the grain of a community. For many Welsh people society was too well-integrated for the crudely exclusive tactics of Labour whilst others resented the politicisation of all aspects of life. At the time of the 1906 debate one miner complained that it seemed to him 'that we are going Parliament mad'.[27]

This preoccupation with Parliament was not to last, and the poor performance of Labour in the various elections of 1910 was both a reflection and perhaps a cause of a sharp decline in ILP activity and enthusiasm. One has the feeling that the party was already somewhat becalmed in the months before the great outburst of industrial unrest in the autumn of 1910. The Osborne Judgement came at a time when industrial matters were already edging out political activity and, as the economic pressure on the miners' wages increased and as the courts and coal-owners seemed to be restricting the miner on all fronts, the only really important question became that of whether the miners' leaders could deliver the goods by defending living standards and working conditions. During the two years of industrial turmoil that south Wales now experienced it became impossible to sustain any meaningful party political propaganda and ILPers began to look back with nostalgia to the days of 1908. This was partly a question of organisational disruption but there was also a new mood which was not conducive to political organisation. There were genuine syndicalists in south Wales but in general 'Syndicalism' was a press term for a range of responses, one of which was a new impatience with those existing procedures much vaunted by established leaders. Conciliation was the main target but 'Labour Partyism' was coupled with it in the literature of the new militants. There was a new prophet now and a native son at that. 'Why cross the river to fill the bucket?' demanded Noah Ablett as he pointed to the twenty-five year battle to win the eight hour day. He advocated instead a short sharp industrial battle to win the minimum wage. Syndicalism was an argument for miners and other unions to play to their strengths and quite evidently parliamentary representation was not seen as a winning card.

For a moment the ILP was eclipsed but it was certainly not replaced. For a moment Keir Hardie looked irrelevant and the propagandists were silenced but at the local level there was considerable consolidation. Whatever the short-term industrial tactics the local ILP branches and the local Labour Party advocates could only benefit from the new disillusionment with Lib-Labism and the new mood of trade-union solidarity. The "Great Unrest" may well have interrupted ILP propaganda but there is no doubt that it finally clinched the argument for a Labour Party. Representation was now to be altogether a more serious business.[28]

These were strange years in which an apparent lack of progress really disguised the vital changes within communities. Of course the Osborne Judgement had acted together with the general unrest to hold up political developments and yet both these influences were really improving the Labour Party's chances of ultimate success. The new militant determination of Welsh Liberals to take the initiative against Labour candidates might well have paid off in 1910 but it probably also inspired union branches to think in terms of improving Labour's organisation. The sudden appearance in valley towns of Young Liberal branches acted as sure incentive to Labour men. Above all, the decisions of the miners not to contest East Carmarthenshire in 1912 and then to curtail their own registration scheme suggested that Labour's advance was somewhat becalmed but in fact all over Wales foundations were being laid.[29]

In April 1912 Llais Llafur thought the local government election results made 'heartening reading'; there were Labour gains in several areas and it was thought that the three gains in the Rhondda marked a significant turning-point. In the following month the ILP held its national conference at Merthyr and amongst the delegates were 73 from some 58 Welsh branches. They were given a report that spoke of 'the awakening of Labour', and of how members had aided 'the organised workers in their splendid industrial battles'.[30] In south Wales there were some hopeless areas and The Labour Leader reflected on how fifteen years of vigorous propaganda had not produced a single Labour councillor in Cardiff and things were thought to be sluggish in the Swansea Valley. During 1913, however, the paper frequently commented on the vitality of many south Wales ILP branches. Swansea was regarded as the model branch, followed by Briton Ferry, Merthyr and Cardiff but there were active and newly re-invigorated branches in all areas.[31] Writing in February 1913 a writer describing himself as 'John Blunt' confessed that he thought of the ILP as being 'more or less inactive' especially when compared to the years before 1908 but nevertheless he maintained that all that earlier work was now bearing fruit. He calculated that there were 'at least 200,000 out-and-out Socialists in South Wales' and that 'of young miners there was not 1 in 10 who was not Labour and Collectivist'; Lib-Labism was 'slowly and steadily dying' and 'young men had no time for Liberalism'.[32]

As local council seats and now even county council seats were gained, the need was for all this activity to be pulled together. The challenge now was an organisational one. In July 1913 it was reported that the Labour Party was taking a special interest in south Wales and making 'elaborate preparations with a view to strengthening her political power especially by stepping up registration through local Labour committees'.[33] In August a Labour conference was held in Cardiff and Ramsay MacDonald, Keir Hardie and other speakers stressed the importance of organisation whilst Mr. Peters of the ILP described what could be learned from German political organisation. Stress was placed on the need for every town to have its own ILP branch (the ILP 'is the petrol of the Labour Party'), its own Women's Labour League and its own local Labour Party, although Hardie conceded that it was up to each constituency to decide whether it could contest elections.[34] One senses that thoughts of the '1915 General Election' were concentrating minds wonderfully and suddenly in 1913 we can begin to identify the reality of a Labour Party presence in south Wales. The new Trade Union Act of 1913 regularised and sanctioned political activity and the SWMF took advantage of the new dispensation by determining that all future elections fought by miners' candidates would be fought 'on strict Labour lines'. During the "Great Unrest" the SWMF had quietly passed into Labour's hands.[35] In the summer of 1913 the federation decided that it would contest eight constituencies in the next election but this decision was a far more momentous one than that taken in a very different era back in 1902. It was accepted that the necessary corollary of this new Parliamentary Scheme was 'that a Labour Organisation be formed for each constituency composed of Miners Lodges and other Trade Organisations for Labour Representation purposes'.[36] The miners were now actually committed to creating Labour Parties, and by early 1914 a significant amount of SWMF time was taken up dealing with the local Labour Parties which were either springing into existence or becoming really active for the first time. What is most noticeable now as compared to just a year or two earlier is that the miners were working amicably with other unions within constituencies. In February 1914 the SWMF Executive even agreed to a suggestion of the Monmouthshire Constituency Labour Party that unions other than the miners could take part in the ballot to select a candidate.[37] At the same time in Caernarfon the North Wales Quarrymen's Union brought other unions together to form a Caernarfon Labour Council. In many areas of Wales the meaningful existence of a local Labour Party dates from 1913.[38]

A significant corner was being turned and we can see this most clearly in the experience of William Brace. He was now a fully-fledged Labour MP but in his South Glamorgan constituency he had always relied on the Progressive vote. At meeting after meeting Brace's position was criticised and obviously for the next election he would have to try to develop his own local Labour Party. At this point Brace decided that he had little chance of winning on a purely Labour ticket and so he made it known, in yet another controversial action, that he would not contest the seat at all in the next election. By his own confession he had always given 'to the constitution of the Labour Party a very generous interpretation' but nevertheless he was now eager to be adopted as a candidate in one of the seats that the miners had designated in their scheme.[39] His name went on the ballot papers along with those of other aspirants; he was unsuccessful in North Monmouthshire but successful in neighbouring West Monmouthshire. The Labour logic had won out and now all the considerable experience and know-how of an established pattern of leadership could feed into the Labour Party. Late in their careers Mabon and Brace had to reconcile themselves to Keir Hardie's party. Meanwhile in East Glamorgan the local Labour Party chose as its candidate Alfred Onions, an Englishman who had come to south Wales in 1883. He had been a checkweigher, then a miners' agent and he had been treasurer of the SWMF since its inception in 1898. For twenty-seven years he had been a Labour representative on various local authorities, he had been a county councillor for twelve years and for four years he had been a magistrate, an honour that many Welsh labour leaders had thought to be beyond their reach. There was a hint of the old politics in Onions's welcoming 'the additional support of every Progressive' and the press gave him the old Lib-Lab accolade when it described him as 'reliable, moderate and cautious', but there was no mistaking the fact that in East Glamorgan the miners had opted for a Labour man. Onions had always been in favour of affiliation and it was made clear that his views 'entirely accorded with the policy of the Labour Party'. Mardy Jones, a political organiser for the SWMF, reported that in 1910 there had been no organisation in the constituency although there had been a Labour candidate but 'now they had an effective organisation with a committee at work in every polling district and practically all the Trade Union branches in the division affiliated to the local Labour Party'.[40]

What we can detect now is a coming together of the right men and the appropriate organisation. In North Monmouthshire the Labour candidate was James Winstone, miners' agent, Baptist preacher, ILPer and Monmouthshire County Councillor. In 1914 he presided over what was - significantly - the first meeting ever held in Wales for Labour representatives on public bodies. He told the assembled gathering of county and local councillors and guardians that 'he was sometimes afraid that the majority of workmen had not yet fully appreciated the enormous power which they possessed through industrial and political organisations' but he reminded them that 'their destiny was in their own hands'. He urged trade unionists 'to broaden their scope and extend their influence' for in his view there 'was not a city, town or village where workers could not if they wished elect their own representatives and make the desert blossom like a rose'.[41] If there had been an election in 1915 there would have been miners and other trades unionists who thought that the ILP was rather 'too advanced' and that Vernon Hartshorn was not quite regular enough in his chapel attendance, but on the whole that election would have seen a significant number of miners' leaders sucessfully standing for Labour and pointing to the future. At the local level there was now a significant Labour presence on most urban district councils and for the first time local government control was becoming a reality. The political side-effect of industrial unrest was perhaps first evident at the local level. The war that intervened in this story was at first to give the old politics one last chance but in effect the battle had been won. Wales was a democratic country covered by a network of public bodies and by 1914 it had already been determined that all the energy and ambition of those working-men who would inevitably dominate those bodies would be put at the disposal of the Labour Party. In those last years before 1914 it was a question of waiting for the men and the organisations to arrive. The war was just to speed up the whole process by giving Labour men a new prominence.

In areas like south Wales the rise of working-class politicians had been inevitable; they would willy-nilly have swamped elections. The issue to be determined was the way in which those working-class representatives were to be organised. The bitter fight-back by the Liberals in 1910 and the last ditch complaints of the Lib-Labs give the superficial appearance of a close-run struggle. In fact deep currents were always taking things Labour's way. Keir Hardie offered a vision of independence and small groups of ILPers did the spade work but they had several very important things going for them. At a vital moment personal life-styles and a lack of organisation made it impossible for the Liberal Party to concentrate exclusively on economic and industrial issues whilst at every stage the logic and actual experience of trade unionism was sanctioning political independence. Economic pressures were clinching the role of unions and then taking working-men into a new politics. As the case for independence was accepted so working-men found that they already had whole cadres of their own men ready to take over every aspect of political and social life. We can talk of men being converted to a belief that independent political action could improve the well-being of working people but that belief came at the very moment in which a whole army of would-be councillors and politicians were offering their services. The patterns and psychology of working-class life were demanding a new agency and in truth the most telling arguments were the very careers and energy of the new men. The great struggle in north and south Wales had been the battle over a whole generation to establish meaningful trade unions. In truth Labour's case was won in the Edwardian years far more easily than we suspect. At the 1906 conference of the SWMF a delegate from the floor, Mr. Alfred Willis of Abertillery, pointed to the MPs on the platform and argued, 'You must be Labour men pure and simple . . . Good heavens is there not enough dignity attached to Labour for us to stand on our own legs?'. There were some prejudices to be overcome but was there ever any real doubt as to how that last question would be answered?[42]

NOTES

1. _Labour Leader_, 8 June 1906.
2. _South Wales Daily News_, 21 July 1907.
3. In 1909 the South Wales miners voted 74,675 to 44,616 in favour of affiliation.
4. In general terms the SWMF with a membership of 121,000 in 1906 dominated social and industrial matters in Wales. R. Page Arnot, _A History of the South Wales Miners Federation 1898-1914_, (Allen and Unwin, London, 1967). The electoral significance of the SWMF vote has been carefully examined in Roy Gregory, _The Miners and British Politics 1906-1914_, (Oxford, University Press, 1968). Gregory estimates that in the south Wales of 1910 the mining vote constituted over 70 per cent of the electorate in one constituency, between 60-70 per cent in one constituency, between 50-60 per cent in two, between 40-50 per cent in one, between 30-40 per cent in one, between 20-30 per cent in two, and between 10-20 per cent in a further three.
5. _South Wales Daily News_, 9 June 1908.
6. _Llais Llafur_, 26 Feb. 1910.
7. K.O. Morgan, _Rebirth of a Nation, Wales 1880-1980_ (Clarendon Press, Oxford, 1981), p. 26 _et seq_.
8. _Llais Llafur_, 14 May 1910.
9. For the defensive attitude of the Lib-Labs see Peter Stead, 'Working-Class Leadership in South Wales, 1900-1920', _Welsh History Review_, vol. 6, no. 3 (1973), and 'The Language of Edwardian Politics' in David Smith (ed.), _A People and A Proletariat_ (Pluto Press, London, 1981).
10. _Glamorgan Gazette_, 17 Aug. 1906.
11. _South Wales Daily News_, 17 July 1906.
12. _Ibid._, 23 July 1906.
13. J. Roose Williams, _Quarryman's Champion, the Life and Activities of W. J. Parry of Coetmor_ (Gwasg Gee, Denbigh, 1978).
14. _South Wales Daily News_, 10 June 1911.
15. Jack Jones, _Unfinished Journey_ (Hamish Hamilton, London, 1938),p.86. For Hardie and Merthyr see Henry Pelling, _The Origins of the Labour Party_ (Macmillan, London, 1954) and K. O. Morgan, _Keir Hardie_, (Weidenfeld and Nicolson, London, 1975).
16. ILP, _General Conference Reports_, and _Labour Leader_, 20 Nov. 1908.
17. _South Wales Daily News_, 30 Dec. 1907 and _Llais Llafur_, 30 May 1908.

18. Llais Llafur, 18 Apr. 1908.

19. Ibid., 2 Oct. 1909.

20. Ibid., 16 Oct. 1909.

21. South Wales Daily News, 1 Jan. 1908.

22. Cambrian, 23 Feb., 23 Mar. and 22 June, 1906.

23. Llais Llafur, 21 May 1910.

24. Peter Stead, 'Vernon Hartshorn', Glamorgan Historian, vol. VI (1970).

25. Cambrian, 8 Nov. 1907.

26. South Wales Daily News, 17 Apr. 1908.

27. Ibid., 28 July 1906.

28. Hywel Francis and David Smith, The Fed, A History of the South Wales Miners in the Twentieth Century, (Lawrence and Wishart, London, 1980) p. 1 et seq., David Smith, 'Tonypandy 1910: Definitions of Community', in Past and Present, no. 87 (1980), and L. J. Williams, 'The Road to Tonypandy', in Llafur, vol. 1, no. 2 (1973). Also R. McKibbin, The Evolution of the Labour Party 1910-1924, (Oxford, University Press, 1974).

29. Gregory, The Miners.

30. ILP, General Conference Reports.

31. Labour Leader, 24 Apr. 1913.

32. Llais Llafur, 1 Feb. 1913.

33. South Wales Daily News, 3 July 1913.

34. Ibid., 12 Aug. 1913.

35. SWMF, Minutes, Annual Conference, 31 Mar. 1913.

36. SWMF, Executive Minutes, 9 Aug. 1913.

37. Ibid., 23 Feb. 1914.

38. Cyril Parry, 'Gwynedd Politics, 1900-1920: The Rise of a Labour Party', Welsh History Review, vol. 6, no. 3 (1973). See also Merfyn Jones, The North Wales Quarrymen, 1874-1922 (University of Wales Press, Cardiff, 1981), p. 315 et seq. and Cyril Parry, The Radical Tradition in Welsh Politics – a study of Liberal and Labour Politics in Gwynedd 1900-1920 (University Press, Hull, 1970).

39. South Wales Daily News, 3 Apr. 1913.

40. Ibid., 8 June 1914.

41. Ibid., 3 June 1914.

42. Ibid., 13 Mar. 1906.

Chapter Four

LABOUR IN THE MUNICIPALITIES

In his <u>History of the Labour Party</u>, published in 1948, G.D.H. Cole remarked that it would be a difficult task to gather the necessary material for a comprehensive picture of Labour's involvement with local government before the first world war.[1] Although the number of local studies of the labour movement in this period has dramatically increased since Cole made this comment it is only in the last few years that attempts have been made to provide a general picture of labour activity in the sphere of local government.[2] This essay reviews the nature of labour and socialist thought about local government before the first world war and the extent to which the Labour Party was successful at the polls.

In 1902 <u>The Times</u> published a series of articles on 'municipal socialism' which detailed the extent to which municipalities were undertaking trading activities and involving themselves in the provision of social welfare.[3] The subsequent scare generated by these articles greatly exaggerated both the influence of socialist representatives in local government and the extent to which councils were committing themselves to collectivism. In reality, Labour was making slow progress at the municipal polls and its programmes contained much that was acceptable to its opponents.

To the late Victorian thinkers whose writings converted many to socialism the new century was destined to bring a transfer of power from the centre to the locality - from Whitehall to the Town Hall. In the writings of William Morris, for instance, decentralisation was a necessary corollary of socialism. In 1893, Morris published a socialist 'text-book', <u>Socialism: its Growth and Outcome</u>, written with Ernest Bax. Morris and Bax believed that the national political system ought to be 'starved out': 'there should take place a gradual and increasing delegation of the present powers of the central government to municipal and local bodies, until the political nation should be sapped, and give place to the federation of local and industrial organisations'.[4] In a more popular vein George Haw's book, Today's Work, Municipal Government, The Hope of Democracy, published at the turn of the century, expressed similar sentiments. In Chapter One, entitled 'The Waning of Parliament', he informed his readers that the best work of Parliament had been done and the era of the municipality had arrived:

> Our local government is as nearly ideal as it can possibly be. Neither America nor France, under Republics, excel our municipal code. We have the largest franchise and the widest powers. Americans themselves admit that our municipal institutions are fifty years in advance of theirs.[5]

Russell Smart of the ILP declared in his pamphlet, Municipal Socialism, that the movement of English democracy was towards decentralisation.[6] It was commonly assumed by socialists in the 1890s that more and more powers would be transferred from central to local government and that any new functions would be entrusted to the municipalities.

The Independent Labour Party was the most successful of the socialist groups which contested local elections in the 1890s. Always a negligible force in London the ILP was rooted in the provinces, with particular strongholds in the West Riding and Scotland. This provincial strength meant its members regarded local politics as of great importance. From its inception in 1893 the ILP realised that it had to be involved in municipal politics if it was to spread the message of socialism to the voter. The emphasis on the importance of local politics became more pronounced after the débâcle at the general election of 1895 in which the party's sole MP, Keir Hardie, lost his seat. In 1898 the party instituted an annual 'Conference of Elected Persons' at which a variety of policy issues of concern to councillors, guardians and school board members were discused. Shortly afterwards a Local Government Information Bureau was opened in conjunction with the Fabian Society to answer queries from local representatives.

In the 1890s the ILP was as convinced as William Morris about the necessity of transferring power to the locality. In their work on town councils, boards of guardians and school boards ILP members promoted measures which would aid the working class. On the school boards they supported the extension of the system of Higher Grade (secondary) schooling so that more working class children would be able to take advantage of it. ILP representatives also pressed for the interests of poor children and campaigned for school baths, schoolfeeding and other welfare measures. The Education Act of 1902 which abolished the school boards and transferred their powers to the local authorities was roundly condemned by the ILP for removing education from direct democratic control.[7]

After the Local Government Act of 1894 extended the poor law franchise the ILP regarded the boards of guardians as local electoral bodies which should be utilised. An ILP leaflet What Boards of Guardians Can Do stated: 'One great reason why workingmen should interest themselves in Poor Law work is that there need be no delay in waiting for new Acts of Parliament'.[8] In the 1890s the ILP was hopeful that boards of guardians could be used to provide work for the unemployed. The failure of these efforts meant that the ILP increasingly looked to local government for the alleviation of the 'social problem'.

The Social Democratic Federation also accorded the municipality a great deal of importance, believing that socialist-controlled town councils would be vivid examples of the superiority of the socialist alternative. Municipalisation was another, and welcome, stage in the development of capitalism as it would make the introduction of complete public ownership under socialism more feasible. As Harry Quelch expressed it, the municipality 'demonstrates the practicality of public collective ownership'.[9]

Trades councils had promoted their own candidates at local elections at various times during the late nineteenth century. After the inception of the ILP this activity declined but the formation of the national Labour Representation Committee in 1900 provoked a similar response in the localities. The trades councils now took it on themselves to run labour candidates. In some places this was done because it was felt that the

ILP was too extreme to reflect the views of labour
accurately. In Leeds in 1908 there was a rift
between the trades council and socialist
councillors with each section appealing separately
to the voters.[10] In many towns a joint list of
candidates would be fielded under the auspices of a
'Workers' Municipal Federation' or similarly titled
body. Until 1905 only trades councils were
permitted to affiliate to the Labour Representation
Committee. In 1905 the LRC permitted local Labour
Representation Committees to be formed but only in
areas where there was no trades council.[11]
    Labour and socialist activists were intensely
idealistic about the possibilities of local
government. This 'civic idealism' was strongest in
the ILP. In the West Riding it clearly stemmed
from the nonconformist culture. When he was first
elected to Leeds City Council D.B. Foster, who was
a lay preacher as well as a member of the ILP,
remarked that: 'The Town Hall became to me the
household of God'.[12] To people brought up in
this tradition plans for municipalisation were seen
as a contemporary equivalent of the early
Christians' belief in holding all goods in common.
Religious imagery was pervasive. Many would have
agreed with these sentiments expressed in the
Municipal Reformer.

> We want a municipal creed with such articles
> as these 'I believe in clean streets and clean
> lives; I believe that what hurts one hurts
> all; I believe in the individual
> responsibility of each man for the collective
> good . . . . A man who does not love the town
> of which he forms a part, and does not take an
> active part in its affairs, is no citizen, but
> a social tramp, an Ishmaelite among the
> people.[13]

Although most frequently expressed by ILP members
such sentiments were not confined to that party.
Dan Irving of the SDF told the readers of his
pamphlet The Municipality, from a Worker's Point of
View: 'The corporation is your corporate self - the
expression of your corporate being'.[14] Appeals
like these were often made to a working class
ignorant of the powers and duties of town councils
and many of whom could not see why they should
bother to register to vote.
    In the 1900s this optimism about the potential
of local government seemed a natural part of the

'evolutionary socialism' which Ramsay MacDonald had popularised. F.W. Jowett's municipal primer, The Socialist and the City, published in 1907, exemplified this approach.[15] Before his election as MP for West Bradford in 1906 Jowett had been an Alderman on the Bradford City Council and Chairman of the Health Committee. Drawing on this experience for his book he acknowledged that public opinion had to be convinced of the importance of reforms otherwise they would be electorally unpopular. To Jowett the 'next step' was always the most important in municipal government:

> The future must grow out of the present; it cannot be created to fit in with a plan. The socialist, in the city life of today, is painfully trying, amid many difficulties and much misunderstanding, unfortunately accompanied also by a considerable amount of misrepresentation to change the municipal institutions at present in existence, to extend their scope and add to their number, so as to bring them in harmony with the social gospel which he preaches in accordance with his convictions.[16]

As might be guessed the kinds of reforms that Jowett advocated in his book - site value rating, more corporation housing - although 'radical measures, were not beyond the pale of political discussion in council chambers. They represented an acceleration of the pace at which many local authorities were already moving in the extension of their powers. Sections of the Liberal Party were not only wholeheartedly committed to such social reforms but were also actively attempting to persuade labour candidates to join 'progressive' alliances. The extent to which such alliances, formal or informal, could lead to major extensions of municipal activity was a source of real alarm to those opposed to the spread of 'municipal socialism'. The gradualism exemplified in F.W. Jowett's approach owed something to Fabian influence. The Fabian Society's tracts on municipal topics were widely read and extensively used by Labour groups on councils.[17] Had the Fabians been prepared to back the idea of an independent labour party in the 1890s then their influence would have been still greater.

Labour proposals on municipalisation fell largely into two categories. First were those which would provide a more efficient service and improve the conditions of staff. Secondly, there were measures designed to improve the health and welfare of the working class. It was the first category, designated 'municipal trading', which attracted the ire of opponents of 'municipal socialism'. They argued that it was no business of the council to run trams and supply electric lighting, gas or other services. This served merely to put private firms out of business and was an unwarranted intrusion into the market. A long-running controversy followed in the wake of the series of articles in The Times which had highlighted this activity, with an Industrial Freedom League being formed in order to co-ordinate opposition to future municipalisation schemes. Understandably there was a fierce reaction from the trades threatened by such proposals. After the plans for the municipalisation of public houses and the coal supply were widely mooted numbers of publicans and coal merchants felt it their duty to represent their fellow citizens as members of the council.

Labour and socialist councillors were particularly keen to introduce measures which would improve the health and conditions of working people. In the 1890s they urged that the Housing of the Working Classes Act should be used by local authorities to clear slum areas and build corporation houses. In the wake of the scare over 'physical deterioration' labour spokesmen demanded that councils start feeding hungry school children. The ILP's Margaret Macmillan played an important role in educating the rank and file to the importance of such issues and after the passage of the Education (Provision of Meals) Act in 1906 she was zealous in her efforts to ensure that ILP branches should press for local authorities to open school clinics. Although there was some opposition from the medical profession to the growth of school and baby clinics there was generally much less opposition to municipal involvement in the sphere of health and welfare, probably because it did not affect so many vested interests. Yet there is some evidence to suggest that social reforms which involved an increase in the number of officials empowered to investigate families' circumstances were not welcomed by the working class.[18] Labour spokesmen were vulnerable to the argument that socialism meant a great increase in officialdom.[19]

Yet it should not be thought that Labour's

approach to municipalisation was non-ideological, merely an acceleration of the reforms proposed by the progressives in the Liberal Party.[20] For Labour and socialist spokesmen did not always respect the proprieties of Edwardian politics. For instance, the municipalisation of hospitals was widely advocated in the labour movement in the 1900s, but this proposal ran directly contrary to the belief in the efficacy of voluntary action which sustained charitable hospitals, and was abhorrent to most Liberals.[21] In Bradford the woolcombing business had long been renowned for its low wages and appalling working conditions, but the Bradford Labour group's proposal that woolcombing should be municipalised in order to end this state of affairs produced a storm of outrage.[22] The Social Democratic Federation, going far beyond the feeding of poor school children by local authorities, espoused the concept of 'state maintenance'. Recognising that many working class parents were unable to afford to feed and clothe their school-age children the SDF proposed that the state should take on the task, with children attending boarding schools set in the countryside, far from the grime and smoke of the industrial cities.[23] Naturally proposals like this were a gift to the propagandists of the Anti-Socialist Union who were able to present them as a plan to remove children completely from the care of their parents and place them in state institutions.

But for the most part Labour councillors expended their efforts in attempting to improve the conditions of the working class. They were especially concerned with the hours and rates of pay of council workmen. Often a Labour councillor would be an official of a union which had corporation workmen among its membership - the Gasworkers Union or the Tramwaymen's Union, for instance. These councillors could sit on the relevant committee and argue their members' case at first hand. As wage rates were negotiated locally some disquiet was felt about this from councillors in the other parties.[24]

This defence of the interests of corporation manual workers was allied with a vigilant scrutiny of the terms and conditions of salaried staff. Pointing to the disparities between the two groups Labour councillors argued on the grounds of 'municipal economy' that salary increases for top officials should be kept to a minimum. Yet parsimony in this area could mean that the best

95

officials would not be attracted to work for the
local authority, a point which came to be
acknowledged by labour groups. Another area where
all labour councillors were active was the question
of 'Fair Contracts'. In the late nineteenth
century, trades councils had been active in
persuading local authorities to adopt 'Fair
Contract' clauses which ensured that municipal
contracts were not awarded to firms which paid less
than trade union rates. Labour councillors were
vigilant in their scrutiny of contracts, wishing
the municipality to become a model employer.[25]
They also advocated that councils start direct
works departments similar to that opened by the
London County Council in 1893.

One of the reasons why the debate over
municipalisation raged was because there was a
severe problem about the financing of local
expenditure in the Edwardian period. The Times'
articles on 'municipal socialism' contained one
recurring theme: the increase in rates brought
about by the growth of municipal expenditure as
local authorities extended their sphere of
operations. The 'burden of the rates' was a real
barrier to the expansion of municipal activity.
Avner Offer has estimated that rates increased four
fold between 1860 and 1912.[26] The brunt of the
increase fell upon the lower middle class, the
owners of shops and small workshops, who were the
section of the population perhaps most susceptible
to arguments which blamed 'municipal extravagance'
for the additional expenditure. The opponents of
municipal socialism characterised labour and
socialist councillors as spendthrifts, careless of
ratepayers' money.

Labour representatives themselves became
extremely sensitive to the charge of 'municipal
extravagance'. There was some attempt to justify
the rate demands of high-spending authorities on
the grounds that many of the services provided –
school meals, and school clinics for instance –
were of direct financial benefit to the working
class.[27] Apart from this 'social wage' defence
of the rates there were two sets of proposals for
the broadening of the revenue base of local
authorities. The first concerned centre-local
relations and called for the extension of the
Grants-in-Aid system. Grants-in-Aid were provided
by central government to local authorities to
supplement their expenditure on certain services,
such as the police. As the activities of local

authorities had grown in the late nineteenth century so the system of Grants-in-Aid had been extended to cover more aspects of expenditure. The grants were not the only way in which central government augmented the budgets of local authorities. There was also a system of 'assigned revenues' by which central government allocated a certain percentage of particular taxes. But these were often used to reduce the general rates burden and gave central government no opportunity of ensuring that there was a minimum standard of service. Sidney Webb was particularly involved in efforts to get the system of Grants-in-Aid extended. For Webb their attraction was that they would enable central government to supervise services and refuse payment to authorities which did not provide a minimum standard. Webb saw it as a way by which a 'national minimum' might be gradually introduced.[28] He proposed that the system of Grants-in-Aid cover fifty per cent of local authorities' expenditure on such services as education and public health.[29]

The second set of proposals for expanding the municipal budget put forward by Labour and socialist representatives concerned local taxation. Labour had long supported the radicals' case for site-value rating, whereby local authorities would be able to gain from the increased value of the land. Another proposal to raise additional revenue was the call for a municipal income tax. Of the two, site-value rating was the most politically feasible. The constraints of municipal finance represented a real check on the extent to which Labour and socialist representatives could argue for an extension of the role of the municipality.[30]

The extent to which Labour councillors could get their proposals accepted depended primarily on their electoral support but also on the degree to which such measures were acceptable to the other parties. Adversarial politics, although not absent from the council chamber, were less in evidence than at Westminster because the committee system afforded even minority parties like Labour some say in policy formation. The best known examples of co-operation between Liberal and Labour representatives were perhaps in London where in the early 1890s the alliance between Labour councillors, led by John Burns, and Progressive representatives on the county council proved to be very fruitful.[31] Progressive and Labour groups had remarkably similar programmes. Much the same set of reforms was introduced by the Progressive Alliance in Battersea as the Labour-dominated West Ham Council pushed through after it gained power in 1898.[32]

Although its opponents made much of Labour's ambitions and the threat of municipal socialism, the reality was far different. Relatively few constituencies fielded Labour candidates in the Edwardian period as the party was generally unable to incur the expense. Consequently the electoral work of the Labour activists consisted mainly in fighting municipal contests and the elections for the board of guardians. These elections were important in themselves but they also served the function of keeping the Labour case before the electorate and were useful in 'nursing' a constituency for a general election. Labour's activity at municipal elections was fragmented and ill-co-ordinated. Its presence on town and city councils was seldom substantial - even in large cities usually a mere handful out of a council of seventy or eighty.

One of the major handicaps for Labour was the size and extent of the municipal franchise. Many working class electors were disfranchised because of the operation of the electoral system. Lodgers were ineligible to vote and as the register for the November municipal election was drawn up in the July of the previous year many working class people were disfranchised because they subsequently moved. Married women who owned property were included in this franchise but few of these would have been likely to vote Labour. It has been estimated that the municipal franchise rarely exceeded twenty per cent of the population.[33]

Despite these hindrances Labour made a steady advance at municipal elections in the early twentieth century. M.G. Sheppard has analysed the distribution of the Labour vote at municipal elections in the period 1901-1913.[34] He demonstrates that despite some temporary setbacks the size of the Labour vote increased as did the number of successful Labour councillors. The contrast between 1901 and 1913 is revealing. In 1901 Labour's 116 candidates won 21 municipal seats, whereas in 1913 171 out of 426 were successful. The number of municipalities fought increased from 52 to 123.[35]

Sheppard's analysis does not include London or Scotland but within England and Wales he shows that the Labour vote was concentrated in northern England, Yorkshire, Lancashire, Peak Don and the east and west Midlands. These regions accounted for almost four-fifths of the municipalities fought by Labour in the period and slightly more than four-fifths of all candidates put forward.[36] Yorkshire and Lancashire predominated in Labour's municipal successes. Together the two counties contained almost one third of all municipalities fought by Labour and more than one third of all Labour candidates.[37]

The controversy over 'municipal socialism' and the exaggerated scares as to the intentions of Labour representatives were the probable causes of a decline in the number of candidates elected between 1906 and 1907. There was another decline in 1910 when the effect of the Osborne Judgement, and the fact that the trade unions and Labour forces had to fight two general elections in one year, left little money or energy available for the municipal elections.

In aggregate in 1913, Labour presented candidates in one third of the municipalities in England and Wales studied by Sheppard. Although there had been significant advances, when examined city by city the Labour position still looks fragile. Even in the 'municipal beacon' of Bradford, after the elections of 1913 which brought it forty-three per cent of the poll, the Labour-Socialist group was still the smallest party on the council with twenty seats to the Liberals' thirty-one and the Conservatives' thirty-two.[38] In large part this was because of an electoral pact reached between the Conservatives and Liberals which ensured Labour had to face straight fights. This was an increasing pattern across the country. In some towns there would be an anti-Labour electoral agreement which covered all the municipal contests in a particular year. In 1913 Labour faced such alliances in twelve towns.[39] While there had been continuous Labour representation on the Bradford council since 1892 this had only been the case in neighbouring Leeds since 1903. By 1913 Labour had fourteen seats in Leeds which was two more than the Liberals but dwarfed by the twenty-five seats held by the Conservatives.[40] In Birmingham there was no Labour representation until 1911 when six councillors were returned. In 1914 this number had increased to eight but on a council of 120.[41] In Sheffield there was no Labour presence on the council until 1905 and by

1912 this had completely disappeared.[42] These were all major cities which possessed identifiable working class cultures and institutions. In smaller towns the position of Labour was much weaker. Chris Cook has remarked that: 'In the smaller boroughs, in the county towns and cathedral cities, Labour's impact had been virtually non-existent'.[43] By 1914 at the level of local government, Labour was still a struggling third party which had failed to 'break the mould'.

By 1914 there was, therefore, a greater realism about the potential of municipalities. Labour remained a minority party on town and city councils and even in its areas of greatest strength it lacked the necessary electoral support to win control of councils. There was a growing recognition that some problems, notably unemployment, could only be tackled by the national government. Equally there was a greater sophistication in relation to policy. This can be clearly seen in the ILP.

After 1909, the year of the publication of the Report of the Royal Commission on the Poor Laws, social policy measures began to predominate in the programme of the ILP and the influence of the Fabian Society became more pronounced. The ILP enthusiastically backed the Webbs' proposals for the abolition of the poor law and the transfer of responsibilities from the boards of guardians to town councils. By this time most Labour and socialist representatives had despaired of being able to utilise the powers of the guardians on behalf of the unemployed as had been envisaged in the 1890s. By 1912 the ILP and Fabian Society were actively co-operating in a 'War on Poverty' campaign aimed at establishing the 'national minimum'. This extensive programme called for 'healthy homes for all', complete provision against sickness (as opposed to the limited coverage of the 1911 National Insurance Act), child welfare measures, a 48 hour week and the abolition of the poor law.[44] In reply to criticisms that this was to substitute social reform for socialism the ILP chairman, W.C. Anderson, remarked that: 'If the socialist city is to have firm foundations we must drain the bogs and swamps'.[45] Although much of this programme was designed to be implemented at the municipal level it had to be passed at Westminster and there was scant chance of this happening.

After 1910 there was some disillusionment with

the parliamentary route to socialism being pursued by the Labour Party. In the ILP this found expression in the shape of the 'Bradford resolution' which was debated annually from 1911 at that party's conference. Essentially this called for a complete overhaul of the machinery of government which could best be accomplished by replacing the cabinet by a committee system. Each minister would be chairman of a committee composed of MPs who were specialists in the area covered by his ministry. The 'Bradford resolution' was proposing then that the Commons be remodelled along the lines of the council chamber.[46]

Although the 'Bradford resolution' became ILP policy in 1914 the plan was soon forgotten after war was declared. The centralisation of state power brought about by the war also ended the hopes of those who believed in a devolution of power to the municipality. By 1913-1914 twenty-four per cent of local authority expenditure was financed by central government.[47] As this percentage rose after the first world war municipal autonomy declined and Keir Hardie's contention of 1906 that 'it became increasingly evident that socialism in this country would come through the municipality' seemed to belong to another age.[48]

NOTES

1. G.D.H. Cole, A History of the Labour Party from 1914 (Routledge, Kegan Paul, London, 1948), p.445.
2. See, in particular, C. Cook, 'Labour and the Downfall of the Liberal Party, 1906-14', in A. Sked and C. Cook (eds.), Crisis and Controversy (Macmillan, London, 1976), pp.38-65 and M.G. Sheppard, 'Labour at Municipal Elections 1901-1913', unpublished M.A. thesis, University of Warwick, 1976: also, M.G. Sheppard and J.L. Halstead, 'Labour's Municipal Election Performance in Provincial England and Wales, 1901-13', Bulletin of the Society for the Study of Labour History, vol. 39 (1979), pp.39-62.
3. The first article was published on 19 Aug. 1902. For an early response see J. Keir Hardie, 'The Times versus Divinity', Labour Leader, 30 Aug. 1902.
4. William Morris and E. Belfort Bax, Socialism: its Growth and Outcome (Swan Sonnenschein, London, 1893), p.282.
5. George Haw, Today's Work. Municipal

Government. The Hope of Democracy, (The Clarion Newspaper, London, 1901), p.15.

6. H. Russell Smart, Municipal Socialism (Manchester, Labour Library, n.d.).

7. ILP, Annual Report, 1902.

8. ILP, What the Boards of Guardians Can Do (1897).

9. H. Quelch, The Social Democratic Federation: its Objects, its Principles and its Work (Twentieth Century Press, London, 1905), p.13.

10. See George L. Bernstein, 'Liberalism and the Progressive Alliance in the constituencies, 1900-1914: three case studies', Historical Journal, vol. 26, no. 3 (1983), p.628.

11. See A. Clinton, The Trade Union Rank and File: Trades Councils in Britain, 1900-40 (Manchester, University Press, 1977).

12. D.B. Foster, Socialism and the Christ: My Two Great Discoveries in a Long and Painful Search for Truth (Leeds, 1921).

13. Municipal Reformer, Mar. 1902.

14. Dan Irving, The Municipality, from a Worker's Point of View (Twentieth Century Press, London, n.d.), p.15.

15. F.W. Jowett, The Socialist and the City (George Allen, London, 1907).

16. Ibid., p.3.

17. See A.M. McBriar, Fabian Socialism and English Politics 1884-1918 (Cambridge, University Press, 1962).

18. On this see Henry Pelling, 'The Working Class and the Origins of the Welfare State', in his Popular Politics and Society in Late Victorian Britain (Macmillan, London, 1979); see also Stephen Yeo, 'Working Class Association, Private Capital, Welfare and the State in the Late Nineteenth and Twentieth Centuries', in Noel Parry, Michael Rustin and Carole Satyamurti (eds.), Social Work, Welfare and the State (Edward Arnold, London, 1979).

19. For a defence see J.B. Glasier, 'The Plague of Officials. How Capitalism Creates it. How Socialism Would Abolish It', Labour Leader, 20 Dec. 1907.

20. Derek Fraser argues that 'There was . . . no greater ideological thrust from municipal labour than from elsewhere in the political spectrum'. See Derek Fraser, 'The Edwardian City', in Donald Read (ed.), Edwardian England (Croom Helm, London, 1982), p.65.

21. A theme vividly illustrated in Stephen

Yeo, <u>Religion and Voluntary Organisations in Crisis</u> (Croom Helm, London, 1976).

22. Bradford City Council, <u>Proceedings,</u> 1907-8, 29 Sept. 1908

23. See J. Hunter Watts, <u>State Maintenance for Children</u> (Twentieth Century Press, London, 1904).

24. See E.P. Hennock, <u>Fit and Proper Persons</u> (Edward Arnold, London, 1973), pp.326-32.

25. See Clinton, <u>Trade Union Rank and File</u>, pp.16-18.

26. Avner Offer, <u>Property and Politics,</u> 1870-1914 (Cambridge, University Press, 1981).

27. See, for instance, Philip Snowden, <u>A Straight Talk to Ratepayers</u> (ILP, London, 1907).

28. See Sidney Webb, <u>Grants-in-Aid: A Criticism and a Proposal</u> (Longman, London, 1911).

29. See the paper Sidney Webb gave to the Conference of Elected Persons in 1913 entitled 'Municipal Finance and Municipal Autonomy', <u>Labour Leader</u>, 27 Mar. 1913.

30. See F.W. Jowett, 'The necessity of state assistance towards the expenditure of local authorities', <u>Labour Leader</u>, 28 Oct., 4 Nov., 11 Nov. 1910.

31. See Kenneth D. Brown, 'London and the historical reputation of John Burns', <u>London Journal</u> (Nov. 1976), pp.226-38.

32. On Battersea see C.J. Wrigley, 'Liberals and the desire for working class representation in Battersea, 1886-1922' in K.D. Brown (ed.), <u>Essays in Anti-Labour History</u> (Macmillan, London, 1974); and on West Ham see Paul Thompson, <u>Socialists, Liberals and Labour: The Struggle for London 1885-1914</u> (Routledge, Kegan Paul, London, 1967), p.133; also see Edward G. Howarth and Mona Wilson, <u>West Ham: A Study in Social and Industrial Problems</u> (J.M. Dent, London, 1907), pp.312 ff.

33. Cook, 'Labour and the Downfall of the Liberal Party', p.39. On the conditions for obtaining a vote at municipal elections see A. Lawrence Lowell, <u>The Government of England</u> (Macmillan, New York, 1908), vol. II, pp.146-48.

34. Sheppard, 'Labour at Municipal Elections, 1901-13'.

35. Ibid., p.17.

36. Ibid., p.21. The regions used are those employed by Henry Pelling, <u>Social Geography of British Elections 1885-1910</u> (Macmillan, London, 1967).

37. Sheppard, 'Labour at Municipal Elections', p.21.

38. See Cook, 'Labour and the Downfall of the Liberal Party', pp.45-7.

39. According to Labour Leader, 6 Nov. 1913 these were: Barnstaple, Birmingham, Bradford, Brighouse, Colchester, Dukinfield, Halifax, Keighley, Leeds, Morley and Stockport.

40. See Labour Leader, 16 July 1914. Also Tom Woodhouse 'The Working Class' in Derek Fraser (ed.), A History of Modern Leeds (Manchester, University Press, 1980).

41. Labour Leader, 30 July 1914.

42. H.E. Mathers, 'Sheffield Municipal Politics, 1893-1926', unpublished PhD thesis, University of Sheffield, 1979.

43. Cook, 'Labour and the Downfall of the Liberal Party', p.58.

44. See Labour Leader, 5 Sept. 1912 and subsequent issues.

45. ILP, Annual Report, 1913, p.43

46. For a complete exposition see F.W. Jowett and Robert Jones, The Parliamentary Labour Party and the Bradford Resolution (ILP, Manchester, 1914).

47. See W.A. Robson, 'Labour and Local Government', Political Quarterly, vol. 24, no. 1 (1953), pp.39-55.

48. Labour Leader, 2 Nov. 1906.

Chapter Five

THE LABOUR PARTY PRESS

'If we wish to maintain our movement intact and preserve its independence, we can only do so by possessing a Press which represents the principles for which the movement stands.'[1]

With these words at the 1911 Trades Union Congress at Newcastle upon Tyne, T.E. Naylor explained to delegates the reasons for the imminent appearance of the Daily Herald, a daily strike sheet which had briefly appeared during the printers' strike of 1911 and which it was now proposed to relaunch as a daily newspaper. An explanation was certainly needed. Prominent members of the TUC were at that very moment engaged in preparing for the launch of another Labour daily newspaper, an official paper for the labour movement, to be called the Daily Citizen, and a number of trade unions were contemplating substantial investments in it. It was a profoundly disturbing situation.

The history of the Labour press in Britain is a history of struggle, with much failure and little success. Judged by the criteria of conventional publishing, there is no doubt that the British labour movement has never succeeded in developing a viable press.[2] To some degree this may have been the inevitable consequence of the political fragmentation which underlay the apparently monolithic structure of the movement; each section jealously developed and cultivated its own press and there was little co-operation between the different elements. Another explanation, much favoured by leaders of the movement, is that the mass of the British public preferred to be entertained rather than be informed, that the 'softer' approach of the commercial press was more palatable than the necessarily rigorous content of theoretically-committed newspapers and journals.

Why then did the Labour Party, a federation of different groups bound together by a common interest in winning parliamentary representation and less hide-bound to a particular political theology than many other political groups, not develop a successful and vigorous press? It is not easy to find a single answer, but an examination of the periodical press of the LRC and the early Labour Party provides some pointers to an answer.

The Labour Party lacked, in its earliest phase, the structural coherence of conventional political parties, even of parties such as the ILP or the SDF. Similarly, its press was less homogeneous than its counterparts in the other socialist and labour groups. In a sense it is difficult to talk of a specifically Labour Party press before 1914. Instead the party benefited from the support of a variety of periodicals, most of which claimed primary loyalty to parties or groups affiliated to the Labour Party. In 1900 around forty periodicals published in various parts of Britain supported the newly established Labour Representation Committee. During the next fifteen years, a further 113 periodicals were started, and most of these gave support to the LRC. There were few periodicals in this period produced specifically for the party, but taken as a whole the Labour Party press was by no means insignificant, consisting of around fourteen local papers and one national daily newspaper. Yet the whole was no greater than the sum of the parts. The Labour Party press was, in the period up to 1914, a disappointment.

From the outset, the leaders of the Labour Party were fully aware of contemporary developments in the press. They were living in an age which was discovering the power of the press. New commercial papers were being launched at an unprecedented rate, the weekly press was flourishing and the reviews were still holding their own as the required reading of educated and intelligent opinion makers.[3] Both in Britain and in the United States the age of the press barons had already dawned and within a few years leading politicians would be expressing their own concern at the irresponsible and unaccountable influence wielded by men such as Alfred Harmsworth and the Kemsleys. Even before this latest development in the history of the British press socialists had realised the importance of cultivating their own media. From the earliest days of the socialist movement, periodicals and journalism had played a crucial part in articulating the aims and objectives of socialism. Many of the leaders of the labour movement were themselves journalists in the sense that they wrote regularly in the press and often helped to organise it; after all, the press was the major mass medium available to politicians. Moreover, socialists had long suspected that their progress was hampered not only by the weakness of their own press but by the way their opponents deployed theirs. Despite the disadvantages of the lack of money, skill, experience and even market, these socialist pioneers invested prodigious amounts of time, energy, and whenever possible money as well, in launching and sustaining a variety of weekly and monthly papers. In its first decade the ILP alone, to which many of the leaders of the Labour Party belonged, published over seventy papers as far afield as Musselburgh and Plymouth.[4]

The establishment of the Labour Representation Committee in theory offered new prospects for the Labour press; a potentially greater readership, greater resources and a more widely dispersed and effective organisational support. In the event the Labour Party failed to fulfil this early promise.

Conventionally the provincial labour weeklies and monthlies played an important part in the corporate life of the socialists of their district and as cogs in the political and administrative wheels of party branches. They were noticeboards for party activity, which is why the appearance of a local paper was usually the reflection of the vigour of the branch itself. It is not altogether surprising therefore that so few papers were produced in this period specifically for the Labour Party. Its branch network was slow to develop. Neither Glasgow nor London, for example, had central Labour Parties before 1914 and elsewhere the organisation was patchy.

The appearance of Labour Party papers falls approximately in two periods. There was a burst of activity around 1904, just at the time when affiliations to the LRC began to climb rapidly. Between 1902 and 1904, the number of affiliated trades councils increased from 21 to 76, affiliated trade unions from 65 to 165 and the membership from 469,000 to 970,000.[5] Although this growth was not mirrored by a commensurate growth in the Labour press, nine new LRC papers were launched, in

Jarrow, Leeds, Eccles, Barrow, Bradford, Newport, Croydon, York and Wakefield. Thereafter there was a lull. The Labour breakthrough at the general election of 1906 did not produce a significant increase in the number of local papers being produced though, as we shall see, it did stimulate interest in the potential of the press more widely. By the end of 1907 there were only four LRC papers in circulation though to these should be added the dozen or so local ILP papers which were in existence. From the end of 1909, however, there was a new spate of activity. A number of local ILP papers were started and between 1910 and 1912 six more LRC papers were launched, in Bow, Manchester, Barrow, Bradford, Leeds and Blackpool.[6]

The geographical distribution of Labour Party papers no more reflects the pattern of the party's real strength than the distribution of ILP or SDF papers is an index of the local strength or weakness of those parties. Some of the new Labour Party papers, it is true, appeared in areas noted for their tradition of labour journalism. Leeds, for example, where there had been no fewer than six ILP papers prior to 1900 saw the appearance of two LRC papers before 1905, the Armley and Wortley Pioneer and the East Leeds New Times. Neither paper appears to have been successful but in 1911 a new paper was launched under the auspices of the LRC to serve the whole of the Leeds labour movement, the Leeds Weekly Citizen which became in time the longest serving labour paper in Britain. Bradford, another major centre of ILP journalism since the early 1890s, saw the appearance of another ILP paper, the Bradford Pioneer, in 1912 but this soon became the organ of the local LRC as well. Under the editorship of F.W. Jowett it became one of the best known local Labour papers of the inter-war years.

Elsewhere in Yorkshire the LRC was active and enterprising. The short-lived York Labour News of 1904 was followed by the York Daily Labour News which was published in support of G.H. Stuart, the LRC candidate in 1906. In Wakefield the local LRC conducted a most interesting experiment when it purchased in 1905 a long established local commercial paper, the Wakefield Echo, which had first appeared in 1874.[7] Either the paper was already in difficulties when the LRC stepped in, which is likely, or the party's handling of the paper's affairs was less than skilful but the paper ceased publication within a year. It should be borne in mind that at this time two of the most successful ILP papers were also being published in Yorkshire, the Sheffield Guardian and the Huddersfield Worker, while the ILP's own national paper, the Labour Leader was circulating widely in this area.

Elsewhere in the north west the vigour which had been so characteristic of the ILP press in the 1890s was sustained in the LRC. There were several attempts to create local LRC papers, usually in association with the local ILP. The Eccles Pioneer, for example, which appeared in 1905, was produced by the same Peter Lindley who published the Pendlebury Pioneer and several other Manchester ILP papers; indeed it appears to have coexisted with an ILP paper of the same name.[8] The Stockport Herald lasted for three years from 1904 to 1907 while in 1911 an attempt was made, in conjunction with colleagues in Leeds and with the support of the National Labour Press, to establish a weekly paper for the whole of the Manchester area. The Manchester Weekly Citizen, however, was distinctly less successful than its Leeds counterpart.

Further north, the creation of the LRC seemed to have breathed new life into the movement. There was a revival in labour publishing in Barrow and this bore fruit in two papers, the Barrow Pioneer from 1905 to 1908 and the Barrow Guardian after 1910. In Blackpool, however, there was no history of any previous socialist activity and here the LRC successfully ran a monthly paper for almost five years from 1910 onwards. Across the Pennines in Jarrow the local LRC launched the only Labour paper which has been recorded for that borough, the Jarrow Division Labour Herald from 1905 to 1907.

In London the trades councils, which played a key role in founding the London Labour Party, also sustained the local labour press.[9] Four of the five papers in the period up to 1914 which were associated with the LRC were established in areas where the trades council had been particularly active. Islington, where one major initative had been started to establish a federation of London trades councils, saw an attempt in 1906 to run a broad labour paper, the Islington Labour Argus. In three other districts where an attempt had been made to create a rival Federation of Trades and Labour Councils, there were local papers associated with the LRC. Both in West Ham and in Croydon, these were essentially private ventures, the <u>West Ham Citizen</u> being owned and edited in the interest of the LRC by Martin Judge. The <u>Croydon Citizen</u>, published for five years from 1904 to 1909, was run by two individuals in close association with the local trades council, which played an important part in the politics of London trades council movement.

The most successful London paper was the Woolwich <u>Pioneer</u> which had been appearing in one form or another since 1898, though largely under the auspices of the local ILP. In 1904 a new company was formed, the Borough of Woolwich Labour Representation Newspaper and Publishing Company, and though the main motivators were members of the ILP, the list of 636 shareholders is a roll-call of local labour activists and trade unionists.[10] With the support of generous gifts and loans from the American soap millionaire, Joseph Fels, and others, the paper managed to transcend the boundary between the different socialist sects in the borough and stayed afloat, though often with great difficulty, until 1922. A less catholic paper was the <u>Bow and Bromley Worker</u> whose first editor in 1909 was George Lansbury. Though less ambitious, and long-lived, than the Woolwich <u>Pioneer</u>, the <u>Worker</u> played a leading part in labour politics generally in London.[11]

Elsewhere in Britain, the situation was very different. In the midlands there was little activity, as had been the case for the ILP. The <u>Leicester Pioneer</u>, which was established originally by the local ILP in 1901 but taken over by a broadly-based LRC publishing company in 1904, was, it must be acknowledged, a highly successful paper, appearing continuously for 27 years. It was alone in the area, however, apart from a very small number of ILP papers such as the <u>Coventry Sentinel</u> and the <u>Nottingham Labour Journal</u>. In Wales, too, the LRC press made little headway. At the very beginning of the period there was a small flurry of activity in Wales. The Cardiff <u>Labour Pioneer</u> was to all intents and purposes an ILP paper but its editorial board contained members of the local trades council and trades unions in a way highly typical of many local LRCs. The same was true of the <u>South Wales Worker</u> published by the South Wales Labour Press Association, which was organised by many of the individuals who in 1906 formed the Swansea Labour Association. The power-house of the local socialist movement, however, remained the Swansea Socialist Society and when the <u>Swansea</u>

Labour Journal appeared in 1910, it was announced as the organ of the Swansea ILP.[12] Only in Newport did a specifically LRC paper appear at the end of 1905, the Labourite, though this did not last beyond the 1906 election. No such papers were produced either in Scotland or in the great tracts of the west midlands, the south east or the south west of England. In all these places there had been some ILP press activity in the past but no LRC papers appeared there.

The aims and objectives of local LRC and Labour Party periodials were broadly similar to those of the ILP and SDF press. They were intended both as propaganda sheets and as instruments of organisation. However, most were published either during an election campaign or in anticipation of one, and disappeared as soon as the election was over. To that extent, it may be argued that most local LRC papers existed for rather different reasons from the papers of, say, the ILP or the SDF. Reflecting the paramount concern of the Labour Party with winning parliamentary elections rather than breaking new theoretical ground or competing with its affiliated political groups in programmatic politics, the local Labour Party press was very largely concerned with elections. This was an inevitable consequence both of the relationship the LRC had with its component groups and of the fact that its own local structure was rudimentary. The local Labour Party rarely had the same corporate or institutional life as the ILP or SDF; there were no Glee Clubs, Socialist Sunday Schools or orchestras, no Cinderella clubs or cycling groups. The Labour Party's press was rarely called upon, therefore, to perform the same function as its counterparts in other parties. This is not to minimise the role of the local Labour Party press but to suggest that in this period it was qualitatively different from that played by other elements of the socialist press.

As was always the case in labour journalism, however, the party press depended a great deal on the enthusiasm and drive of particular individuals. It is this, more than anything else, which explains the pattern of distribution of the papers, though a local tradition of labour publishing or the particular impetus provided by an election clearly helped. In Barrow, for example, the Barrow Guardian, which lasted from 1910 to 1947, was the third in a line of labour papers beginning with the weekly Barrow ILP Journal which appeared in 1895. Uniquely, the Barrow Labour Party was organised by two men who subsequently became National Agents of the party, Arthur Peters and Egerton Wake, and it was they who organised the publication of the local papers. One of the key figures in the Bow and Bromley Worker was George Lansbury, while Ramsay MacDonald played a leading role in the launching and maintenance of the Leicester Pioneer. Elsewhere, the names of the journalists are more obscure but everywhere there were one or two individuals who undertook the bulk of the work. In Woolwich it was William Barefoot and the indefatigable C.H. Grinling, who devoted his life savings to keeping the Pioneer afloat; in Eccles, Peter Lindley, in Swansea, John Littlejohn; and in Croydon, H.T. Muggeridge, George Gliddon and Harry Sidey. In their localities these were often very well-known people, active in a number of organisations and often serving as local councillors as well.

Financing the local Labour Party press seems to have been no easier than, and indeed no different from, the conventional methods used by the ILP or SDF press.[13] A variety of methods were used. At the simplest level, a local branch or a group of individuals provided the finance on an ad hoc basis. This seems to have been true of the Jarrow Labour Herald, which was run for much of its life by one man. Other papers, unfortunately no longer extant, may well have been organised on an issue by issue basis. On a more complex level, the promoters of a paper could choose either to register their enterprise as a friendly society, as in the case of the South Wales Worker, or, even more ambitiously, as a fully fledged company. The Leicester Pioneer and Woolwich Pioneer were two such companies, the former with 68 shareholders and the later with over 600. They could raise mortgages, issue new stock, arrange debentures and conduct themselves in every way like a commercial business with none of the limitations which were imposed on friendly societies. For a prospering or ambitious paper this was clearly the way forward, but the risks were great, as the stockholders of the Woolwich Pioneer discovered when faced year in, year out by fresh demands for money. Rarely were these companies involved in printing or technical work, though a number of ILP branches did own their printing presses. Instead they dealt with commercial firms, usually sympathetic to their views. One of the most important presses was owned by the ILP, the National Labour Press, which undertook a wide range of business well outside the orbit of the party which owned it.

On the whole the promoters of local Labour Party papers were unambitious. They were modest in their objectives, and when their ventures did survive longer than a few issues, they tended to live from hand to mouth. As George Lansbury put it, describing the Bow and Bromley Worker, which was probably typical:

> This ran until all of us were double bankrupt and had exhausted every avenue for begging or borrowing money. Finnis, Annie and Jessie Johnston were our millionaires, and they were just black-coated workers.[14]

The impecunious state and amateurish conduct of Labour's local press contrasts sharply with the condition of the party's national press, for the most important development in this period was the establishment, for the first time, of a daily Labour newspaper. From the earliest days of the Labour Party, indeed long before that in radical circles, there had been a dream that there should be such a paper. Lack of resources, recognition of the limited market for such a paper and the absence of an appropriate organisational platform from which to launch it had prevented the dream becoming a reality. The birth of the LRC transformed the situation. A vast new readership seemed to be beckoning, the resources of the trades unions were greater than anything available to labour journalists in the past, and the new challenges to the organized workers posed by the Taff Vale case and the increasing power of the commercial press put the idea of a Labour daily paper high on the movement's agenda. Early in 1903, the Parliamentary Committee of the TUC began, therefore, to consider the question seriously.[15]

To some extent the labour movement was simply responding to the trend of the age and, as it believed, following belatedly in the footsteps of its European counterparts. The halfpenny press had only recently begun to make its impact, and the advent of new technology and an aggressive new journalism made socialists acutely aware both of the vulnerability of their own position and also of the possibilities opening up before them. They could look abroad at successful ventures such as Vorwarts which was continually referred to in the socialist press as a paradigm. Above all, they believed that newspapers could not but be profitable. The leaders of the Labour Party were quick to observe that if only some of the one and a half million or so affiliated members of the TUC bought their paper they would immediately be challenging the largest circulating papers of Fleet Street. The Daily Mail's circulation had leapt from 400,000 to 989,000 in only two years, heralding the arrival of a new era in the press. By 1903 there were almost as many people affiliated to the Labour Party as there were readers of the Daily Mail. It is hardly surprising, therefore, that the idea of starting a daily newspaper took on a new urgency at this time.

True, an early initiative at the 1903 LRC Conference failed but the trade unions soon grasped the notion.[16] At the TUC Congress in September 1904 a resolution was carried instructing the Parliamentary Committee to begin negotiations with the LRC and the General Federation of Trade Unions to prepare and submit a scheme for a daily newspaper. A joint committee was established and concluded that in view of the need to raise £150,000 for such a paper, it might be wiser to begin with a weekly paper which would, even then, cost £50,000. In May 1904, a joint circular was issued by the TUC and LRC, canvassing support and soliciting money from the unions. The response was very disappointing. Only 29 replies were received from the 204 unions affiliated to the TUC. Of these fourteen favoured a weekly paper, none wanted a daily and six opposed any paper at all. More important, only three offered any financial support.[17] Undeterred, in 1904 the TUC instructed the Parliamentary Committee to establish a Co-operative Printing Press, in the hope that this positive approach might encourage the more reluctant unions to change their minds. In 1905, however, this scheme was abandoned for lack of support.

In the meantime, a number of private ventures were launched. In 1904 a number of Lib-Lab MPs and trade unions leaders supported the publication of the Weekly Tribune which was directed by Richard Bell and Edmond Browne, a member of the London County Council. The Parliamentary Committee gave its blessing and the paper was financially supported by several unions, including the electricians and the railwaymen. The editorial policy was to support the LRC but its appearance prompted a considerable controversy. Richard Bell, the Labour MP for Derby and leader of the railwaymen, had recently come under fire for his unorthodox dealings with the Liberals and both he and his paper were widely criticised within the LRC. The paper succumbed in May 1904 after just seventeen issues. Ruefully the editors declared:

> We have tried to provide a genuine labour paper in which all shades of opinion might find a common meeting ground and which should make labour news a special feature, but owing to the lack of support from the workers we are unable to carry on any longer [18]

A more promising venture was F.W. Pethick Lawrence's Labour Record and Review which was launched in May 1905 and lasted for over two years before being incorporated in the New Age. The New Age provided an important intellectual forum for the emerging Labour Party though it was even more notable for its literary and artistic commentary.

Soon after the 1906 general election, when it appeared that a new political situation was developing in Britain as a result of the Labour Party's electoral breakthrough, new initiatives were begun. One group of Lib-Lab MPs and trade unionists launched their own daily labour newspaper, The Majority, which appears to have had close links with the Labour Record and Review. The LRC, however, was deeply suspicious of this venture largely because of the intimate connections some of the proprietors appeared to have with the Liberal Party. Within a week the paper was dead, amidst some recriminations.[19]

A more promising initiative was launched by Ramsay MacDonald, now the MP for Leicester. Immediately after the election, a number of letters had begun arriving at LRC headquarters urging the establishment of a party daily.[20] It is possible that MacDonald had been actively pursuing an idea of this kind even before 1906 but from March there was a crescendo of activity. The most practical idea seemed to be to buy and develop an existing newspaper, the most obvious candidate appearing to be the Daily News. A highly respected Liberal paper launched in 1846 and dedicated to Cobdenite ideals of free trade and social justice, among its illustrious former staff were Charles Dickens, Frederick Hunt, Harriet Martineau, Frank Hill and, more recently, Edward Cook. By 1900, however, it was in dire financial straits and David Lloyd George, anxious for a paper to support his beleaguered pro-Boer campaign, engineered a take over with the backing of George Cadbury and his partner Franklin Thomasson, each of whom invested £20,000. Within a year, Thomasson had withdrawn leaving Cadbury to bear the brunt of the paper's continuing financial losses. Over three years he invested £135,000 in the paper, but the losses continued at around £20,000 a year.[21]

Aware, but undeterred by the scale of the losses, Ramsay MacDonald began to explore the possibility of buying the paper from Cadbury, who had already shown sympathy for the Labour cause. The key figure in these negotiations was Henry Wigham, a wealthy Labour Party sympathiser, who offered to invest £10,000 himself and raise a further £15,000 from friends, purely as a commercial stake.[22] Cadbury, however, refused to sell although he was pressed to do so several times over the next three years. Using Edward Pease, Secretary of the Fabian Society, as an intermediary, MacDonald sought the advice of experienced journalists and close associates of Cadbury. A detailed report from P.J. Reid of the North East Daily Gazette was pessimistic, not only over the prospect of Cadbury ever selling the paper, but of the Labour Party ever being able to run it. He wrote:

> The whole affair bristles with difficulties . . . . To attempt to run a national and imperial daily newspaper in London is a titanic task nowadays; to run a socialist daily n and i [sic] daily paper - words fail to describe the difficulty. The thing is this; you need such an efficient organisation and for a time at least unlimited financial resources. Even the Daily News would be a pure speculation if it got into socialist hands. The trading community would boycott it.[23]

With this avenue closed MacDonald sought other alternatives. His closest adviser was Robert Donald, the editor of the Daily Chronicle, who prepared a detailed memorandum on the range of alternatives.[24] The conclusion was unequivocal and similar to the conclusion drawn up by the TUC and LRC some years earlier. Unless the party could persuade Cadbury or another proprietor to part with an established, albeit loss-making, daily paper, the party should contemplate starting nothing more ambitious than a weekly, and even here the best alternative was to buy an existing paper. A blunt and tactless approach to the proprietor of the Reynold News elicited an angry response with demands that the 'source' of the rumours about that paper's financial difficulties should be revealed.[25] Nevertheless, and an indication that Reynolds was looking for work, the paper did offer to place its own printing presses at the disposal of the party, at the appropriate rate of course. Presently a tentative name was mooted, The Morning Herald.

As soon as news of these initiatives became known, LRC headquarters were inundated with unsolicited applications for positions on the new paper from journalists.[26] Heading the queue were those who had been associated with previous ventures of this kind. Arthur Lawrence, the editor of the ill-fated Majority, and Sidney Foxwell, its business manager, both offered their services. Among the other applicants were Charles Sarle, former editor of the Midland Express, and Arthur Welland, former circulation manager of the Daily Chronicle, both of whom had recently lost their jobs as a result of the collapse of the Tribune, Franklin Thomasson's ill-fated Liberal weekly.

By 1910, the scheme was beginning to gain momentum. In 1908 there was a long and detailed discussion of the idea of a Labour daily at conference, and later that year a special meeting was held at which delegates from the London Society of Compositors outlined a detailed plan.[27] Yet progress was still too slow for some of the movement's leaders. Early in 1909 Keir Hardie, whose experience of newspaper publishing was wider than most, began his own initiative, proposing a daily paper on the lines of L'Humanité.[28] As ever, his plans were hopelessly optimistic. He wanted the ILP to maintain full control and he argued that only £10,000 would be needed in the first instance, with options on a further £15,000 if needed. This could be obtained, according to Hardie, by a levy of ten shillings on each member of the ILP. In the pages of the Labour Leader and in the meetings of the ILP's National Administrative Council he argued his case vigorously.[29] From the outset, however, he encountered stiff opposition from Ramsay MacDonald and other NAC members. At a crucial meeting in May 1911 Hardie was outvoted; his colleagues agreed that the new newspaper should only be run under the joint auspices of the Labour Party and the ILP, and that its nominal share capital would be £100,000. Hardie resigned.[30] Henceforth the plans for a Labour daily were conducted without Hardie's participation, advice or help. Eventually, the ILP itself would be displaced by the Labour Party and the TUC in these negotiations.

By August 1911 a special committee of the Labour Party was well advanced in its discussions and plans. The share capital of a proposed new company was set at £150,000 with a target of £50,000 in the first instance.[31] A prospectus was issued and money began to trickle in. Inhibited by the Osborne Judgement and numerous threats of injunctions against them, many trade unions were reluctant to become involved. Nevertheless, by October 1911 a total of £26,000 had been raised or firmly promised and this reached £40,000 by the end of the year.[32] Encouraged by this response, the committee was transformed into the board of directors of Labour Newspapers Ltd.

From the outset, the company had ambitious plans.[33] Much to the disappointment of some ILP members on the board, Ramsay MacDonald was elected chairman and he spared no efforts in his attempt to make the new paper a major undertaking. A special report by Mr F.R. Roberts of Manchester estimated that £25,000 should be spent in setting up and equipping the new paper, and over £250 a week for employing the fifty journalists and technical staff who were needed. These were unprecedented figures for a labour paper in Britain but the committee pressed on. In his report, moreover, Roberts stressed the need to adopt a commercial approach to the new publication. He argued:

> In my opinion the success or failure of the proposed paper depends entirely upon its policy and on the character of the news it provides. I am convinced by experience that the reader wants his news first and his politics after. I would, therefore, strongly advise that it be run on the most up-to-date morning newspaper lines, to contain a good racing and commercial service; in fact differing only from the other successful half-penny morning papers in policy only; which you would deal with in your leaders, special articles and reports of meetings. If you attempt to run it on any other lines by

which I mean to entirely specialise in Labour politics, I am strongly of the opinion that you would fail where you would otherwise succeed.[34]

Early in 1912 a young Cambridge graduate, Clifford Allen, was appointed full-time Secretary of the Company and he bore the brunt of the preparations for the establishment of the paper's offices.[35] In the summer of 1912 a professional journalist, Frank Dilnot, was employed as editor of the new paper at the rather unsocialist salary of £1100 a year. Other professionals were employed in key positions, much to the dismay of many socialists, though there were some committed men on the management, notably the young Herbert Morrison in the Circulation Sales Separtment. Early in October 1912 the first issue went on sale. It was a disappointment.[36] Not only did the paper strike no new or exciting chords, but it was distinctly duller than the average Fleet Street product. The early sales figures were by no means disastrous, and for a time the advertising revenue was reasonably buoyant. Moreover, capital continued to arrive. Nevertheless, it is clear that the paper was undercapitalised from the start, unable to develop the extensive news service and scoop journalism which was now the staple of Fleet Street and the expectation of readers. In competing directly with the other national newspapers the Daily Citizen put itself at an immediate disadvantage; incurring all the expense of a national paper with none of its ability to generate real income.

It is also unfortunate that the Daily Citizen should have appeared at the very time as the revived Daily Herald.[37] It is a piece of supreme irony that after twenty years searching for one labour daily, the movement should have been presented with two simultaneously. The irony was not lost on the people involved. Late in 1912 the proprietors of the Daily Herald offered its copyright to the board of Labour Newspapers, thus providing a clean and obvious solution to the embarrassing confrontation.[38] Astonishingly, the board rejected the offer by five votes to four; either the price of £2500 was deemed too high, or members of the board had become convinced that the Daily Herald would in any case soon pass away.

In the event, it was the Daily Citizen which lost the battle. The demand on capital was insatiable. By the end of May 1914 the company had spent £150,000, and losses which had been running at almost £1800 a week were only marginally less disastrous at £1400 a week. Circulation revenue was steady at between £950 and £1000 a week but advertising revenue was declining. Small amounts of capital continued to arrive but the full amount was never raised and the board of directors was continually going cap in hand to the TUC or to individual unions for loans. A special conference of trade unions at Caxton Hall in March 1913 agreed on a scheme for levying one shilling per year on members for three years to help the paper. Guarantee funds were a lifeline for the paper and by June 1914 £62,000 had been raised this way.

Even this was not enough once the first world war began. Newsprint and other materials were in short supply, while advertising and circulation revenue dwindled. Only the fact that the paper itself was now smaller in size contained the weekly losses and late in 1914 the directors launched one more guarantee fund, the '100,000 shilling Fund'. A new round of negotiations opened with the TUC to try to raise more money and increase capital investment. A joint meeting of the Parliamentary Committee and the board of the company agreed on drastic expenditure cuts, the discontinuation of printing in London and an outline scheme for a new trade union levy.[39] These plans were thrown in utter confusion when, in February 1915, Mr Justice Warrington ruled in the High Court that an investment by the National Amalgamated Society of Operative House and Ship Painters in the Daily Citizen was contrary to the constitution of the union.[40] This was a final, fatal blow for the paper. A last attempt was made at a special trade union conference immediately after the High Court decision to raise money by other means and an attempt was made to transform the registered company into a friendly society in order to evade the new legal restrictions, but to no avail.[41] In June 1915 it was announced that the Daily Citizen had ceased publication. Giving the announcement, the editor of the paper wrote:

> From the start there have been heavy difficulties to contend with because, while a great many of the heavy expenses inseparable from the conduct of a modern daily newspaper had to be incurred in common with other national daily newspapers the Daily Citizen

with a social mission as its mainspring could never, from its very nature, adapt itself to many of the purely commercial methods which are brought to play by other popular halfpenny newspapers. It was further handicapped by a very small capital from the start, and by a constant struggle for fresh capital throughout its existence. Among the effects of this was the continual cutting down of outlay in various directions where a freer spending of money, had it been possible, would have been in the long run a business economy.[42]

Why did the Daily Citizen fail? In hindsight it is possible to argue that the paper was too ambitious, too costly and too complex an organisation, and that the unfortunate coincidence of war and an adverse legal judgement made any attempts at reorganization impossible. Certainly the paper became unpopular among some sections of the labour movement, chiefly the ILP, because of its patriotic stance over the first world war. The editorial decision to give coverage to military news was regarded, together with the earlier decision to include horse racing news, as an indication of the paper's failure to serve the socialist community in an appropriate way.[43] Yet it is by no means clear that deferring to these views would have saved the Daily Citizen. The contrast with the Daily Herald is instructive. Where the Daily Citizen began from the assumption that a daily labour paper should compete directly, both in editorial approach and in infrastructure, with the commercial Fleet Street press, differing only in editorial opinion, the promoters of the Daily Herald seemed to have assumed that a socialist daily paper could operate on quite different principles, financed in a less ambitious way and staffed at a minimal level. Where the Citizen sought £150,000, the Herald settled for little more than an initial £300.[44] In the absence of archival material for the Herald comparable to the Citizen it is not possible to say how much money was raised for the former paper over three years.[45] There was certainly no long list of shareholders and few institutional backers. The paper seemed to have survived through the efforts of a few wealthy sponsors and the activities of local fund raising committees.[46] Yet, it was the small scale of the Herald's operations and the consequent low costs, that gave it the resilience to survive the exigencies of war in 1914. It was possible for the _Herald_ to become a weekly and survive, whereas the _Daily Citizen_, far more cumbersome in organisation and costly in operation, could not make such an adaptation. No doubt, too, the relative uniqueness of the _Herald_'s position in opposing the war gave it a small but loyal band of supporters, whereas the _Citizen_ was indistinguishable from the rest of the Fleet Street press.

Yet this is only part of the answer. At no time before the war did the _Daily Citizen_ show any real signs that it was moving to profitability. The estimates for an improvement in the paper's circulation and advertising revenues proved unfounded and throughout its history it was bedevilled by lack of funds, brought on in part by costs but largely through its failure to attract advertisers or readers. It is this which is most perplexing. Did the working class, as a whole, not want a socialist daily paper? Did not the organised trade unionists at the very least, feel impelled to buy one? It is difficult to avoid the conclusion that, at root, the problem lay in the relationship between the leadership and active section of the labour movement on the one hand, and the mass of ordinary working people on the other. Arthur Henderson had a simple explanation. Writing to an anguished Clifford Allen after the collapse of the _Daily Citizen_ in 1915, he said:

> If resolutions could have saved the _Daily Citizen_ it would have had a long life ... The plain, blunt fact is the Labour Movement does not want a daily newspaper and is not prepared to regard such a weapon as necessary in the Labour fight.[47]

It is clear that at a local level socialists saw little need to discontinue their own publishing efforts simply because there was now a daily labour paper. Indeed, new papers continued to be launched even while the _Daily Citizen_ scheme was being actively and publicly pursued. In 1912 alone twelve new local labour papers were started and this number rose to fourteen the following year, and these included major undertakings such as the _Bradford Pioneer_ and the _Leeds Weekly Citizen_. This can be partly explained by the relationship between the ILP, which started both papers, and the Board of Labour Newspapers Ltd. By 1912, the ILP was feeling less enamoured of the new paper. The

City of London Branch, for example, had protested very early on at the decision to press ahead without taking seriously Keir Hardie's ideas and throughout the paper's existence there were complaints from ILP branches about different aspects of its editorial presentation, chiefly its political and parliamentary coverage.[48] It is also fair to say that the Daily Citizen could never fulfil for a local branch what its own paper could do, any more than The Times could offer a comprehensive coverage for every locality. The role which a local paper performed for a local socialist movement was quite different to that performed by a national daily.

Few historians have managed to write successfully about the impact of the editorial activity of newspapers.[49] What impact, for example, did the LRC press have on the politics of the party? What impact, indeed, did the Daily Citizen have, bearing in mind that at one point it had a circulation of some 250,000? It is difficult to measure this impact in terms purely of electoral success or failure. In the period 1910 to 1914 there were three-cornered by-election contests in fourteen seats where the Lib-Lab pact had previously operated and in none of them did Labour do better than third. There is some evidence, according to Dr Peter Clarke, of a small advance in the Labour vote, but there is also strong evidence that Labour was hitting a ceiling of thirty per cent.[50] This has given rise to the argument, most cogently advanced by McKibbin, Matthew et al, that the main inhibition on Labour's development in these years was the restraint imposed by a restrictive and exclusive franchise.[51] Certainly there is no empirical evidence, from this quarter, that the possession of a daily paper made any difference. In any case, it is not surprising that this should be so. If the total membership of the Labour Party in the period between 1910 and 1914 was between 1,500,000 and 1,800,000, its vote in the second election of 1910 was only 371,000. The Daily Citizen, from a purely statistical point of view, could have made little impact outside the ranks of firm Labour voters.

It is equally clear that the local Labour press performed only a limited function. Many areas where the Labour Party made significant electoral headway never once possessed a local paper and there are grounds for arguing that the main benefit of local papers accrued to the individual journalists and local politicians associated with them. For some people, writing was a necessary part of politics. Furthermore it may be argued that the advantages of a Labour press are most obvious when it does not exist. It was always the complaint of socialists that their activities and views were misrepresented or ignored by the non-socialist press, but it is by no means clear that the situation was much improved when a Labour press existed. Mass communication required mass readership and this has been conspicuously absent, with one notable example in the history of the Daily Herald, in the Labour press as a whole. The electoral advance of the Labour Party in the years from 1906 onwards does not seem to have been hampered because the Labour press was struggling. Yet, without even this fragile network of local Labour papers, and without the strenuous efforts which lay behind both the local and national Labour Press, how much poorer would the movement have been, how much less effective would the journalist-leaders of the movement have been and how much less successful in electoral terms would the Labour Party ultimately have been?

NOTES

1. TUC, Annual Report, 1911, p.172.
2. See R. Harrison et al (eds.), The Warwick Guide to British Labour Periodicals, 1790-1970 (Harvester, Hassocks, 1977). For an overview of the labour press in this period see D. Hopkin, 'The Socialist Press in Britain, 1890-1910', in G. Boyce et al (eds.), Newspaper History from the Seventeenth Century to the Present Day (Constable, London, 1978), pp.294-306. One paper has recently been studied in detail in F. Reid, 'Keir Hardie and the Labour Leader', in J.M. Winter (ed.), The Working Class in Modern British History (Cambridge, University Press, 1983), pp.19-42. For a hagiographical account which nevertheless underlines the sense of vain struggle see S. Harrison, Poor Men's Guardians (Lawrence and Wishart, London, 1974).
3. A. Lee, The Origins of the Popular Press, 1855-1914 (Croom Helm, London, 1976), pp.179-80 ff. See also the same author's essay on the press in the period 1855 to 1914 in Boyce et al (eds.) Newspaper History, pp.117-129.
4. D.R. Hopkin, 'The Newspapers of the ILP, 1893-1906', unpublished PhD thesis, University of

Wales, 1981. Especially Appendix A.

5. These figures are obtained from LRC, Annual Report, 1902, 1903, 1904.

6. The majority of the titles mentioned in this chapter can be consulted in the Labour newspapers microfilm archive at the Hugh Owen Library, University College of Wales, Aberystwyth.

7. See the new company's prospectus in Wakefield Echo, 8 June 1906.

8. J. Smethurst, 'The Pioneer Press', Bulletin of the Society for the Study of Labour History, vol. 31 (1975), pp.59-62.

9. For the politics of the London trades councils see P. Thompson, Socialists, Liberals and Labour. The Struggle for London, 1885-1914 (Routledge and Kegan Paul, London, 1967).

10. The shareholder list is in the company file at the (P)ublic (R)ecord (O)ffice, BT31/17292/81915. The occupational structure of the shareholders is examined in D. Hopkin, 'The Membership of the ILP, 1904-1910', International Review of Social History, vol. XX (1975), pp.175-97.

11. G. Lansbury, My Life (Constable, London, 1928), pp.170-71.

12. For an account of the Swansea Labour Party and its publishing activities see D. Cleaver, 'Swansea and District's Labour Press, 1888-1914', Llafur, vol. IV, no. 1 (1975). See also S. Awberry, Labour's Early Struggles in Swansea (Swansea Labour Party, Swansea, 1949).

13. Hopkin, 'Newspapers of the ILP'.

14. Lansbury, Life, p.170.

15. The main sources for examining the various attempts to establish a daily Labour newspaper are Annual Reports of the Trades Union Congress and the Quarterly Reports of the Labour Party, the Minutes of the National Executive Committee and the Newspaper Sub-Committee; Labour Party Archives, Walworth Road, London SE9 (henceforth LP.Arch.). There is considerable correspondence on the subject in the LRC letter files. See for example LP.Arch./LRC 11/145, 363-4; 12/27, 138, 222-4.

16. There was an early attempt to persuade the Weekly Times and Echo to become an organ of the LRC. See LP.Arch./LRC 17/551-5, Nov. 1904. Even earlier the Railway Review had urged the establishment of a labour daily; quoted in Cardiff Labour Pioneer, Feb. 1902.

17. Memorandum entitled 'Labour Newspaper'; LP.Arch./NEW/06/91i.

18. Weekly Tribune, 28 May 1904.

19. See the attacks in the Labour Leader, 20 July 1906; 14 Sept. 1906. The leaders of the ILP issued a warning about the paper which was widely published in the local Labour press; see for example Jarrow Labour Herald, June 1906.

20. See for example the letters from Arthur Bullivant, Newcastle and District LRC and W.C. Hendry, January to March 1906 in LP.Arch. General Correspondence, 1/225,228 and 2/147-8. See also ibid., 1/238-42 for other letters.

21. Stephen Koss, Fleet Street Radical. A.G. Gardiner and the Daily News (Allen Lane, London, 1973). See also A.G. Gardiner, The Life of George Cadbury (Cassell, London, 1923).

22. H.J. Wigham to Ramsay MacDonald, 22 Mar. 1906; LP.Arch./NEW/06/1. See MacDonald's reply insisting on the Labour Party retaining political control of the paper; 28 Mar. 1906; LP.Arch., ibid.

23. Ibid., NEW/06/30.

24. Ibid., NEW/06/15-17.

25. John Dicks to Ramsay MacDonald, 11 Jan. 1908; ibid., NEW/06/32.

26. Ibid., NEW/06/38,41,43,45.

27. TUC, Annual Report, 1908; ibid., 1909, pp. 73-4, 142-4.

28. See Hardie's speech at the inauguration of the National Labour Press. Labour Leader, 5 Nov. 1909.

29. By October 1910, for example, he had raised £2134 in guarantees for the new daily paper; Labour Leader, 14 Oct. 1910. For more details of Hardie's scheme see ibid, 7 Oct. 1910, 4 Nov. 1910; 18 Nov. 1910.

30. There is a detailed account of this in L. Thompson, The Enthusiasts, A Biography of John and Katharine Bruce Glasier (Gollancz, London, 1971), pp. 178-87. See also K.O. Morgan, Keir Hardie: Radical and Socialist (Weidenfeld and Nicolson, London, 1975), pp. 234-37.

31. The company file, containing prospectus, share register and details of the company's incorporation is in PRO BT 31/119898/20435 (Labour Newspapers Ltd). The financial registers and day books, including analyses of the balance sheets are in LP Arch/Daily Citizen. Many of the earlier papers, including the weekly balance sheets and inventories of equipment and stock are in the British Library of Political and Economic Science, R(SR) 1143, Coll G, 1972, (henceforeth BLPES DC Arch).

32. The two largest individual shareholders

were T.D. Benson, former Treasurer of the ILP and W.E. Balston, each of whom invested £10,000 in the paper. There are no indications of what conditions applied but one investor had offered a similar sum under certain unspecified conditions in 1911; BLPES DC Arch, f.16.

33. For a detailed account of the establishment, management and performance of the Daily Citizen see T. Ichikawa, 'The Daily Citizen, 1912-15', unpublished MA thesis, University of Wales, 1984.

34. Report dated June 1911; BLPES DC Arch, f.M 282.

35. M. Gilbert, Plough My Own Furrow. The story of Lord Allen of Hurtwood as told through his Writings and Correspondence (Longman, London, 1965), pp.24-34.

36. For Bruce Glasier's reaction see Thompson, Enthusiasts, p.185. The editor of the rival Daily Herald was even less charitable; R. Kenney, Westering (Dent, London, 1939), p.190.

37. An interesting comparison of the two papers is R.J. Holton, 'Daily Herald v Daily Citizen', International Review of Social History, vol. XIX (1974), pp.347-376.

38. Minutes of the Board of Labour Newspapers Ltd., 4 Nov. 1912; BLPES DC Arch f.60.

39. NEC Minutes, 6 Jan. 1915; LP Arch.

40. Bennett v. National Amalgamated Society of Operative House and Ship Painters and Decorators, High Court, Chancery Division, 2 Feb. 1915; Weekly Notes, 1915. 6 Geo V, p.73.

41. See TUC, Annual Report, 1915.

42. Daily Citizen, 5 June 1915.

43. See for example the resolution of No. 6 Division of the ILP condemning the pro-war stance of the Daily Citizen; BLPES DC Arch Misc 314, IV b (23 Jan. 1915). This is in sharp contrast to an earlier resolution praising the paper by the same group of ILP branches; ibid., Misc 314, IV b (13 July 1913).

44. G. Lansbury, The Miracle of Fleet Street (Labour Publishing Co., London 1925), p.171.

45. The only company records available are a few papers relating to the Limit Printing and Publishing Company which was registered in June 1913 with a capital of £2000; PRO BT31/21545/129717.

46. In 1913 there were only four shareholders, George Lansbury, Charles Lapworth, Sime Williams and Francis Meynell; ibid. For a discussion of the activities of the Daily Herald League, which

combined a servicing role, see Holton, 'Daily Herald v Daily Citizen', p.368.

47. Gilbert, Plough My Own Furrow, pp.33-34.

48. For example, see the complaints of No. 6 Division at a conference in July 1913. BLPES Misc. 314, iv b.

49. Splendid but rare examples are Lee, Popular Press, and S. Koss, The Rise and Fall of the Political Press in Britain (Hamilton, London, 1981), vol. 1.

50 See P. Clarke, 'The electoral position of the Liberal and Labour parties, 1910-1914', English Historical Review, vol. XC (1975), pp.828-36. See also C. Cook, 'Labour and the Downfall of the Liberal Party', in C. Cook and A. Sked (eds.) Crisis and Controversy: Essays in Honour of A.J.P. Taylor (Macmillan, London, 1976), pp.38-65.

51. H.C.G. Matthew, R.I. McKibbin and J.A. Kay, 'The franchise factor in the rise of the Labour Party', English Historical Review, vol. XCI (1976), pp. 723-752. See the rejoinder by P.F. Clarke, 'Liberals, Labour and the franchise', ibid., vol. XCII (1977), pp. 582-90. For an interesting study of the regional dimension as opposed to the franchise factor, see J.P.D. Dunbabin, 'British elections in the 19th and 20th century', ibid., vol. XCV, (1980), pp. 241-267.

Chapter Six

LABOUR AND THE TRADE UNIONS

In Britain in the fifteen years before the
first world war the dominant Lib-Labism of the
trade unions was replaced by a socialist-flavoured
Labourism. That this occurred without causing any
major schisms is perhaps the most striking aspect
of the history of the British trade union movement
in the period. It was furthermore, in marked
contrast with the experience of several other
European countries. In France, Italy, Spain and
Switzerland, for example, serious divisions arose
between syndicalist or anarcho-syndicalist trade
union groupings and the socialist parties. There
were also Catholic unions in Italy, France,
Belgium, the Netherlands, and Switzerland, the last
two also having Protestant unions. The
'confessional unions' often had direct links with
the anti-socialist parties in Parliament.[1]
Nevertheless, there were pressures between 1906 and
1914 to steer British unions away from the link
with the Labour Party. These included strong
efforts to maintain the old Lib-Lab politics as
well as various efforts to set up Conservative
trade unions and more generally to encourage
Conservative trade unionists.

One attitude in the French labour movement, an
attitude which could be resistant to radical ideas
or, in syndicalism, could be very radical, was
ouvriérisme. At the first French national workers'
congress in 1876 this was given expression as
follows:

All the systems, all the utopias for which the
workers have been blamed have never come from
them at all. They have all come from the
middle class people, no doubt well
intentioned, who have sought the remedies for

our ills in their own ideas, burning the midnight oil instead of looking at our needs and at reality.[2]

Such suspicions were also deep within the generation of British trade union leaders which was prominent in the last two decades of the nineteenth century and the first few years of the twentieth century. The Independent Labour Party leaders had to tread exceedingly warily in order not to stir up such feelings on the trade union side of the Labour Party. Indeed, in 1904, as one of the first group of fraternal delegates from the Labour Representation Committee to the TUC, Ramsay MacDonald assured the trade unionists, 'The Labour Representation Committee is neither sister nor brother to the Congress, but its child. We come therefore to offer our filial respects'.[3]

After the 1906 general election the Labour Party was not the trade union movement's only political mouthpiece. Whilst, in 1904, the TUC and the General Federation of Trade Unions had agreed to support LRC candidates, the LRC had agreed to support candidates approved by the Parliamentary Committee of the TUC. This primarily meant the Lib-Labs who had worked together in the 1900-06 Parliament as the Parliamentary Trade Union Group. In the latter days of that Parliament, under John Burns' chairmanship, they had scored some successes in debates on trade union matters and in particular on the Trades Disputes Bill.[4] After the 1906 election the group continued, comprising thirteen miners, four from other trade unions, Henry Broadhurst (soon to retire) and William Cremer (who was to die in 1908). Burns was now in the Liberal Cabinet.

On the whole relations between the two trade union groups were good; though some of the older Lib-Lab members such as Fred Maddison and Charles Fenwick could be difficult. The latter's suspicion of the socialists could readily surface among the Trade Union Group, as happened in May 1906 when Keir Hardie and Shackleton tried to get a Labour Party member onto the House of Commons' Select Committee which was being set up to look at amendments to the Housing of the Working Class Acts. Fenwick took umbrage when Hardie asserted, '. . . as a Labour Party, paid by Labour organisations and directly representing Labour opinions, they were entitled to representation on a Committee of this kind'. Fenwick complained with vigour,

> What special right had his hon. friends on the
> other side to be considered as the representa-
> tives of Labour that they who sat on the
> Ministerial side of the House had not an equal
> claim to? They were trade unionists, they
> stood at the head of large Labour organi-
> sations which they had built up. Their claim
> in both these respects was infinitely superior
> to the claim of some of those who claimed to
> be members of the Labour Party. They had
> worked in the mine and in the factory side by
> side with those who sent them to this House.

William Brace, a miner, observed that 'this
discussion was to him one of the most painful
experiences of his life' and added that his group,
like the Labour Party, did not always vote with the
government even if they did take the Liberal
whip.[5]

For some of the miners' MPs the situation was
happily resolved when the Miners' Federation of
Great Britain resolved to affiliate to the Labour
Party after a ballot in May 1908. Up until then
the miners (apart from the Lancashire and Cheshire
miners who had affiliated to the LRC in May 1903)
had been the main industrial group affiliated to
the TUC which did not support the Labour Party. In
areas such as the east midlands Lib-Labism was
especially strong amongst the miners, and in that
area there were strong votes against affiliation to
the Labour Party both in the unsuccessful MFGB
ballot of 1906 and the successful one of 1908.[6]

Naturally the Liberals made the most of such
trade union support. In the Loughborough
constituency which covered a large section of the
North-West Leicestershire-South Derbyshire
coalfield, one finds that in the 1906 general
election the Liberals made much of John Burns'
membership of the cabinet and of the miners'
support. Thus at one big public meeting in
Loughborough the main support speaker was
W.E. Harvey, a leading figure in the Derbyshire
Miners' Association and soon to enter Parliament
himself with Liberal aid. Harvey informed the
meeting that he was there to support Maurice Levy,
an east London clothing manufacturer, 'as the agent
of a very large organisation for the reason that Mr
Levy on the floor of the House of Commons had aided
and assisted the Labour party in dealing with

measures for the welfare of the workers'. The
mention of Burns' name by the local Liberal Party
President was received with cheers - and they were
told 'that an honour had been done to every worker
in the country by placing him in the Cabinet. He
hoped that every worker would be able to appreciate
that and would do his level best' to get Burns and
the Liberal Government returned to power.[7]

After all but three longer serving miners' MPs
had accepted the Labour whip in Parliament at the
start of 1909, the Lib-Lab Trade Union Group of MPs
faded away. However, there were to remain tensions
between many of the trade unionists and the ILP
wing of the Parliamentary Labour Party. Indeed,
the accession of the miners strengthened those
elements within the Parliamentary Labour Party
which were almost indistinguishable from the
Lib-Labs. In 1914 the Labour whip was withdrawn
from two of the miners' MPs for repeated disregard
of the Labour Party constitution.

At the outset of 1906 there had been a
contested election for the chairmanship of the
Parliamentary Labour group between Keir Hardie and
David Shackleton, each representing a different
wing of the party. Snowden wrote of this:

> The trade union members, knowing Mr Keir
> Hardie, had no objections themselves to his
> appointment to the leadership. But they felt
> that the selection of a purely trade union
> member was justified by the numerical strength
> of the trade unions in the party, and that
> such an appointment would prevent any
> suspicion among the trade union members that
> the Socialist section was using the movement
> for its own purposes.[8]

Many trade unionists in the decade and a half
before the first world war were highly suspicious
of socialists. In many unions there were factional
struggles between the Lib-Labs and the socialists.
Such strong divisions were particularly apparent in
the Amalgamated Society of Railway Servants (ASRS),
where Lib-Lab supporters could rally behind the
union's secretary and MP, Richard Bell. Before the
1906 general election Bell had fallen out with his
fellow Labour Representation Committee MPs and
throughout the 1906-1910 Parliament he acted
independently not only of the Labour Party but also
of his union's policy.

The divisions of opinion in that union were

highlighted by the Osborne Judgment in 1909. Walter Osborne provides the most obvious example of a determinedly non-Labour Party trade unionist of the 1900-1914 period.[9] His views deserve serious attention. George Alcock later recalled,

> For some years Osborne was at the same station as myself, and for some years a lodger in my house. Knowing the man, though I disagreed with his actions in this matter, I always defended him from imputations of having a warped character. I knew him to be a man of . . . upright character, and whilst regretting his opinions and actions defended his moral character. He was a lodger with me up to the time of his marriage.[10]

By the early years of the twentieth century Osborne, a former member of the Social Democratic Federation, was holding strong views on trade unionism which were more in line with the thinking of Herbert Spencer than of Karl Marx. In a series of books, pamphlets and other writings Osborne propounded a view of trade unionism which followed on from that of George Howell, as expressed in his various books and in an essay in A Plea for Liberty (1891), a strongly individualist set of essays organised by leading figures of the Liberty and Property Defence league.[11] Indeed, on several points, Osborne followed Howell's views and words very closely indeed.

Osborne argued that the way foward for the unions was an accommodation with capital, to achieve high output, high wages and industrial peace. Thus in his Sane Trade Unionism he wrote:

> In view of the present fierce world-competition, Trade Union leaders bear an almost appalling responsibility. . .. . The only road to real advancement lies through higher wages and greater purchasing power. The application of science and machinery has both increased and cheapened the output, and articles which were the luxuries of the rich a century back are now the everyday necessities of the poor. Good work adds to the wealth not merely of one class, but of the nation, and the duty of the Unions is to see that workmen get their full share of the fruits of their labour.

> Just as national peace is necessary for national advancement, so is industrial peace essential for industrial progress. Every day lost by a strike is a loss to the nation.

Osborne praised the old skilled unions, which he felt inculcated good moral values into their membership as well as good workmanship. For Osborne, trade unionism began to go wrong after the 1889 London Dock strike. That strike he regarded with approval, not least because it 'was carried through without any outbreak of violence, and tens of thousands of strikers marched through London streets as orderly as an army of soldiers, a thing which would have been impossible without Trade Union influence'. However, like Howell, he was vehemently opposed to the eight hour day movement. 'New unionism', he held, 'had a deteriorating effect upon the character of the workmen who, instead of being taught the advantage of thrift and self-help, and reliance on their Unions for the regulation of their conditions of employment, were now advised to appeal to Parliament for everything.'[12]

For Osborne, and those Liberal trade unionists whose views were akin to his, the committing of the unions to socialism seemed likely to undermine their ability to carry out collective bargaining effectively. He wrote:

> When the Unions confined themselves to purely industrial affairs they could meet the employers on an equal footing; their bargain being merely for the rightful division of the profits as between the two partners - capital and labour.
>
> When the Unions openly proclaimed that it was no longer their policy to bargain as between employer and employed, but rather to exterminate the former, who were recognised only as the natural enemy of the worker, then an atmosphere was created which tended to make the true functions of Trade Unionism difficult if not impossible.

Osborne went further, observing that 'there can be no liberty apart from private property. Property and the means of existence in many hands guarantee independence and freedom, but when all means of existence is centred in one set of men, then the nation will touch the lowest depths of slavery'.

Given such opinions it is clear why a man like Osborne should have been so strongly opposed to his union being able to enforce its political levy and to subscribe to the funds of the Labour Party. He felt, 'It is contrary to all human justice that men should be compelled to join an association to promote political and religious views which they believe erroneous, and to oppose those principles which in their individual capacity they are supporting with time, money and effort'.[13] He went on to set up a 'Trade Union Political Freedom League', using his house for its headquarters, and by November 1910 he was supporting a Conservative in a parliamentary by-election. Attempts to gain support for a non-socialist Labour Party, however, came to little. The British Labour Party of 1911, which aimed 'to secure direct parliamentary representation, not in antagonism to capital, but as a joint partner with capital, demanding equal right and equal voice', was a failure.[14]

Whilst Osborne, having failed to win his case within the union by speeches at its conference, resorted to using the law, ILP activists pursued their aims by taking over branch organisation within the union. One socialist activist, J. Phipps of Ormskirk, wrote to Ramsay MacDonald in 1912 telling him that MacDonald's call to Labour to 'fight for independence' had delighted 'nearly all our ASRS socialist secretaries', and reported a good response from Preston, Barrow, Whitehaven, Workington, Maryport, Carlisle, Glasgow, Edinburgh, Newcastle, Leeds, Bradford, Wakefield, Doncaster, Sheffield, Manchester, Wigan and Chesterfield. Earlier Phipps had supplied more details, which give a rare view of a socialist pressure group's activities in a union in this period:

> The Socialist Branch Secretaries in the ASRS are organised for the purpose of ensuring, as far as possible, the election of known and tried socialists for all positions in our Society, and I, as Secretary of this socialist organisation often have to adopt a policy which does not cause me to be a favourite with Unity House (the ASRS headquarters).

> Unity House has been supporting for years a South Wales member named Charles who is a Bellite and an Anti-Socialist.

We have defeated him on every occasion, and now - in spite of the support of Unity House he is being again beaten by a young socialist named Brown of Hull, a Ruskin Hall student.

Our man Brown beat Charles for the position of organiser by 132 votes. Unity House then allows certain South Wales branches to send in votes of nine numbers <u>after</u> the date for votes to be received, which caused our man Brown to be beaten.

The case has been relegated to our annual meeting at Carlisle. <u>Our</u> men at Carlisle are going to make things warm for Unity House people. I am sorry that (J.H.) Thomas M.P. has become suspect in our Society, and <u>not</u> through idle rumour.

We <u>know</u> for certain that Bell's influence is one of the guiding factors in our Society, through (J.E.) Williams (his successor as Secretary); also that Osborne obtained his information direct from Bell. <u>Our</u> men have little faith in our leaders, for though paid to lead, they have to be <u>pushed</u> by the rank and file.

The young ILP element in our society is in favour of energetic methods, whereas Unity House wishes to lead a comfortable life, and we are eager to accelerate this Resolution by Evolution.[15]

If Osborne's objections to the trade union link with the Labour Party were essentially Liberal, there were also trade unionists who were members of the Unionist Party or who at least voted for it. The Unionists appear to have been keener to organise Conservative trade unionists than to get Tory working men elected to Parliament. In the debates on what was to be the Trade Union Act (1913), Labour MPs spoke of these attempts to set up Conservative trade unions. John Clynes informed the House of Commons that 'Conservative agents are known to be endeavouring to organise and establish rival trade unions - constitutional trade unions, non-political trade unions, and all you have to do to be a non-political trade unionist is to be a Tory, and generally to associate yourself with the party of that name'. Such activity had become very

important in the eyes of some Unionists after the
electoral disaster of 1906, and such efforts were
usually focused on Lancashire. In denouncing the
proposed trade union legislation in 1911 F.E. Smith
had made much of the Weavers' Protection
Association of Blackburn voting by 2009 to 466
against legislation to reverse the Osborne
Judgment. Clynes later could comment of Smith,

> He did not tell the House, probably he did not
> know, that this is really a Tory organisation
> established some twenty years ago for
> absolutely partisan reasons. It is not
> representative of the textile workers or the
> weavers' organisation, that class of work
> being represented by the very much larger
> body, the Weavers' Amalgamation.[16]

However, with the rise of Labour, the
Unionists made greater efforts to win working men
to Conservative and Unionist bodies. The National
Conservative Party had been set up in 1904, and,
after the 1906 election, Blackburn was one of its
centres in Lancashire.[17] 1904 was also the year
in which the Trade Union Tariff Reform Association
had been organized to assist Chamberlain in his
crusade. Winston Churchill appears to have felt,
in late 1905, that these moves posed a challenge.
A Liberal official noted, 'Churchill is most
anxious that the Liberal Party will capture the
Trade Unions. He says that if they don't,
Chamberlain, or someone else arising out of the
wreck of The Unionist Party, most certainly will'.
Unionist efforts in this direction revived again
after the Osborne Judgment. Leo Amery and some of
the more fervent tariff reformers placed great
emphasis on creating 'a real Unionist Labour
Party'.[18]

Whilst there remained many Tory working men in
trade unions, the attempts to create Conservative
Labour unions, like the attempt to create a
Unionist Labour Party, were unsuccessful. Tariff
Reform succeeded in attracting glassmakers, who
felt threatened by imports; but that was the only
industrial group. In urging the reversal of the
Osborne Judgment Ramsay MacDonald could taunt the
Unionists with the observation that 'This is no
party measure, although it happens that up to now
we, being most active in the matter, have got the
affiliations. There is no reason why, say,
a glass-bottlemakers' society that thinks its

interest is wrapped up in Protection should not affiliate with the party opposite'.[19]

Tory working men also disliked paying political levies to help other parties. Before Osborne's action was first heard in the High Courts in July 1908, some Welsh miners took their union to the High Court to test the legality of political expenditure by trade unions. This action in 1907 was unsuccessful.[20] However, one very interesting feature of it has not attracted attention. That is that the Conservative miners were objecting to the political levy at the time when the South Wales Miners' Federation was supporting the Liberal Party.

When Osborne's action was first turned down in 1908 Mr Justice Neville, influenced by the case concerning the South Wales miners, observed on the political levy:

> The trade unions, if they please, are at liberty just as much to affiliate themselves and to support the Socialist Party as they would be to affiliate to and support, if they pleased, either the Unionist Party or the Liberal Party. Once given the right to spend their money to promote their interests in the House of Commons, I think the question of how they could do so is surely a question of policy with which the court will not concern themselves.

Osborne then found that the Miners' Federation was to affiliate to the Labour Party and this apparently ensured that he went to the Court of Appeal.[21] There, and at the appeal to the House of Lords, the Law Lords came down firmly against the ASRS and in favour of Osborne. They were either against trade unions being entitled to levy money for political purposes or felt that the commitment to the parliamentary Labour discipline was unconstitutional.[22] As Labour Party speakers repeatedly observed, labour representation was only deemed illegal when it was independent. Clynes observed in the House of Commons, 'From 1871 down to 1908 the trade unions, without any interference and without any alleged illegality, have been quite free to spend their money by the votes of majorities for the purpose of sending their men here. Conservative working men and Socialist working men have been contributing towards the support of Liberal working men who have sat on

these benches'. As to Labour Party organisation
threatening the constitution, the growth of party
politics was well established well before the turn
of the century. All three of the Law Lords who
took exception on these grounds had been Liberal
MPs in the past (though one had become a Liberal
Unionist).[23] Little wonder that Labour MPs asked
whether there would be objection if they still were
Liberal MPs or, as Clynes asked, '. . . if there
would be any objection if we could be induced to
sit on the other side of the House, and if we could
adopt the views of hon. and right hon. Members
opposite on Imperial, fiscal and other matters, and
range ourselves generally on their side?'[24]

The Osborne Judgment put both the Liberal and
the Unionist Parties into a dilemma as to what
extent they could resist trade union pressures to
reverse it and yet ensure labour representation in
Parliament. On the one hand resistance could help
to separate the trade unions from the Labour Party;
on the other too great intransigence could annoy
those trade unionists who might vote for their own
party.
    Liberal cabinet ministers were careful not to
rush into committing themselves as to what they
would do about the judgment. Thus Churchill, when
questioned in his constituency during the January
1910 election, replied:

> . . . he was not prepared without a great deal
> more consideration than he had given to the
> question to say that he would support a Bill
> to reverse the Osborne Judgment. It was a
> very strong order to say that the con-
> tributions of Conservative, Liberal and
> Socialist trade unionists were to be taken
> against their will to maintain a Parliamentary
> candidate with whom they did not agree. He
> was in favour of the payment of members as he
> thought it was better that members should
> represent constituencies than they should
> represent special interests.

Rufus Isaacs in October, similarly, would go no
further.[25]
    However the Liberal Ministers had to be wary
of antagonising the Labour MPs. Since the 1906
election there had been occasional talk amongst
Liberals of the dangers of the Irish and Labour MPs

ganging up together. From 1910 this became more of
a threat, especially the possibility of them
combining to insist on a higher priority being
given to Home Rule and action on the Osborne
Judgment.[26]

In September 1910 the Unionists were also
trying to decide what line to take on the Osborne
Judgment. Balfour and Bonar Law consulted Austen
Chamberlain. Chamberlain informed Law of Balfour's
view on the payment of members: 'I gather that he
dislikes it very much in itself but thinks it might
possibly strengthen our hands in upholding the
judgment if we offered payment of members as an
alternative to its reversal'. This, Chamberlain
observed, was the view of F.E. Smith as well as
Law. He himself felt it was 'infinitely preferable
to the reversal of the Osborne Judgment'.
Chamberlain then emphasised that Unionist tactics
should be to ensure that the Liberal Cabinet did
not reverse it.[27]

Bonar Law, however, viewed with equanimity the
prospects of the government trying to reverse the
judgment. 'It would, I think, split up their Party
to some small extent; but what is more important, I
think our view would be popular even with a very
large number of trade unionists, providing we gave
good reasons for the belief that we were not really
opposed to any form of working class representation.' His comments on the case for supporting
payment of members are interesting as a leading
Unionist politician's views on trade unions and
politics at this time. He commented to Austen
Chamberlain:

> There is undoubtedly a great deal of fear of
> the effect of the Osborne Judgment on the part
> of Unionist Members for the industrial
> centres. This was shown very clearly at the
> time of the debate last session, when at least
> a dozen of those Members came to me urging me
> not to say anything definitely hostile, for I
> think some of them have been foolish enough at
> the election actually to commit themselves to
> approving the reversal of the judgment. They
> fear a new Taff Vale agitation, but in this I
> am sure they are mistaken, for there is a
> great difference as the Labour leaders will
> find out between the legal decision, which
> takes money away which the Trade Unionists
> have already subscribed, and the decision
> which saves them from the necessity of

subscribing.

On the other hand, the country has become accustomed to direct representation of working men in the House of Commons, and there is not, I think, any doubt that the working classes approve of it. The Osborne Judgment, however, destroys the means by which this representation in the past has been secured. The Unionist Party is unanimous in the determination to uphold the judgment; but that being so, we as a Party are faced with one or two alternatives: either we must be prepared to support some real alternative by which labour representation can be secured; or we must take up the attitude that we are for practical purposes opposed to it. The last alternative is impossible; and so far I have seen no other method is suggested which seems to me feasible, except payment of members.

Now what is likely to be the real effect of payment of returning officers' expenses and a salary not exceeding at the outside £300 a year? Its first effect, in my belief, would be that members of Trade Unions would not see the fun of subscribing for political purposes, and that therefore the political influence of the Trades Unions would be destroyed. It always seemed to me that the only sign of anything approaching statesmanship of any of the Socialist leaders was the way in which Keir Hardie collared the Trades Unions and made them serve his purpose. If payment of members did have the effect of killing the purely political influence of Trades Unions, that would simply be of incalculable advantage to our Party, and would also, I am sure, be of great advantage to Trade Unions in the long run.[28]

Balfour, himself, spoke publicly on the issues, denouncing 'the enforced subscriptions and the tyrannical methods' of the unions and, indeed, of trade union representation in Parliament, as well as dismissing the idea of payment of MPs. Beatrice Webb felt he had been so negative on these points and the constitutional issues that she wrote in her diary, 'A.J.B. has done for the chances of a Tory Party at the next election, if this takes place in January . . . . Now is Asquith's chance!

Break up the (constitutional) Conference, and go to
the country on House of Lords and Labour
representation'.[29]

However, the Liberal leadership was also in a
dilemma as to how to respond to the Osborne
Judgment. Thus Asquith observed, characteristically, to Lewis Harcourt, 'The Osborne affair
requires a good deal of careful thought'. After
the cabinet had discussed it in mid-October,
Asquith informed the King that 'Some diversity of
opinion appeared in the course of the discussion'.[30] Part of this was between those who
favoured almost complete reversal, such as Lord
Loreburn, and those who favoured payment of members
only, such as Lord Carrington.[31] Part also was
over the political implications for the Liberal
Party. Samuel argued that if the Osborne decision
was not reversed then new forms of working class
organisation would emerge and 'they would lack such
steadying influences as many of the Trade Unions
are now able to exercise on the labour movement.
Existing for one purpose only, they would probably
tend to emphasise their raison d'être, to increase
the separation between Labour and Liberalism, and
continually to become more socialistic'. In
contrast, Sir William Robson (Attorney General
until a few days before) expressed views not
dissimilar from Osborne's and urged resistance to
reversing the decision. He argued:

> No amount of compliance on our part now will
> affect the determination of the Labour Party
> to oppose Liberal candidates wherever they can
> find the money to do so. Sooner or later,
> therefore, the Liberal Party will be driven to
> more open and direct battle with the
> Socialists in the constituencies. Nothing can
> avoid this conflict. It is also unfortunately
> too clear that the Socialists are in effective
> command of the Trade Union organization, and
> if they are at liberty to draw on that
> organization for funds they may do so up to
> £80,000 or £100,000 per annum . . . .
>
> The question is whether we should recognise
> the inevitable at once, or try to stave it off
> for yet a little longer until the socialist
> organisation, by our own assistance, have got
> command of this enormous war chest.
>
> In giving the Labour Party battle now we shall

have the following advantages:

(1) We shall have a just and intelligible argument against their immediate demands.

(2) We shall be defending the bulk of Trade Unionists from an impost which is obviously unpopular, although it is due to their own inert assent.

(3) The rest of our programme, e.g. Free Trade and the House of Lords, appeals strongly to the artisan sympathy, and the working men will be indisposed to let their food be taxed in order that they may declare in favour of a compulsory levy they do not like.[32]

Against this background it may well be reasonable to give greater emphasis to non-reversal of the Osborne Judgment as one attraction in Lloyd George's package of policies in his secret coalition talks with the Unionist leaders. Whilst Lloyd George drew up the proposals in August, the approaches to the leading Unionists took place at about the time the two party leaderships were agonising over their response to Labour's demands for the reversal of the judgment.[33]

Surely this was one of the matters that was in Lloyd George's mind when he wrote in his memorandum, 'Extreme partisans supporting the Government often drive it against its better judgment to attempting legislation on lines which are the least useful in dealing with a question . . . . Joint action would make it possible to settle these urgent questions without paying undue regard to the formulae and projects of rival faddists'. In his supplementary memorandum of 29 October 1910 it featured, along with Welsh, Irish, temperance and educational matters: 'Whilst the Osborne Judgment is not to be completely reversed, inasmuch as its effect at the present moment is rather obscure, a Declaratory Bill to be passed, making quite clear what political functions Trade Unions may exercise. Provision also to be made for Payment of Members of Parliament'. Certainly Lloyd George's talk of a deal including the Osborne Judgment was a major attraction to F.E. Smith. Smith eagerly informed Austen Chamberlain such a coalition government could impose a compromise on the Irish Nationalists and also could 'absolutely refuse reversal of the Osborne Judgment, which Asquith standing alone cannot'.[34] Equally clear, Lloyd George was talking of a deal between 'both great parties in the State', excluding the Irish and the Labour Party.[35]

The cabinet discussion of 13 October had come to an interim decision to look into reversing the Osborne Judgment, with the proviso that 'it was recognised to be impolitic and impossible to legalise any power in the Trade Unions to impose a compulsory levy on their members for political purposes'. The Lord Chancellor and the Attorney General were asked to prepare further information, including the provision of 'safeguards for the protection of minorities and dissentient members'. The cabinet made its decision after two discussions in mid-November (incidentally, after the secret coalition talks had collapsed). This decision, made 'after an exhaustive debate', went much of the way to meet the Labour Party's wishes, but it did substantially help minorities who did not wish to support the Labour Party. Asquith's report to the King summarises the key points which were to be incorporated in the Trade Union Act 1913:

(1) Payment of members and of official expenses.

(2) Restoration by legislation to the trade unions of the power (which they were understood, prior to the Osborne Judgment, to possess which many of them have exercised for the last 30 years) of providing a fund for Parliamentary and municipal expenditure and representation. But by way of safeguard.

(3) The power not to be exercised until it has been effectively ascertained (by secret ballot, or some other appropriate mode of procedure) that it is the wish of the members of the union, and

(4) In no case is a member to be compelled to contribute to the fund, or to suffer any disability from refusing contribution.

(5) The fund to be kept separate from the general funds of the union.[36]

Whilst the 1913 Trade Union Act did not go as far in reversing the Osborne Judgment as the Labour

Party wanted, nevertheless it was fortunate for Labour that the Liberals did make it easier again for trade unions to finance parliamentary and local elections. Over a period of time the consequences of the Osborne Judgment would have been serious to the funds of the Labour Party, even if, as many historians have remarked, it did not have a great impact on the two 1910 general elections.

Many unions, such as the Amalgamated Society of Engineers and the Typographical Association, kept up a political fund by voluntary subscription after injunctions were brought against them. In most unions the voluntary schemes raised substantially less funds. In some unions, such as the Yorkshire miners, the Osborne Judgment was also an important factor (along with a desire not to split opposition to the House of Lords) in bringing about a reduction in the number of candidates they sponsored for parliamentary elections.[37]

If a skilled union such as the United Society of Boilermakers is anything to go by, then the Osborne Judgment led to a dramatic drop in funds, as compared with what had been raised earlier and what was to be raised in 1918; and it also appears to have encouraged apathy for Labour politics. In the case of the boilermakers the parliamentary levy brought in some £863 in 1906 and about £745 in 1908 (when trade was depressed). With the Osborne Judgment it dropped rapidly to just over £194 in 1910, almost £87 in 1911 and fell to £27 in 1912. Far from the union being in 'the political vanguard of trade unionism' as its socialist secretary, John Hill, had hoped in 1910, the members voted in 1912 to opt out of political action. In his annual report for 1912 Hill, noting the members' votes first against financing candidates and then against continuing the affiliation to the Labour Party, wrote of the latter vote: 'The majority against was a small one, and no doubt the illegality of levies for political purposes was the deciding factor'. However, he could add, 'since that vote, however, the law has been altered, and the question of our taking advantage of the new Act, which legalises our activities in public work, will be further considered'.[38]

It seems likely that apathy towards political action was growing among the boilermakers before the Osborne Judgment. Early in 1902 they had voted to affiliate to the LRC by 26,478 votes to 8,905. In the spring of 1904 they voted by 33,044 to 4,611 to pay an additional penny levy (on top of three

pence already) for political representation.
Whilst depressed trade is part of the explanation
for the dip in the political levy after 1906, it is
only part of the explanation. John Hill did not
hide his exasperation at his members' apathy in
1910, which deprived the union of its first
sponsored MP. He wrote in his annual report:

> Early in the year a vacancy occurred in the
> Jarrow Division and Bro. John Barker was
> selected by the Labour Party to contest the
> seat. His name was submitted for the votes of
> all members. Out of our total membership of
> nearly 50,000 only 5,299 troubled themselves
> to record their votes, and 1,928 of that
> number voted against his candidature. The
> votes of our members who were actually
> residing in the Jarrow Division were even more
> unsatisfactory, as out of seven branches there
> were only 265 members voted, 137 in favour and
> 128 against. In view of such a vote Bro.
> Barker wisely relinquished his candidature.

After commenting on the small amount subscribed to
his union's political fund that year, Hill
caustically observed:

> Until our members are prepared to pay for
> their politics we must continue to go cap in
> hand to other politicians - Cabinet Ministers
> and Members of Parliament, sent even by
> Labourers' Unions supported by the pennies of
> men whose average earnings all the year round
> are less than £1 per week. Our 50,000 skilled
> artisans have paid much less than one penny
> each during 1910 for political purposes.

After the passing of the 1913 Trade Union Act
the boilermakers remained affiliated to the Labour
Party, voting by 2,764 to 1,542 to re-establish a
political fund. By 1915 the political levy was
back up to over £800; in 1917 it brought in £1,533;
in 1918 it was just short of £3,000 and the union
had in that election year an overall balance of
over £8,100. As a result it ran five candidates in
the 1918 election, one of whom was successful.[39]
Such was the importance of the passing of the 1913
Act in the case of that union.

Whilst the boilermakers' union may not have
been typical, it was not unique. Other unions'
political funds dipped down after 1909 and other

societies were embarrassed at their inability to
finance their members as candidates. Thus the
Carpenters and Joiners' were unable to support
their member in the Keighley by-election of
November 1913 as its labour representation fund
stood at a mere £46 and its affiliation fee to the
Labour Party for 1913 was still outstanding.[40]
    The Osborne Judgment also threatened the
Labour Party at the local level. Ramsay MacDonald
wrote in his diary in June 1910, 'The Osborne
decision is . . . paralysing us especially in our
local organisations, which are suffering from want
of money'.[41] This was a point also emphasised by
many trade union leaders at the time.[42] Without
further studies, it is hard to assess the local
impact accurately. However, it is clear that
trades councils in many areas lost the support of
railwaymen's branches for some time. Also, in some
areas at least, there was a rapid rise in trade
union affiliations to the local labour
representation committees after the 1913 Trade
Union Act.[43] If the Osborne Judgment affected
funds for local politics, it does not appear to
have diminished enthusiasm. Indeed this legal
intervention, like the Taff Vale decision,
encouraged trade unionists to support the Labour
Party.


    Trade Union support was, of course, crucial
for the Labour Party at the local level, in terms
of finance and often in terms of organisation.
Thus in Dundee local activists raised money for the
local electors 'by sales of work and such efforts'
but the money for the parliamentary elections came
from the unions, and in particular the union that
sponsored the local Labour MP.[44]
    At the local level, just as at the national
level, the history of the Labour Party in the years
before the first world war is very much a history
of a struggle between socialist trade unionists and
Lib-Lab trade unionists to win working class
support. In Sheffield it appears that the divide
between the two groups followed industrial lines,
with workers in the modern heavy industry being
more likely to support socialists and with those in
the old light crafts being more likely to support
Liberal-Radical groups. It is also a history of
local tensions, as well as the tensions of national
level, between the ILP activists and the local
trade unions. In industrial areas the trade union

delegations could often outvote the ILP activists. This is well illustrated by a plaintive letter Ramsay MacDonald received in February 1908 from the Secretary of the Oldham branch of the ILP, concerning a selection meeting between the ILP nominee, Smart, and the card room workers' candidate, Crinion. MacDonald was informed,

> Both candidates were asked to address a meeting of delegates. Smart turned up, Crinion was absent through illness. We know as a matter of fact that the textile delegates present had instructions in their pockets to vote for Crinion. This of course made our nomination abortive, and our work useless and foolish. The textile trade had a majority of votes. We strongly object to Crinion on two grounds. (1) His personal character is repugnant to us and (2) he is a strong anti-socialist.

MacDonald naturally rebuffed firmly the local ILP's view of delegates and suggestion of selecting their own candidate, observing that if they did so 'instead of helping yourselves and the Labour and Socialist Movement you would only damage it for another generation in your town'.[45]

However the ILP activists and the trade unionists did stay together in the Labour Party. Part of the explanation from the trade union side was the value the party could be to the unions. This is true of weaker unions as well as the stronger. Thus as their MP Ramsay MacDonald could help the boot and shoe workers and the hosiery workers of Leicester, both in industrial and in social matters. A downtrodden group such as shopworkers could benefit from broad local trade union and socialist support in winning public opinion to support improved working conditions. Those employed by municipal authorities could also hope for a better deal through the labour movement being involved in local politics. This could be true also of industrial disputes, as James Sexton emphasised in commenting on a Liverpool dock dispute in his annual report to his members:

> The value of direct labour representation on our City Council will also be recognised in the case of the flagrant prostitution of our civic authority during the dispute in the South End. Here it was proved, beyond the

shadow of a doubt, that local laws were deliberately set aside in the interests of employers. We, at the time, had no opportunity of putting our case to the public, being debarred from direct representation on the Council.[46]

Trade unionists also moved towards the Labour Party as the Liberal government became more involved in industrial disputes. Too often government intervention in strikes and lock-outs could appear to trade unionists to favour the employers.[47] The labour unrest of 1910-1914 was marked by a ferocity of feeling, especially among unskilled workers whose real wages, often not far from subsistence level, had been eroded in the preceding decade. The disputes in the docks, the mines and elsewhere in 1911 and 1912 polarised local society. The New Statesman observed of the midland strikes amongst unskilled and often unorganised workers in the summer of 1913, 'We cannot recall a more remarkable instance of working class solidarity (as distinguished from mere trade solidarity), and the employers will be very unwise if they underrate its significance'.[48] The strikes and the authorities' responses in places such as Tonypandy in 1910 were powerful recruiting agents for the labour movement.

However, the industrial unrest of 1910-1914 also fostered challenges to the links between the trade unions and Labour Party politics from the left. This was notably the case with the syndicalists and those close to them. At first there was a blurring of the issue by some as to whether parliamentary action, as a minor adjunct to industrial action, was acceptable in the short term. The authors of The Miners Next Step (1912) and even some writers in The Syndicalist in early 1912 suggested that parliamentary action could accompany industrial action but that in due course Parliament would wither away. In The Miners' Next Step it was argued:

Political action must go side by side with industrial action. Such measures as the Mines Bill, Workmen's Compensation Acts, proposals for nationalising the Mines etc. demand the presence in Parliament of men who directly represent, and are amenable to, the wishes and instructions of the workmen. While the eagerness of Governments to become a bludgeoning

149

bully on behalf of the employers could be somewhat restrained by the presence of men who were prepared to act in a courageous fashion.

It also suggested rules by which union sponsored MPs would become truly accountable to the union membership.[49]

However, Tom Mann, Guy Bowman (editor of The Syndicalist) and others outrightly condemned parliamentary moves ('We are ourselves non-parliamentarians'). Tom Mann, who returned from Australia in 1910, could testify that 'his hopes for working class success from political methods had suffered a rude and killing shock' from his experiences of Labour in power in several Australian states. Before the TUC debated the merits of parliamentary action at its meeting in Newport in September 1912 The Syndicalist appealed to delegates, 'There never was, and there never will be "independence" in parliamentary politics. Even with a separate Labour Party, compromise reigns supreme; there are conferences, committees, bargainings, and what not, with the political parties of our employers . . . . Down with parliamentary politics that divide the workers, and Up with Direct Action that unites them'.[50]

The TUC reaffirmed its support for Labour politics, both nationally and locally, by 1,123,000 to 573,000 votes. After this, syndicalism did not fade away. Syndicalist thinking continued to challenge the existing trade union orthodoxies, and it gained more adherents beyond the mines and transport, its early strongholds. However, syndicalism after 1912 did not have the unity and, perhaps, impact that it had when the government gratuitously publicised The Syndicalist and made martyrs of Tom Mann, Guy Bowman and others over the publication of 'The Open Letter to British Soldiers' in The Syndicalist in January 1912.[51]

By 1914 British trade unions were firmly identified with the Labour Party. The parliamentary Labour Party appeared even less effective and independent after 1910, when it was fearful of pushing the Liberals from power and precipitating another general election. The People's Budget, the clash with the House of Lords, the social reforms, the charisma of Lloyd George and Churchill all overshadowed the parliamentary Labour Party. W.S. Sanders of the Fabian Society was not alone in his thoughts when he wrote in

1912, 'The Labour Party is getting more and more uninteresting. It is undramatic and dull. MacDonald appears to be taken in by (Lloyd) George every time he sees him on business'.[52]

Yet in the trade unions support remained strong for the links with the Labour Party, and there was no fragmentation of the trade union movement on political lines. As The New Statesman commented of the 1913 Trade Union Act, it would 'involve a new campaign among the trade unions up and down the country in favour of Labour representation. This represents a task of no small magnitude for the Labour Members and trade union leaders, but, by reawakening popular interest and making trade union action in politics more real, may ultimately benefit the trade unions and the Labour Party'.[52] Whether or not the campaigns were very effective, the various trade union ballots very nearly all resulted in majorities in favour of a political levy.[53] These votes ensured Labour's post first world war electoral finances, and in themselves reflect an element of the explanation for the rise of the Labour Party and the decline of the Liberal Party in the early twentieth century.

Ballots to establish Union Political Funds 1913

| Name | Number of members at 31 Dec 1912 | Votes in favour | Votes against | Votes rejected |
|------|------|------|------|------|
| Nat Assoc of Operative Plasterers | 7,918 | 1,183 | 657 | 18 |
| Amalg Soc of Carpenters and Joiners | 78,965 | 13,336 | 11,738 | 266 |
| Amalg Assoc of Operative Cotton Spinners etc | 23,500 | 4,826 | 3,376 | 73 |
| ASLEF | 26,500 | 7,839 | 3,841 | 9 |
| Friendly Soc of Ironfounders | 24,200 | 6,854 | 2,576 | 188 |
| ASE | 143,998 | 20,586 | 12,740 | 29 |
| Nat Union of Boot and Shoe Operatives | 41,440 | 6,085 | 1,935 | 108 |
| Ship Constructors and Shipwrights Assoc | 26,223 | 7,446 | 5,487 | 59 |
| Amalg Soc of Gasworkers, Brickmakers and General Labourers | 7,146 | 7,248 | 1,108 | 113 |
| Nat Union of Dock Labourers and Riverside Workers | 44,227 | 4,078 | 501 | 34 |
| United Machine Workers Assoc | 7,269 | 2,673 | 1,686 | 25 |
| Amalg Musicians Union | 6,745 | 1,661 | 688 | 23 |
| Nat Union of Clerks | 8,840 | 1,844 | 540 | 42 |
| Amalg Assoc of Card and Blowing Room Operators | 51,914 | 2,293 | 1,437 | 53 |
| British Steel Smelters etc | 29,299 | 5,705 | 1,400 | 88 |
| Railway Clerks Assoc | 19,151 | 15,496 | 1,340 | 123 |
| General Union of Assocs of Loom Overlookers | - | 1,966 | 1,228 | 21 |
| Amalg Assoc of Beamers, Twisters etc | - | 1,409 | 828 | 23 |
| Miners Federation of GB | - | 261,643 | 194,800 | 20,223 |
| Amalg Weavers Assoc | - | 98,158 | 75,893 | 367 |
| Operative Bleachers, Dyers etc | - | 1,864 | 964 | 60 |
| TOTAL | 1,207,841 | 298,702 | 125,310 | |

This list of individual unions includes only those of over 5,000 members. The source is Hansard, 5th series, vol. LVIII, cols. 613-4, 16 Feb. 1914. See also Report of the Chief Registrar of Friendly Societies for the Year 1912 (London, HMSO, 1914). The discrepancy in the Gasworkers' figures where the votes cast considerably outnumber the union's total membership is not explained in either source.

NOTES

1. V.R. Lorwin, The French Labor Movement (Harvard University Press, Cambridge Mass., 1954), pp.17-46; M.J. Neufeld, Italy: School for Awakening Countries (Greenwood, Westport Conn., 1961), pp.339-58; P. Reymond-Sauvain, Le Syndicalisme en Suisse (Editions Générales, Geneva, 1966), pp.43-66; W. Kendall, The Labour Movement in Europe (Allen Lane, London, 1975), pp.213-17 and 249-51; J.A. Moses, Trade Unionism in Germany from Bismarck to Hitler (Prior, London, 1982), vol.I, pp.140-162.
2. Lorwin, French Labor, p.18.
3. Quoted in H.A. Clegg, A. Fox and A.F. Thompson, A History of British Trade Unions since 1889 (Oxford, University Press, 1964), p.380.
4. F. Bealey and H. Pelling, Labour and Politics 1900-1906 (Macmillan, London, 1958), pp.210-211; and K.D. Brown, John Burns (Royal Historical Society, London, 1977), pp.99-102.
5. Hansard, 4th Series, vol. CLXV, cols. 1275-1281. 8 May 1906. Keir Hardie's move was heavily defeated. The Labour Party was supported by some Radicals but also by some Tories, such as Sir William Bull, later of the Anti-Socialist Union. The Times, 9 May 1906.
6. In the Derbyshire, South Derbyshire, Leicestershire and Nottinghamshire areas the vote against was 24,088 to 9,617 in 1908, whilst in 1906 it had been 23,504 to 3,791. R. Gregory, The Miners and British Politics 1906-1914 (Oxford, University Press, 1968), pp.28-34.
7. Loughborough Herald, 11 Jan. 1906.
8. Quoted in Bealey and Pelling, Labour and Politics, p.278.
9. For Osborne, see P.S. Bagwell, The Railwaymen (Allen and Unwin, London, 1963), pp.336-353 and H. Pelling, 'The Politics of the Osborne Judgment', Historical Journal, vol.25 (1982), pp.889-909. G.W. Alcock, Fifty Years of Railway Trade Unionism (N.U.R., London, 1922), pp.336-43. See also the University of Warwick Library publication, The Osborne Case Papers and Other Records of the Amalgamated Society of Railway Servants, compiled by Christine Woodland, ed. R. Storey (Coventry, 1979).
10. Alcock, Fifty Years, pp.340 and 236.
11. G. Howell, 'Liberty for Labour' in T. MacKay (ed.), A Plea for Liberty (Murray, London), which has an introduction by Herbert Spencer. As one would expect the brief

bibliography to Osborne's _Sane Trade Unionism_ (Collins, London, 1913) contains three books by Howell. See also N. Soldon, 'Laissez-faire as Dogma: The Liberty and Property Defence League 1882-1914', in K.D. Brown (ed.), _Essays in Anti-Labour History_ (Macmillan, London 1974), pp. 208-233, and F.M. Leventhal, _Respectable Radical_ (Weidenfeld and Nicolson, London, 1971), pp. 196-209.

12. See in particular Osborne, _Sane Trade Unionism_, pp. 252-253, 54-55, 228, 62-63, 58.

13. Ibid., pp. 69-70, 232 and 221. The reference to religious views is to Labour's support for secular education. It was a point made much of by F.E. Smith in the Commons in 1911.

14. Bagwell, _Railwaymen_, p. 255. H.V. Emy, _Liberals, Radicals and Social Politics 1892-1914._ (Cambridge, University Press, 1973), p. 253.

15. J. Phipps to Ramsay MacDonald, 31 July 1912 and 4 Oct. 1911. Ramsay MacDonald Papers. PRO 30/69/1156, ff. 156-9 and 1155, ff. 316-20. For Osborne's comments on socialist activists in the ASRS, see Osborne, _Sane Trade Unionism_, pp. 66-68.

16. For Smith see _Hansard_, 5th Series, vol. XXVl, col. 934. 30 May 1911. For Clynes see ibid, vol. XXXXl, cols. 3015-16. 6 Aug. 1912.

17. For this response in Lancashire see P.F. Clarke, _Lancashire and the New Liberalism_ (Cambridge, University Press, 1971), chapter 12, especially pp. 332-6. See also P. Joyce. _Work, Society and Politics_ (Harvester Press, Brighton, 1980), especially chapter 9.

18. K.D. Brown, 'The Trade Union Tariff Reform Association, 1904-13', _Journal of British Studies_, vol. IX (1970), pp. 141-153. A. Sykes, _Tariff Reform in British Politics 1903-1913_ (Oxford, University Press, 1979), pp. 220-223. For Churchill's views, W.M. Crook to L. Harcourt, 14 Nov. 1905. Bodleian Library, Harcourt Papers. Box 29.

19. Brown, 'Trade Union Tariff Reform Association', pp. 143 and 146. Ramsay MacDonald, Hansard, 5th Series, vol. XXVI, col. 949. 30 May 1911.

20. For the Steele v. SWMF case see K.D.Ewing, _Trade Unions, The Labour Party and the Law_ (Edinburgh, University Press, 1982), pp. 21-3.

21. Bagwell, _Railwaymen_, pp. 249-250.

22. See Ewing, _Trade Unions_, pp. 23-37, for a detailed discussion of the Osborne Judgment.

23. Lord James of Hereford had been a Liberal MP 1869-1886, then Liberal Unionist MP 1886-1909; Lord Shaw of Dunfermline had been Liberal MP for Hawick District 1892-1909; and Lord Moulton had been Liberal MP for these seats between 1885-1906.

24. Hansard, 5th Series, vol. XXVI, cols. 3012 and 3014. 30 May 1911.

25. At Dundee, 15 Jan. 1910; The Scotsman, 17 Jan. 1910. The Marquess of Reading, Rufus Isaacs (Hutchinson, London, 1942,) vol. I, pp. 198-199.

26. See, for example, the memoranda by successive Chief Whips: Pease, 18 Dec. 1906. Herbert Gladstone Papers, B.L. Add. MS.46022, f. 157; and Elibank, 29 Mar. 1910. National Library Scotland. Elibank Mss. 8502, f. 38. In the latter Elibank observed, '. . . socialists and Labour and Irish and extreme Radicals if joining in one party would make Liberalism impossible and must give Tariff Reformers better opportunity than they could ever have expected'.

27. Austen Chamberlain to Bonar Law, 29 Sept. 1910. House of Lords Record Office. Bonar Law Papers. 18/6/125.

28. This is about half of Bonar Law's lengthy letter to Chamberlain, 1 Oct. 1910; ibid., 18/8/12. Bonar Law's views may have in part been influenced by the journalist H. Gwynne; see ibid., 20/19.

29. The Times, 6 Oct. 1910. Beatrice Webb's diary, 6 Oct. 1910; B. Webb, Our Partnership (Longman, London, 1948), p. 461.

30. Asquith to Harcourt, 3 Oct. 1910. Harcourt Papers, Box 27. Asquith to the King, 13 Oct. 1910. Bodleian Library. Asquith Papers, vol. 5, ff. 242-243.

31. This is to judge from the Cabinet Papers by Loreburn, Carrington, Haldane, Robson, Samuel and later by Buxton. PRO CAB 37/103/44-52. For a survey of the government's view see Ewing, Trade Unions, pp. 40-44.

32. Robson's memorandum, 10 Oct. 1910. PRO CAB 37/103/45.

33. For the secret coalition proposals of autumn 1910 see G.R. Searle, The Quest for National Efficiency (Blackwell, Oxford, 1971), chapter 6, and R.J. Scally, The Origins of the Lloyd George Coalition (Princeton, University Press, 1975), chapter 7. For Lloyd George's two memoranda, see Scally, Origins, pp. 375-386.

34. F.E. Smith raised this issue in his letters to Chamberlain on 20 and 21 Oct. 1910; See

the Earl of Birkenhead, Frederick Edwin, Earl of Birkenhead (Thornton Butterworth, London, 1933), vol. I, pp. 205-8. See also Sir Austen Chamberlain, Politics From Inside (Cassell, London, 1936), pp. 279-294.

35. A point well emphasiscd by Dr. Scally, Origins, 189.

36. The key elements in the Act were agreed at the Cabinet meeting of 22 Nov. 1910. The matter had also been discussed five days earlier. Asquith to the King, 13 Oct. 17 Nov. and 22 Nov. 1910. Bodleian Library. Asquith Papers, vol. 5, ff. 242-243, 246, and 248-249.

37. W.B. Gwyn, Democracy and the Cost of Politics in Britain (Athlone Press, London, 1962), pp. 191-197; Gregory, Miners., pp. 111-115; Pelling, 'Osborne Judgment', pp. 894-6.

38. United Society of Boilermakers, Annual Report, 1906, 1908, 1910, 1911 and 1912.

39. United Society of Boilermakers, Monthly Report, Mar. 1902 and June 1904; and Annual Report, 1909, 1910, 1915, 1917 and 1918.

40. ASCJ, Monthly Journal, Jan. 1914, p. 27. The Amalgamated Society of Railway Servants was relatively successful, its political fund dropping from £4,187.6s.2d. in 1909 to £2,386.17s.4d. in 1911. ASRS, Reports and Financial Statements, 1909 and 1911.

41. Cited in Pelling, 'Osborne Judgment', p. 897.

42. See, for example, the President of the ASRS's address at the union's annual general meeting, 3 Oct. 1910, ASRS., Annual Report, 1910, p.5. Parliamentary Committee, Quarterly Report, Dec. 1910, p. 31.

43. On the railwaymen see A. Clinton, The Trade Union Rank and File (Manchester, University Press, 1977), p. 20 and J. Mendelson et al., The Sheffield Trades and Labour Council, 1858-1958 (Sheffield Trades and Labour Council, Sheffield, 1958), pp. 59-60. For the rapid increase in affiliations to the Liverpool Labour Representation Committee see P.J. Waller, Democracy And Sectarianism (Liverpool, University Press, 1981), p. 267.

44. Details in letter by J. Duncan, Secretary of the Scottish Steam Fishing Vessels' Enginemen's and Fireman's Union, to Ramsay MacDonald, 16 Jan. 1911. Ramsay MacDonald Papers, PRO 30/69/1155, f. 123.

45. H. Chadderton to Ramsay MacDonald, 6 Feb.

1908, and MacDonald to Chadderton, 6 Feb. 1908. ibid., 30/69/1152, ff. 65-66.

46. For MacDonald see ibid. 30/69/1150-1158. For shop workers see, for example, National Amalgamated Society of Shop Assistants, Warehousemen and Clerks, Annual Report and Balance Sheet 1906 (1907), p. 5. For Sexton's report, see National Union of Dock Labourers, Report of Executive 1905 (1906); and for the background to the dispute see Waller, Democracy, pp. 214-216. See also Clegg, Fox and Thompson, Trade Unions, pp. 88-90.

47. I have argued this in some detail in C. Wrigley, David Lloyd George and the British Labour Movement (Harvester Press, Hassocks, 1976), chapter 3 and in my essay in C. Wrigley (ed.), A History of British Industrial Relations, 1875-1914 (Harvester Press, Hassocks, 1982).

48. New Statesman, 1, 10, 14 June 1913.

49. In fact within The Miners' Next Step there are different emphases as to the role of political action. For The Syndicalist arguing 'we do not think Parliament as at present composed can ever do much if anything toward preparing the way for the future industrial society' see the March-April 1912 issue (published when the usual editor was in gaol over 'The Open Letter to British Soldiers').

50. The Syndicalist, Jan., Feb., and Sept. 1912.

51. The Syndicalist itself became sectarian. Thus in February 1914 under a front page headline of 'Trite and Tripe: A Collection of Fakes for Mugwumps', it dealt with industrial democracy, industrial unionism, guild socialism, Daily Heraldism, Larkinism and the SLP. For the case for emphasising the continuing importance of syndicalism 1912-1914 see B. Holton, British Syndicalism, 1900-1914 (Pluto Press, London, 1976).

52. The New Statesman, 1, 4, 3 May 1913, p. 103.

53. See Table 1. See also Pelling, 'Osborne Judgment', pp. 906-907 and M. Pinto-Duschinsky, British Political Finance 1839-1980 (American Enterprise Institute, Washington, 1981), pp. 67-71.

Chapter 7

LABOUR AND EDUCATION

At the 1906 conference of the Labour Party
Pete Curran of the Gasworkers' Union moved
a resolution on education which began, '. . . this
conference condemns the Educational policy of the
Government as laid down in the Act of 1902
. . .'[1] A similar response to Balfour's
Education Act had occurred at the Trade Union
Congresses of 1904 and 1905, echoing opposition
declared in the very year of the act.[2] Hence the
Labour Party began with antagonism towards past
Conservative legislation and believed that the new
Liberal administration of 1906 would provide the
necessary measures to reverse it in the same
forthright manner they promised to use in dealing
with trade union grievances arising out of the Taff
Vale dispute of 1901.[3]

The rising Labour Party knew it could not
carry either of these measures by itself. Even
after the 1906 election when it held a respectable
29 seats and could usually count on the support of
a further 25 Lib-Labs, the party was in no position
to force the Liberal pace. Elements within the
government, including the Prime Minister, felt some
obligation to support Labour's Trade Disputes Bill
in 1906, if only because of the backing apparently
given to it by many Liberal candidates during the
election campaign.[4] On the other hand
indifference could best describe the Liberal
attitude towards the Education Bill drawn up by the
TUC and introduced by Will Thorne in the same
year. It may be that the issue of trade union
funds was more simple. The Liberals knew that for
the trade union movement it was vital to survival.
The 1902 Education Act was a more complicated
matter in that there was considerable room for
disagreement as to how best to tackle the many

issues involved. The interests of the Liberal Party and the new Labour Party were not identical in the field of education. For the labour movement the school board era, which lasted from 1870 to 1902, had been looked upon as a period of slow but steady improvement in the education provided for the majority of children; compulsory attendance in 1880, free education in most elementary schools in 1891, a gradual raising of the school leaving age from ten years in 1876 to twelve years in 1899 and the development of some kind of secondary education in the form of higher grade schools.[5] Moreover, the school boards were elected bodies for which working men and women could vote and stand as representatives. This had provided some members of the labour movement with their first opportunity to have a say in the running of the schools which were intended primarily for their children. The unsectarian school boards were paid for by the rates but they were directly responsible to elected representatives within the community. The religious schools which pre-dated them formed a separate but parallel system which was neither in receipt of rate aid nor directly accountable to the community. The 1902 Education Act abolished the school boards and provided rate aid to religious schools. It was the former measure which brought most protests from the labour movement; it was the latter action which provided the spur to much of the nonconformist objection within the Liberal Party.[6] Because of the growing strength of organised labour there was little incentive for the Liberals to restore a situation in which increased numbers of labour representatives might gain influence at local level in the education system but they did feel a greater necessity to try to tackle the religious issue which had bedevilled the development of elementary education in England and Wales throughout the nineteenth century. This difference in interests may explain why the new Labour Party in Parliament had more success in the welfare aspects of education than in matters involving its political and financial control.

The party did not develop a distinctive education policy of its own immediately. It directly imported the policy of the TUC and this is made clear by an examination of the detailed items listed in the resolutions adopted at their respective conferences. A summary shows the following common points:

## Labour and Education

| Item | Labour Party 1906[7] | TUC 1905[8] |
|---|---|---|
| | Education Resolution | Education Resolution |
| Condemnation 1902 Education Act | Introductory Paragraph | Introductory Paragraph |
| 1 free meal per day | Clause 1 | In separate resolution on physical deterioration |
| All grades of education free, state maintained | " 2 | Clause 1 |
| Secondary & Technical education with bursaries for all children who would benefit; 16 years to university | " 3 | " 2 |
| Capable students to go to university | " 4 | " 3 |
| Continuous assessment to replace exams | " 5 | " 4 |
| Secular education | " 6 | " 5 |
| State schools controlled by directly elected representatives | " 7 | " 6 |
| Each educational district to establish teacher training colleges | " 8 | " 7 |
| Education authorities to feed children without reference to Board of Guardians | " 8a | |
| Cost of educational reforms to be met by National Exchequer and restoration of misappropriated endowments | " 9 | " 8 |
| TUC Parliamentary Committee to formulate these proposals in a bill to be laid before Parliament | | " 9 |
| No parliamentary candidate to be endorsed who does not accept/promote above educational policy | " 10 | " 10 |

At Labour's conference in 1910 I.H. Gwynne of the Tin and Sheet Millmen moved, 'That this Conference demands that efforts shall be made by the Labour Members in the House of Commons to secure an Educational Policy passed at the last TUC at Ipswich, and which includes a National System of Education under full popular control, free and secular from Primary School to the University'.[9] Will Thorne seconded and after a brief word of clarification from the chairman it was passed by 650,000 to 120,000 votes without further discussion. However, it needs to be pointed out that there were two other resolutions on education discussed that year at conference, one concerning secular education and another dealing with school meals and child welfare.

There was nothing strange about the adoption of TUC education policy because often the same prominent trade unionists and Labour MPs were likely to attend both annual gatherings. Indeed it would have been stranger if their policies had not been similar. Neither is it surprising that whilst there was a general unanimity of views concerning education throughout the organised labour movement the few points of contention were raised by the same personalities at various conferences; secular education and the agreed minimum school leaving age. Tracing back Labour Party education policy to the much older TUC is only the first step back to the source of these ideas. At the TUC resolutions on education were brought forward by a few trade unionists, especially members of the Gasworkers Union, such as Will Thorne, Pete Curran and J.R. Clynes. They in turn often gained their ideas from the smaller socialist parties of the time, Thorne being a member of the SDF and the other two members of the ILP. This source of ideas partly explains why TUC views on education were radical in an organisation heavily influenced by liberalism. It also explains the near consensus of views on education within the labour movement.[10]

Three main strands can be detected in Labour Party education policy. There was the philosophical which considered the kind of education to be provided, and this could be seen in ideas concerning secular education, who should receive secondary education, and the role of technical education. Often these ideas were little more than responses to the system as it was. Secondly, there was the political view which demanded to know who was to have financial and political control over the various sections of the education system. Finally, there was the sociological approach which sought to change the social circumstances of working class children so that they might be in a position to take advantage of the educational opportunities offered. All three were of course closely related.

Widespread agreement among most sections of the labour movement on educational ideas was partly explained by the fact that many people were fully aware of their own limited formal education and the manner in which it had contributed to their restricted job opportunities. They were therefore determined that their own children and those of other working class people should have better chances so that in turn they might enjoy improved working and living conditions. This was because success in formal education was seen as one of the few ways in which working class children might gain social mobility. Hence free education financed by the state and maintenance grants received overwhelming support. So too did demands to return to the principle of educational organisation established by the previous school board system; namely that local education be controlled by elected representatives from the community. There was also a demand, based perhaps more upon feelings of injustice than hard evidence at the time, for, '. . . the restoration of misappropriated educational endowments . . .' held by numerous private schools and the universities of Oxford and Cambridge.[11] Many of these endowments, it was believed, had originally been intended for the children of the poor and were now used almost exclusively to help pupils from families enjoying well above average incomes.

Two other issues worth recording are those concerning the curriculum and assessment although they were rarely referred to under these titles. Organised workers had long recognised that skilled jobs received better pay and were less likely to suffer the unemployment frequently experienced by the unskilled. Attempts to cater for this problem were expressed in early demands, '. . . that secondary and technological education be placed within the reach of every child . . . .'[12] By 1912 it was argued that, '. . . there is urgent need for a generous measure of educational reform in the direction of providing for liberal, as distinct from technical education, thus laying the basis of national life in a democracy'.[13]

Education in the 'duties of citizenship' now seemed to be as important as the impartation of knowledge directly related to work. Workers were demanding to know how the social and political system worked with the expectation that they would be taking part in it sooner or later. There was also some evidence to suggest that it was now felt that the new secondary schools might provide greater opportunities for social mobility than increased information concerning technology; the latter might provide promotion to the rank of foreman but it also seemed to restrict any advance further; secondary education promised the chance of a secure white-collar job and sometimes the potential for promotion to the managerial side in industry or commerce.

Assessment was also related to this theme. In 1906 it was suggested that '. . . standards of capacity to be judged by work previously accomplished and not by competitive examination', in other words a system of continuous assessment.[14] Yet there was always a measure of ambiguity over Labour policy towards selective education. It was clear that working class children were often held back because of the financial circumstances of their parents, hence the call for maintenance grants and more scholarships. Such feelings of injustice were bluntly expressed by A. Hayday of the Gasworkers, '. . . if education through a university was good enough for the children of the idle rich it was not too good for the children of the very poor wage earners'.[15]

At the same time there was a general acceptance that there should be some form of competition for secondary school places. Skilled workers in particular often held meritocratic views but wished selection to be based upon ability rather than social privilege. In the early years of the twentieth century elementary and secondary schools were not progressive stages of education through which all children passed, but separate forms of schooling distinguished largely by the social origins of the children. Most children attended elementary schools, the majority of which had stopped charging fees in 1891, but secondary school fees of approximately one pound per term put such institutions well beyond the means of working class parents unless their child was one of the few to win a scholarship.[16] In addition the schools differed in the curriculum taught with elementary schools restricted, as their very name implied, to arithmetic, writing, English, some basic history, geography, with perhaps a little science and physical exercise which might take the form of military drill.[17]  By contrast secondary schools taught mathematics including geometry and algebra, the traditional three sciences and at least one foreign language.  Intelligent working class children who stayed on at school after twelve years of age did so in the senior forms of elementary schools, denied access to a wider curriculum because it was illegal to teach such material at elementary schools.[18]  From 1902 some scholarship places were offered at secondary schools but these were usually gained by children from either middle class or skilled artisan backgrounds.  One requirement was that a successful child should stay at school until 16 years of age and it was almost impossible for poor parents to manage without the small income a youngster could bring to the family upon starting work.  The prospect of a job inevitably put pressure on both parents and child to let the latter leave school at an early age.

The Liberal government of 1906 was more responsive to pressure concerning privilege in education than the previous Conservative administration and in 1907 Reginald McKenna, President of the Board of Education, introduced the Regulations for Secondary Schools which provided additional money to those schools willing to offer at least twenty-five per cent of their places without fees to pupils from elementary schools.  A qualifying test was to be passed to ascertain whether a child was capable of benefitting from secondary education.  Labour's main efforts at that time were directed towards ensuring that as many free places as possible were offered and to gaining some form of maintenance grants which would allow poor children to take up a place if it was offered.  The acknowledgement that not all children could receive secondary education was made explicit in the language of the resolution passed at Labour's conference in 1906.  Secondary education, it argued, should be available '. . . to all children whose usefulness would be enhanced by such extended education'.[19]  The following year, however, Will Thorne's resolution broke with this general view and demanded 'That secondary and technical education be an essential part of every child's education, and secured by an extension of the scholarship system as will place a maintenance scholarship within the reach of every child, and thus make it possible for every child to be a full-time pupil up to the age of 16'.[20] Whilst Thorne's resolution was readily agreed to at the time, when the party's Memorandum on Education was issued in 1914 it illustrated an acceptance of limited secondary educational provision in its very first sentence. 'In view of the fact that the education of the mass of working class children to-day begins and ends at the elementary school . . .' and went on later to suggest, 'At whatever age full-time attendance ceases, it will still be necessary to provide continued education for the vast majority who do not pass to a secondary school'.[21] For most working class children it was therefore proposed that some form of part-time secondary education through continuation classes was the best that could be hoped for at this time.

Two issues which did lead to some controversy by small minorities at Labour conferences were the raising of the school leaving age and secular education. In 1906 and 1907 a clause was passed suggesting, '. . . adequate provision be made for children to continue at school until the age of sixteen years, or until such age as the university course begins'.[22] This raised no opposition but there was a certain ambiguity here because the stress seemed to be on financial provision to enable youngsters to stay on until sixteen or later. However in 1909 the call for maintenance grants and raising the school leaving age were separated into two distinct clauses and the latter now demanded 'The abolition of the half-time system and the raising of the School age to 16'.[23] The half-time system by which children worked in a factory in the morning and attended school in the afternoon one week and reversed the process the following week had developed out of the factory acts passed early in the nineteenth century. In fact when the hours were added up over a fortnight it soon became apparent that twice as much time was spent in the factory as in the school room, sixty six and thirty hours respectively. This system had once been prevalent in agriculture and the textile industry but by the Edwardian period was virtually confined to the Lancashire textile trade. Trade union leaders opposed it but were conscious that it was supported by the majority of textile workers as well as the factory owners. Moreover, in 1909 a ballot taken among the textile workers, including the children, showed a large majority in favour of keeping the present minimum age for half-timers.

D.J. Shackleton MP pointed out his dilemma to the Labour's conference as he had done to the TUC:

> He agreed with Miss (Margaret) Macmillan that education should not finish at sixteen. What was the position of the textile people? During the last summer a conference of textile workers was held to discuss the subject thoroughly, and that conference decided to give a lead to all the members. While they had been doing their best to educate their people up to this level a ballot had been taken which expressed the very opposite view. They, as leaders, believed in the raising of the age and were doing their best to bring about the change. But at the present they had met with a democratic vote which was about six to one the other way. He wanted the Conference to recognise that if they voted against the resolution it was not because they as leaders believed they were doing the right thing but because they were not prepared to vote against the wish of their people.[24]

There were two important issues here. One concerned the role of representatives and whether they should vote according to their own view of the matter.[25] The other was the question of child labour which was strongly opposed by most sections of the labour movement. Bernard Shaw told the same conference that it should oppose the half-time system, '. . . to enable Mr Shackleton to go back to his constituents and say that . . . Conference had backed him up . . . a strong lead had to be given to those people . . . . The capitalist system had got them into a bad habit of selling their children to the capitalist'.[26]

Whilst most condemned the half-time system because it really was by now seen as an anachronism there was not complete agreement on the exact minimum age for children to leave school. It had been raised to twelve years in 1899. To ask for a further four years was considered unnecessary by some.[27] At the Labour conference of 1909 the abolition of the half-time system and the raising of the school leaving age to 16 years were put to the delegates in one clause and was carried by 724,000 to 309,000 votes. This was to be the accepted school leaving age to aim for and when the Memorandum on Education was put before conference in 1914 the committee retained the idea but recommended that it be carried out in stages, the first being to raise the age to sixteen years. By then another related proposal had been agreed; that young people should not be required to work more than thirty hours per week so, '. . . that Classes shall be provided during the day time, to enable students from the age of 16 to 18 years to learn thoroughly the theoretical and practical side of their work; and that employers shall be compelled to allow their employees the necessary time off to attend such classes . . .'.[28] These classes were known as continuation schools and considerable discussion arose over the concept which was sometimes interpreted as a form of technical training and at other times as an opportunity for further education. H.H. Elvin of the Clerks' Union promoted the idea vigorously at the TUC and Labour conferences. He also supported a bill introduced by the Liberal MP, Chiozza Money, to set up such classes in 1908.[29] He argued for them primarily as a substitute for evening classes in the belief that after a day's work most youngsters were too tired to study effectively. This was shown by the rapid drop-out rate each year from 'night school' classes.

The second aspect of education in dispute within the party concerned the demand for secular education. This, too, mirrored a similar disagreement at the TUC, with the opposition led again by James Sexton MP and leader of the Liverpool dockers. Rivalry between the British and Foreign School Society (Nonconformist) established in 1808 and the National Society (Anglican) formed in 1811 had plagued education throughout the nineteenth century. Since 1833 both had received government grants but by the 1860s it was obvious that there were insufficient places for the number of children who ought to be attending school. For a variety of reasons including the persistence of child labour, parental indifference, inclement weather and the need to care for younger siblings or parents who were ill, many children failed to attend school regularly. The demand for a national system of elementary education had been repeatedly blocked by Anglican interests in Parliament.[30] The election of a Liberal government in 1868 and an effective campaign led by the National Education League finally enabled W.E. Forster, Vice-President of the Committee of the Privy Council on Education, to carry through the 1870 Education Act which broke the monopoly of religious control over

schools.[31]    Nowhere    could    the    jibe    that    the
Church of England was the Tory Party at prayer have
seemed  to  be  more  relevant  than  in  the  field  of
education.   Here  the  two  became  allies  not  only
within the National Education Union which opposed
the NEL but also in their joint opposition to the
new    school    board    system    which    emerged    from
Forster's Act and was supported in general by the
Liberals,   nonconformists   and   labour   movement.[32]
Their  opposition  to  the  school  boards  continued
throughout the remainder of the nineteenth century
and they gradually gained the support of the fee
paying  secondary  schools  and  the  Roman  Catholic
Church    before    they    finally    witnessed    the
destruction  of  the  school  boards  with  the  1902
Education  Act  brought  in  by  the  Conservative
government.
     Forster's  Act  laid  down  that  school  districts
should  be  established  to  ascertain  the  supply  of
school places and where they were deemed deficient
the religious societies should have six months to
make good the shortcomings.  If they could not, the
rate payers would elect a school board with powers
to raise money from the rates to build and maintain
schools.     No    religious    conditions    were    to    be
attached to attendance at such schools and in the
famous    Cowper-Temple    clause,    an    amendment
introduced during the debate in Parliament, it was
agreed  that  any  religious  teaching  should  be
undenominational.   The  Anglicans  had  argued  that
there was already sufficient schooling provided but
the    school    building    programme    which    followed
illustrated    the    fallacy    of    this    suggestion.
Between   1870   and   1895   school   boards   provided
accommodation for 2,211,299 pupils and during the
period  from  1870  to  1891  religious  societies
provided places for a further 1,475,000 pupils.[33]
     To  a  large  extent  the  working  classes  were
indifferent  to  the  religious  squabbles  of  the
nineteenth century.  Certainly those in towns had
largely given up the habit of church attendance
long ago.  Those who became leaders in the labour
movement during the Edwardian era often looked back
upon the Anglican Church as an organisation which
had rarely supported trade unions and often denied
working  class  children  good  educational  opportunities.   This  outlook  was  based  upon  their  own
school experiences and the manner in which the
Anglicans had fought to undermine the school board
system   which   trade   unionists   had   seen   as   a
substantial  improvement  on  the  voluntary  system  of

education which had preceded it. The Anglicans and Tories combined in the Church Party at school board election time and claimed that religious schools were cheaper for the town because they relied upon voluntary subscriptions whereas school boards were a charge upon the rates.[34] This was true but the corollary was that church schools could not compete with the better equipped school boards which attracted the best teachers by paying higher salaries. Given the part that the Anglicans had played in trying to undermine the school boards it can be no surprise to find that whilst individual members of the labour movement were to be found as practising members of various religious faiths there was a general feeling that the only way to avoid the disputes was to keep denominational religion out of schools altogether. It was for this reason rather than any strong support for atheism that secular education had become a firm demand within the labour movement.

In 1906 the Labour conference agreed that, 'All State supported schools to be secular' but this clause was responsible for the longest argument on education and just as Shackleton argued with his textile workers in mind so James Sexton knew that the dockers of his Liverpool constituency with its strong Irish links and influential Catholic Church would not agree to secular education. He argued that:

> In the rank and file of the unions of the country there were men and women of different political and religious persuasion. They contributed their mite to the Parliamentary levy for purely Labour representation . . . if the levies of the men and women in the Trade Union movement were to be used for the purpose of what they considered the abolition of religious principles from the schools, they would not only withdraw their levy, but also withdraw their membership from the union.[35]

Sexton received little support for his views. There were those who wanted secular education simply in order to avoid religious arguments arising in the party. J.H. Thomas claimed, 'He knew of nothing that was more calculated to split the Labour forces than to depart from the known policy of secular education. They found today that their council chambers were turned into theological battlegrounds, and the best interests of the children and of the community were being neglected'.[36] Others thought the religious lobby was one of self interest. 'They had had enough fighting over the children', W.B. Parker of Islington Trade Council told delegates, 'They heard parsons and ministers delivering sermons for God and the children, while it was nothing but for themselves and their own creed'.[37] As for Sexton's threat that members would leave the unions if secular education was introduced, Pete Curran drew loud applause when he declared, 'Well, if any people were prepared to secede because the movement pledged itself to the diverting of money wasted over religious scrambles, to higher forms of education, the sooner such people were out of the movement the better'.[38] The complete education resolution including secular education was passed by 817,000 to 76,000 votes, nearly all the opposition being accounted for by the religious dispute. The secular issue arose again at conference in 1907, 1909, 1910 and 1911. In 1910 W. Marshall proposed that the issue be put to a ballot of all party members but his suggestion was rejected, 99,000 to 810,000 votes. In 1911 the resolution on secular education, 'fell to the ground the representative of the organisation responsible for it not being present'.[39]

From outside, meanwhile, the Catholic Federation tried to put pressure upon the Labour Party just as it had upon the Parliamentary Committee of the TUC.[40] A circular on secular education from the trade union section of the Catholic Federation was sent to the Labour Party Executive in 1907 and the following year the Executive rejected a request to receive a deputation from the Catholic trade unionists.[41] The Federation lobbied the party conference annually from 1907 and in 1909 produced a lengthy open letter to delegates which restated the views frequently expressed by Sexton, playing up in particular the fears of disunity which might arise from support for secular education.[42] Such special pleading made no more impact upon Labour Party delegates than Sexton had done earlier. Yet when the final Memorandum on Education was published in 1914 there was no mention of secular education. It might be that by then the religious groups were no longer seen as a possible threat to the development of the national education system or that arguments born in the nineteenth century no longer seemed relevant.

The areas discussed so far relate largely to proposed changes in the structure of the school system, emphasis upon what should be taught and who should control the schools. With the exception of McKenna's Free Place Regulations little progress had been achieved. The second major strand to the Labour Party's education programme was that concerning the social conditions which prevented children from gaining the most that the educational system had to offer. One item was the maintenance grants already mentioned. Another was the concern for ill-nourished and sick children who were too hungry to concentrate on lessons or frequently absent because of illness. There was little need to convince Labour Party delegates as to the reality of working class life in which problems of hunger and sickness were common enough, but convincing Parliament was another matter. Yet it was in the area of welfare related to children at school that the Labour Party had most success.

The provision of meals for hungry children had a considerable history. 'In February, 1864, the first of the relatively few stable school meals associations appeared in the Destitute Children's Dinner Society, which had as its chief object the feeding of children at a ragged school in Westminster. This society and others like it grew rapidly in the years at the end of the decade under the stimulus of the interest in education aroused by the Forster Education Act of 1870'.[43] The idea was rapidly taken up by the SDF in the 1880s and later by the ILP and Fabians.[44] It soon became part of the TUC education programme and by 1906 'one free meal a day' had become Labour Party policy. Outside the labour movement there was also some support among charitable societies for the feeding of poor children and attempts were made by the London School Board to coordinate a programme for feeding children but this met with little success. By 1901 an average of just over one meal per year for each child attending school within the board's jurisdiction was achieved.[45]

The SDF, TUC and Labour Party advocated school meals for all children in order to avoid the stigma attached to charitable handouts. Not all agreed with this approach and Sexton expressed opinions that were echoed by Conservative MPs in Parliament over the matter:

He would vigorously support any suggestion that they should feed needy children, whose

> parents could not afford to do it themselves
> . . . but if they extended that they would
> include the children of parents who would take
> advantage of the legislation to evade their
> responsibilities.[46]

He was greeted with cries of 'shame' and was no
more successful over this issue than he was over
secular education. Yet the link between
nourishment and health was obvious enough and two
important reports emphasised it; the 1904 Report of
the Committee on Physical Deterioration and the
1905 Report on Medical Inspection and Feeding of
School Children. The former revealed the existence
of a section of the population, '. . . whose
children are improperly and insufficiently fed and
inadequately housed'.[47] Dr Eichholz pointed to
three aspects of the food problem as he saw it; the
lack of it, the irregularity of meals and the
unsuitability of much of the food. Such reports
provided independent information to support
arguments put forward by labour representatives
based upon their actual experience of hungry
children in the areas in which they lived and
worked.

There were attempts led by Labour and Liberal
MPs with the support of a few Conservatives to
provide legislation for school meals in 1905 but to
no avail.[48] No mention of the matter was made by
the Liberals in the 1906 election but at the
beginning of the new session:

> . . . a lucky draw on the private members'
> ballot enabled William T. Wilson, Chairman of
> the Amalgamated Society of Carpenters and
> Joiners, and a newly elected Labour MP from
> Lancaster, to introduce within days of his
> arrival in London, a Bill for the feeding of
> school children by the local education
> authorities.[49]

It was given a second reading within a week but the
enthusiasm of the Liberal administration for the
measure can be indicated by the fact that it was
then, '. . . pushed by the Government into a Select
Committee backwater . . .'.[50] It finally emerged
for a third reading nine months later but it was
subjected to considerable opposition, largely from
Conservative MPs, which led Major Seely, Liberal MP
for Liverpool, to observe, 'The Committee had seen
a good deal this evening of the opposition of the

over-fed Member to the underfed child'.[51]

Opposition to the measure was usually voiced on the principle of parental responsibility although a year earlier Keir Hardie had pointed to an element of hypocrisy here. 'The provision of school meals for which the parents would pay when able would no more interfere with parental responsibility and family ties than did the provision for hon. Members' families at boarding schools'.[52] Frequently financial interests were closely related to arguments over principle and Sir Fred Banbury, Conservative MP for the City of London, appealed to both tradition and vested interest.

> The Bill would change the practice which had existed in this country for hundreds of years . . . the burden would be put upon the State or the rates . . . he was against the provision of any meal at all . . . no doubt there was a certain amount of misery, although he himself did not think there was so much distress as was represented . . . .[53]

When the bill finally emerged it had been considerably weakened. It no longer required but only permitted local education authorities to provide meals at their discretion. Voluntary efforts were to be encouraged, fees could be charged and as a last resort financial help given provided it did not exceed one shilling and twopence in the pound. Like so much permissive legislation it meant that provision depended upon the area in which a child lived. All sections of the labour movement gave enthusiastic support to the limited legislation and it was no coincidence that Bradford, an ILP stronghold which had benefited earlier from the pioneering work of Margaret Macmillan, soon led the way with a well organised system of school meals. Yet when Pike Pease, the member for Darlington, asked McKenna the following summer how many authorities were providing school meals he was informed that only areas which used money from the rates were obliged to inform the Board of Education and of these there were eleven.[54]

The provision of school meals was haphazard. Within a few years Dr Ralph Crowley's experiments at Bradford revealed a deficiency which had not been considered earlier; namely that in areas with school meal programmes the benefit gained by poor children during the term was lost during the school holidays when there were no meals provided. It was shown that after a four week period in which poor children had gained on average 1lb 14oz in weight, in the following week of school holiday they lost 1lb and it took them a further fortnight when back at school to recover that weight. Quoting from the details of the experiment in 1912, F.W. Jowett, Labour MP for Bradford, supported among others by Ramsay MacDonald, Chiozza Money and James Yoxall, sought to introduce an amendment of the 1906 Act to remedy this problem.[55] At the end of March Prime Minister Asquith expressed sympathy for the bill but gave little hope of parliamentary time being made available, a response which was echoed in July by McKenna and again by the Prime Minister on 11 November 1912.

Frustrated by expressions of sympathy but no active government support Jowett protested a week later at:

> . . . the Adjournment of the House at so early an hour, in view of the fact that there are Order Paper items of very great importance . . . there is an opportunity not only to show sympathy but to give substance . . . there is an amount of poverty in this country that without exaggeration, there are probably at least 120,000 children living in families where the income is so small as not to afford the members of those families as much as 3s per head per week for sustenance, clothing and all the necessary expenses of living including rent . . . . The Christmas holidays are coming on, when those children who are fed when the schools are in session will not be provided for in any way whatever, except where the local authorities risk being surcharged.[56]

J.A. Pease, President of the Board of Education, could only repeat the sympathy of the government and suggested that if only the bulk of Conservatives would drop their opposition the amendment could get through. Sir Fred Banbury told Jowett that he should, '. . . be content with the mischief he and his party have already done . . . on the opposite side of the House in the last two years . . . before they returned to the obscurity from which I am sorry they ever emerged'.[57] It was pointed out to Banbury that although he had backed a bill for the protection of dogs he opposed a bill to feed hungry children.[58] Jowett's bill was lost but just before the outbreak of the war the Education (Provision of Meals) Act of 1914 was passed which gave power to the Board of Education to compel local authorities to feed necessitous children and also authorised feeding children during the holidays. It had taken the Labour Party fourteen years to wring the concession from Parliament.

The complementary measure to school meals was medical inspection and treatment of children. This did not raise the same opposition as school meals although in the long term it was to be a more complex and expensive part of child welfare. One major reason for this greater acceptance was concern expressed at the poor health of potential recruits at the time of the Boer War.[59] Encouraged by the recommendations of the Interdepartmental Committee on Physical Deterioration, by 1905 some eighty-five local authorities appointed school medical officers. Medical welfare was one part of the general education policy discussed at Labour's conference in 1907. 'Scientific physical education with medical inspection and records of the physical development of all children attending State schools; and skilled medical attendance for any child requiring it'.[60] This clause was so developed further over the years to include demands for school clinics, open air schools, and sanatoria that by 1910 the welfare aspects of education policy formed a detailed separate resolution. As with school meals, major stress was placed on the need to remove welfare from reliance upon charities and to have the government and local authorities take over financial responsibility for providing an efficient service. Medical inspection in schools was included in the Education (Miscellaneous Provisions) Act of 1907. Initially children could be examined but not treated. This illogical situation arose from a combination of factors; the belief that it might take away parental responsibility even though it was admitted that children of negligent parents would suffer, the suggestion that some doctors might object to the loss of potential fees and the knowledge that it would increase the cost of the school medical service. Treatment remained permissive until it was enforced in 1918.

What had the Labour Party achieved in the sphere of education with its comparatively small number of MPs in Parliament between 1906 and 1914? In terms of fundamental changes within the education system the answer has to be virtually nothing. If the Liberal government of 1906 with an overall majority of 130 failed to get its own education bill through Parliament it was clear that the TUC Education Bill of 1906 introduced by Will Thorne had no chance of success. Attempts to reverse the 1902 Education Act might make progress in the elected House of Commons but the vested interests of the Anglicans and the Conservatives combined in the hereditary House of Lords ensured that each bill would be transformed into a pro-Anglican measure.[61] The only way forward would have been for the Liberal government to tackle first the House of Lords by reform, abolition or the creation of enough Liberal peers to break the Conservative monopoly. Birrell complained about the treatment of his 1906 bill by the peers. 'What is the good of winning great electoral victories when you find on going a few yards down the lobbies of the House all the foes you routed in the open field, installed, established and apparently unmovable, mutilating all your work and substituting something quite different'.[62] The Liberals failed to distinguish then between being in office and being in power. Labour was to inherit this problem and show just as much reluctance in tackling it.

The welfare bills for school meals and medical help did not arouse the same measure of opposition. Neither threatened Anglican interests and both were reduced in their effectiveness by amendments. The School Meals Act was the one real triumph in education of the Parliamentary Labour Party and whilst the Liberals were able to claim credit for it the government's lack of active support does not warrant the claim. Reform in education was finally spurred on by the first world war when it became so apparent that the manner in which wealth purchased social services in Edwardian Britain could no longer remain the major criteria when all citizens were being called upon to make such terrible sacrifices. The 1918 Education Act was to be the Liberal answer to the problem but the limitations of this measure, especially when it had been amended, only goes to show how their ideas had been overtaken by events. It was not as radical as the Labour Party's Memorandum on Education published in 1914 which had in any case been superseded by the Bradford Charter of 1916 which took Labour thinking on education a stage further. This Charter was adopted by the Labour Party as education policy in 1917.[63] It revealed that whilst the Liberal Party still held to the values of the Edwardian era, Labour had come to adopt socialist ideas for the future in education.

NOTES

1. Labour Party, Annual Report, 1906, p.58.
2. Trades Union Congress, Annual Report, 1904, pp.68-69; ibid., 1905, pp.142-143; ibid., 1902, pp.70-72.
3. P.S. Bagwell, The Railwaymen (Allen & Unwin, London, 1963), ch. VIII.
4. For a discussion of this episode see Kenneth D. Brown, 'Trade Unions and the Law', in C.J. Wrigley (ed.), A History of British Industrial Relations, 1870-1914 (Harvester, London, 1982), pp.126-130.
5. By the 1880s some intelligent working class children with parental support had worked their way through the grades laid down by Robert Lowe's Revised Code. Provision began to be made, especially in northern and midland industrial towns, for such pupils to be taught beyond Standard Vll in Higher Grade classes. In some towns they were transferred to a central Higher Grade School. e.g. Sheffield, Bradford, Birmingham. The Higher Grade Schools were supported by the Board of Education, encouraged by parents and gained grants for successful teaching of certain subjects from the Science and Arts Department of South Kensington. They became secondary schools in all but name with the added advantage of teaching a curriculum which seemed more relevant than that of the fee-paying secondary schools. The latter were antagonised by their success and together with the Church Party which believed only elementary education should be provided for working class children throught the rates, joined forces with the Conservative Party to bring about their demise.
6. C. Griggs, The Trades Union Congress and the Struggle for Education 1868-1925 (Falmer Press, Lewes, 1983), ch. 6.
7. Labour Party, Annual Report, 1906, p.58.
8. TUC, Annual Report, 1905, p.142.
9. Labour Party, Annual Report, 1910, p.86.
10 The Labour Party was the most recently organised section of the labour movement which is

assumed in this study to include the Cooperative Movement, the TUC, trade unions, SDF, ILP, and Fabian Society. People were often members of several of these sections, working through trade union branches, the smaller socialist parties and at the TUC or Labour Party conference. Until the 1902 Education Act there was unanimity on most aspects of education policy but the Fabians supported the Conervatives on this issue, even boasting that they had engineered certain aspects of it behind the scenes. The NUT, which refused to affiliate to the TUC, also supported the Act because it believed that rate aid for religious schools would improve the wages of members in such schools. The Labour Party's ideas need to be put into perspective within the general struggle of the labour movement for better educational opportunities for all children.

11. Labour Party, Annual Report, 1907, p.62; see also C. Griggs, 'The Trades Union Congress and the Question of Educational Endowments, 1968-1925', History of Education Society Bulletin, vol.28 (1981), pp.45-53.

12. Labour Party, Annual Report, 1906, p.58.

13. Ibid., 1912, p 104.

14. Ibid., 1906, p.58

15. Ibid. 1909, p 76.

16. Fees in all Elementary schools were not abolished until the 1918 Education Act.

17. The labour movement was completely opposed to military drill in schools and youth organisations. C. Griggs, 'The Attitude of the Labour Movement towards Drill in Elementary Schools 1870-1925', Bulletin of Physical Education, vol. XVII (1981), pp.21-25.

18. In order to destroy the Higher Grade Schools in 1899 John Gorst, Vice President of the Committee of Council on Education in the Conservative government, secretly arranged for Cockerton, auditor of the London School Board, to challenge their expenditure on education other than elementary. The LSB lost the case in the High Court. Gorst even denied to the House of Commons that he had anything to do with the case. It was another example of Conservatives using the law to undermine working class progress just as had been done in the Osborne Judgement. For full details see E.J.R. Eaglesham, From School Board to Local Authority (Routledge and Kegan Paul, London, 1956).

19. Labour Party, Annual Report, 1906, p.58.

20. Ibid., 1907, p.62.

21. At the Labour conference of 1912 a resolution called upon the party in parliament, '. . . to appoint a small Committee to consider the general question of educational reform and draw up a report thereon'. The result was the <u>Memorandum on Education</u> which was put before conference in 1914. It can be seen as the first attempt of the party to think out an independent education policy although the final product still included most of the stated aims of past TUC and Labour Party policy because of the general consensus of such views within the labour movement. Its main purpose was to provide a programme by which the Labour Party could work towards these aims. Ibid., 1914, pp.40-42. This should not be seen simply as a move back towards the proposals of 1906 but rather a more ambiguous statement brought about by both the terms of reference given to the Committee and the manner in which it tried to react to the complex contemporary education system. In the case of the former, secondary education was not mentioned as such. Instead the Committee was asked to '. . . consider the general question of educational reform' especially the curriculum of primary schools in terms of future citizenship, the raising of the school leaving age to 16 years accompanied by maintenance grants, the limiting of the hours of boy and girl labour up to 18 years to 30 hours per week with provision for 20 hours per week for physical, technological and general training and the establishment of medical treatment centres based upon groups of schools. In responding to these issues the Committee put forward a programme of action to allow elementary, secondary and university education to advance on a broad front for all youngsters. A specific aim for secondary education was not mentioned; instead proposals were made to break down gradually the barriers preventing many children from entering secondary education, the Committee recommending the 'extension of the system of providing free places in secondary schools until they are entirely free and maintenance grants made available in cases of necessity'. To this extent the Committee's proposals need to be seen as a programme for action then rather than a declaration of aims to be worked towards in the future. Ibid., pp.40-41.

22. Ibid., 1906, p.58. The wording of the clause in 1907 was slightly different, '. . . an extension of the scholarship system as will place a

maintenance scholarship within the reach of every child, and thus make it possible for all children to be full-time pupils up to the age of 16'. Ibid., 1907, p.62.

23. Ibid., 1909, p.74.

24. Ibid., p.75.

25. In 1906 Hardie objected to Clause 10 in the Education Resolution which bound parliamentary candidates 'to accept and promote' Labour Party education policy. 'It established a dangerous precedent. He was sure they could trust Members without binding them down to a number of principles . . .'. The question of MPs fully supporting party policy or using their own judgement independently was to be a long-running source of argument within the Labour Party.

26. Labour Party, Annual Report, 1909, p.76.

27. The school leaving age was raised to 14 in 1918, 15 in 1947 and to 16 in 1972.

28. Labour Party, Annual Report, 1911, p.90.

29. R.S. Barker, 'The Educational Policies of the Labour Party 1900-1961', unpublished PhD thesis, University of London, 1968, pp.62-63.

30. Education Bills had been blocked by Anglican opposition in 1853 and 1855.

31. The NEL drew most of its support from Nonconformists but Robert Applegarth (Carpenters) and George Odger (Shoemakers) were both speakers on their platforms. In general the TUC was sympathetic to NEL aims.

32. M. Cruickshank, Church and State in English Education (Macmillan, London, 1963), p.16. This book provides a detailed survey of the arguments and actions of the parties involved in the religious dispute in education in England.

33. G.A.N. Lowndes, The Silent Social Revolution (Oxford, University Press, 1969), p.5.

34. Eastbourne was one of the few towns in England which never developed a school board system. The Church Party was very strong and a Voluntary Schools Building and Maintenance Company was established to keep out the school board. G.F. Chambers, Conservative Party Agent in the town, worked closely on this Committee with the Anglican Clergy and whenever school accommodation was considered inadequate another appeal would be launched. In 1899 the Committee reported, 'The subscription . . . should at least be £100 per annum. This could readily be effected did the Residents more generally realize the benefits accruing to the Schools from the Fund, and the

saving secured to themselves as Ratepayers by staving off the cost of a Board School.' Eastbourne Voluntary Schools Maintenance Fund, Report of the Committee for the year ending 30 June 1899.

35. Labour Party, Annual Report, 1906, p.59.

36. Ibid., p.60.

37. Ibid.

38. Ibid., p.61.

39. Ibid., 1911, p.90. Arguments over the secular issue, though of a shorter length to that of 1906 can be found in ibid., 1907, p.62.; 1909, pp.77-79.; & 1910, p.85.

40. Griggs, The Trades Union Congress and the Struggle for Education, pp.92-93.

41. British Library of Political and Economic Science. The Infancy of the Labour Party. Typescript minutes of the Labour Party Executive Committee, Labour Party Minutes, 18 Dec. 1907. Ibid., 22 Jan. 1909.

42. Ibid. Roman Catholic Federation Circular, 22 Jan. 1909.

43. B. Gilbert, The Evolution of National Insurance in Great Britain (Michael Joseph, London, 1966), p.104.; S. Meacham, A Life Apart: The English Working Class 1890-1914 (Thames & Hudson, London, 1977), pp.208-209.

44. P. Thompson, Socialists, Liberals and Labour: The Struggle for London, 1885-1914 (Routledge and Kegan Paul, London, 1967), p.117.

45. Gilbert, Evolution of National Insurance, p.106.

46. Labour Party, Annual Report, 1906, p.59.

47. [Cd.2175] Report of the Interdepartmental Committee on Physical Deterioration (1904), vol.1, p.15 para. 76.

48. Hansard, 4th Series, vol.CXXXXV, cols. 826 & 827. 3 May 1905.

49. Gilbert, Evolution of National Insurance, p.110.

50. E. Shinwell, The Labour Story (MacDonald, London, 1963), p.62.

51. Hansard, 4th Series, vol. CLXVI, col. 1464. 7 Dec. 1906.

52. Ibid., vol. CXXXXV, col. 556. 8 Apr. 1905.

53. Ibid., vol. CLXVI, cols. 1329-1330. 7 Dec. 1906.

54. They were Aston Manor, Barry, Birmingham, Crewe, Huddersfield, Manchester, Nottingham, Bath, Bradford, Norwich and Cannock. Ibid., vol. CLXXVI, col. 902. 24 June 1907; ibid., vol. CLXXIX, col.

143.   25 July 1907.

55. Ibid., 5th Series, vol. XXXV, col. 1113. 13 Mar. 1912.

56. Ibid. vol. XXXXIV, cols. 1113.  18 Nov. 1912.

57. Ibid. cols. 89-90.

58. Ibid.

59. H.C. Barnard, A History of English Education from 1760 (University of London Press, London, 1966), p.224: Lowndes, Silent Social Revolution, p.174.

60. Labour Party, Annual Report, 1907, p.62.

61. B. Simon, Education and the Labour Movement 1870-1920 (Lawrence and Wishart, London, 1965), p.251.

62. Speech by Rt. Hon. Augustine Birrell at Bristol, 13 Nov. 1906. Quoted in Cruickshank, Church and the State, p.99.

63. Details of the Bradford Charter can be found in Simon, Education and the Labour Movement, pp.346-349.

Chapter Eight

THE LABOUR PARTY AND STATE 'WELFARE'


The attitudes of the Labour Party towards the various early forms of state welfare and its underlying motivations, have been a matter of some contention among historians.[1] This is hardly surprising since these issues, like much else, were highly contentious within the party itself. The party was neither ideologically nor sociologically unitary before 1914, if it ever has been, and certainly no single view of the role of state welfare emerged in its first years. Rather the party was a forum for debate among groups and individuals of different and sometimes incompatible beliefs, which were themselves changing, in res- ponse, above all, to a changed political context - one in which Labour for the first time in history had a significant political voice and plausible political prospects and in which Liberal governments were reshaping the role of the state in unprecedented ways.

This essay will attempt to survey this debate as it concerned welfare, chiefly through analysing the statements of principal spokesmen for the party. The debate necessarily ranged far beyond such technicalities as the desirability, or not, of school meals, pensions, national insurance et. al. Issues of this kind could not be dissociated from such central questions as the views of the Labour Party concerning the relationship of the state to the individual and to the economy, and of the Labour Party itself to the objects of 'welfare' provision - the working class. Such matters had been discussed as abstractions in the labour movement for some decades before 1906, though with increasing concreteness as the 'interventionist' role of the state increased in, for example, such matters as housing, education and industrial relations from the 1870s; also as the participation of Labour representatives in local government and hence in social administration and policy making grew, especially from the early 1890s. They became of immediate importance when the Liberals after 1906 proposed and implemented quite new kinds of measure.[2] In response, the various groups within the Labour Party had to define their positions more clearly. What were these positions? And what was their relationship to radical liberalism which both contemporaries and historians have claimed to be indistinguishable from the views of Labour?

Somewhat paradoxically, L.R.C. candidates at the time of the general election of 1906 were more committed to, and more united on, recommendations for social reform than were the Liberals. This would not have been difficult, because the Liberals were also acutely splintered over a range of views, from progressive 'new liberalism' to the unreconstructed individualism of Harold Cox (MP for Preston). The Liberal leadership gave more prominence in the election campaign to retrenchment than to reform and was notably vague on specific reform proposals.[3] Also the L.R.C. was determined to achieve success in the election, and possessed a strong sense of the need to present the electorate with a corporate identity, distinct from that of radical liberalism. It was aware that, whatever its internal difference, it possessed an essential unity of interests distinct from those of the Liberal Party. Also it had some experience of the processes by which this separate identity could be established, drawn from a decade of Labour organization for local elections, and with fewer candidates to marshal it could exert somewhat greater control over its representatives than could its larger rival. Unlike the Liberals or Conservatives, but like the S.D.F. (with 9 candidates) and the 86 Irish Nationalists, it issued a collective programme, though candidates issued separate election addresses. The L.R.C. programme attacked the 1905 Unemployed Workmen Act, the maldistribution of wealth and income, regressive taxation, slums, and the failure to implement old age pensions. Eighty eight per cent of L.R.C. candidates proposed the reversal of the Taff Vale judgement (relevant to 'welfare', as will be seen, in view of the associated threat to trade union funds from which friendly benefits were drawn, and of the centrally important connection between wages and welfare); 84 per cent supported measures to combat unemployment, 81 per cent old age pensions, 79 per cent educational reform, 60 per cent housing reforms, 16 per cent 'retrenchment'. These categories disguise wide differences of approach, but there is some, very broad, value in comparing them with the equally question-begging profile of the addresses of the 529 Liberal candidates in England, Scotland and Wales. Eighty six per cent of these, not surprisingly, were pledged to amend the Education Act, 69 per cent to pensions and poor law reform, 59 per cent to trade union law reform, 41 per cent to housing legislation, 41 per cent to unemployment legislation, 54 per cent to 'retrenchment'.[4]

The relatively low level of Liberal commitment to new approaches to social reform helps to explain - together with the shadow of the Tory Lords and the considerable problem of shortage of government revenue in a low direct taxation, free trade, economy - the inaction of the Liberal government on 'welfare' matters at the outset. The social issue on which it was most committed, amendment of the 1902 Education Act in the non-conformist interest, was stifled by the Lords. Liberals, however, had two debts to pay to Labour in return for the mutually advantageous electoral pact: reversal of Taff Vale and reform of the Workmens' Compensation Act. Both had priority in the programme of the Labour leadership because they were urgent demands of the leading trade unions and they had, in turn, to pay their dues to the institutions whose affiliation and cash had made Labour's political success possible.

For most trade unionists the capacity to strike or to threaten to do so was a more important guarantor of 'welfare' for themselves and their families than social measures from the state. There can be no serious doubt that most trade unionists would have preferred adequate wages and full employment, advanced through voluntary organization, with the resulting sense of independence and equality with other classes, as the means to acquire and dispose of his (rarely her) income for the security of himself and his family, to dependence upon publicly funded benefits. These were seen as undesirable for the sense of dependence which they created; and, often, also, as employer-inspired alternatives to high wages, full employment and further development of an independent assertive working class movement. To what extent, and for whom, Labour activists thought this ideal realizable is, as we shall see, a different matter, but the right to free collective bargaining was - entirely understandably - seen as the basis for true working class welfare, as their representatives perceived it.[5]

This view was shared by prominent members of the Labour Party. J.R. MacDonald asserted at the second reading of the National Insurance Bill: 'If the employer pays proper wages, or, in other words, if the workers' share of the national income is adequate, then we do not want charity and we do not want assistance at all . . . the prime consideration of everybody who is concerned in raising the status of the working classes is the amount of wages the working class get. You cannot get out of that. We do not want charity and we do not want doles and we do not want grants-in-aid and we do not want relief . . .'.[6] As is well known, the Trade Disputes Act 1906 guaranteed considerable trade union rights. As it was debated in the Commons, Labour members successfully resisted repeated proposals, backed by employer organizations, for the divorce of union strike and benefit funds. To this, unions were passionately opposed. A high proportion of their funds came from contributions for 'friendly benefits' and the existence of such benefits was a major motive for members to remain in a union in periods of industrial peace, especially in unions of skilled workers which offered extensive benefits.[7] Equally important, unions refused to make the distinction between provision of benefits and industrial bargaining strategies which their opponents sought. Benefits included not only sickness and - more rarely - superannuation pay, but, for example, unemployment benefit for men refusing to work at below the trade union rate, or made jobless as a result of a dispute in an adjacent trade - a desirable reciprocal action between unions. Not only were wages believed to be preferable to welfare from any source, even the union, but union welfare was perceived as an indispensable part of the strategy for attaining higher wages.[8] The separation of strike fund from 'friendly' fund was incompatible with this tradition. In 1906 trade unionists successfully repelled the assault, but it was, as we shall see, to recur in the context of discussion of state welfare. The reform of the Workmens' Compensation Act of 1897 was of less urgent significance to the unions and to the Labour Party, but it had been a constant course of union discontent as anomalies and gaps in the legislation became plain. The 1897 Act gave a right to compensation in industrial accidents, but only where the worker could prove that the accident was not due to his own negligence (an inexhaustible source of litigation costly to the union,, in both funds and time, since they alone could or would finance such cases on behalf of workers). The measure applied only to a restricted range of industries and to a restricted list of recognized hazards, which excluded the mass of industrial diseases. It also, of course, effectively excluded workers unable to obtain trade union support (i.e. most of them when there were only a little over two million trade union members in 1911.[9])

The 1906 Workmens' Compensation Act increased the number of workers theoretically covered by six million, broadened the range of recognized hazards and eased the mechanism for further extending those listed. Labour amendments expanded a still more limited initial bill, achieving payment of compensation from the day on which the accident occurred in cases of serious accident or death, fighting off a proposed seven-day gap designed to deter the 'malingerer', though failing to prevent this in respect of less serious cases; similarly they defeated an attempt to disqualify from compensation men seriously injured due to what was claimed to be own misconduct, on the grounds that misconduct was notoriously difficult to define and that serious injury restricted a workers' earning power, whatever the cause. Keir Hardie persuaded Parliament to allow illegitimate children to qualify as dependants for receipt of compensation in cases of death at work.[10] Generally, Labour was satisfied with the Act, which by reason of its wider and more clearly defined coverage, substantially reduced the number of cases requiring litigation, though the party critized the exclusion of many casuals and outworkers, as well as of certain causes of accident and sickness, issues which continued to be raised at trade union and Labour Party conferences thereafter. Workmen's Compensation was, again, an issue which the labour movement had long accepted lay within the desirable confines of government action, since the state alone was capable of forcing necessary concession from employers, and long-term compensation for the injured would have laid a heavy burden upon union funds. These and other debates, however, also revealed a great deal about how Labour members regarded their constituency and about their attitudes to the House of Commons itself.

Historians have, on the whole, understated the drama of the entry into the House of this first band of working class representatives, for the first time a group large, and confident, enough to make an independent impact. More conscious at least at first of what united than of what divided them and of how they differed from the mass of landowners, professional and businessmen around them, the Labour MPs themselves did not underestimate the element of theatre in the events in which they were involved. Their speeches read, throughout the 'welfare' debates of 1906-14, and no doubt in other debates too, as painstaking, conscious, attempts to describe the reality of the experience of the "working classes" (the terms almost invariably used except within the phrase "working class movement") to their fellow Members, often across a gulf of evident incomprehension.

Unlike many Labour MPs of later generations they had all been born in or close to the working class and most had considerable experience of work, trade unionism and working class life. When the opportunity could be created they described to the House conditions of work, of home, of the elementary schools which their children had attended as those of Liberals and Tory Members did not; for example, the 'nasty class feeling' experienced by the daughter of Lib-Lab Member Fred Maddison when she attended a fee-paying secondary school.[11] They spoke, out of direct experience, for, partially to, and in defence of, the mass of respectable workers of all grades, speaking without the different, more distant and patronizing tones audible in the words even of progressive Liberal or Tory MPs. They were defending a sense of the absolute equality of working people with all others, which had long historical roots, in language which also, on occasion, had a much older resonance. J.R. MacDonald wrote in the Labour Leader in 1907:

> Our task is to devise a system of reforms which will advance our general scheme of reconstruction, which will free us of parasites and which will smooth the way for economic liberty. It means that we must improve the machinery of democratic government so that the representing authorities shall be

> in such close touch with the people that they
> will be bound to do the peoples' will . . .
> the grand task of the socialist is to
> establish a co-operative commonwealth and in
> order to do that we must place in the hands of
> the community all the instruments used in the
> creation of wealth.[12]

They were sentiments which were entirely compatible
in Britain with non-revolutionary politics and
belief in gradual, constitutional reform.

Labour Members were, of course, consciously or
not, presenting an image of their party
simultaneously to the House, and to their voters,
and non-voters, outside it. The responses of these
audiences further influenced and refined Members'
perceptions, policies and strategies. This image
was, with extremely rare deviations, not that
familiar from certain text-books of a party
speaking only or primarily for a skilled trade
union elite, sharing a conventional contempt for
their inferiors, even in the case of such prominent
members of elite unions as George Barnes of the
A.S.E.[13] Rather it was close to the real world
of labour in the early nineteen hundreds, in which
the strict division between skilled and semi-
skilled or unskilled workers, and the equation of
each with trade union membership or lack of it or
with a predictable package of political attitudes
and social experiences, was less clear than it has
seemed to more recent commentators. In the
workmens' compensation debates for example, Barnes,
Stephen Walsh of the miners' federation and
J.R. Clynes spoke up for the need to provide for
the non-unionized, 'whose wages were miserably
small and to whom a week on the sick list would be
a serious thing'.[14] Far from sharing the almost
obsessive fear of members of other parties -
apparent in all of these debates - of the
"malingerer", at the bottom of society they
persistently and unanimously denied that working
people had any greater tendency to malinger than
members of other classes. Though, as Barnes put
it, 'workmen were only human beings and sometimes
they tried to get a day's holiday', they did so, it
was argued, remarkably rarely.[15] As Barnes
pointed out on another occasion, 'what right had
they to say that a man had refused to work or had
refrained from working? . . . there were many men
walking about not out of work and some of them
demoralized by want of work, and this (Old Age

Pensions) Bill proposed that now, having been got
down as a result of this demoralization through
want of work, they should turn around and kick them
because they were down'.[16] W. Brace, Labour
member for Glamorgan South, commented in the Right
to Work debate of 1907 that 'in his own division
there were out of employment hundreds of men with
high moral characters, highly skilled, with
respectable wives and families . . . the Bill would
help them through bad times, avoiding
demoralization'.[17] Or, more predictably,
Lansbury in the debate on unemployment insurance
said that 'A sort of uneasy feeling occasionally
goes through this place that there are people who
really will not work, and that in the main they
live among the casual labourers. I have lived most
of my life amongst these men and they are as
industrious a class as any in the whole community.
Many of them are men who have walked mile after
mile for the purpose of getting work';[18] and
later: 'I am bound to say from my knowledge of the
middle and upper classes that they are adept at the
game of malingering . . . when they are a little
run down the doctor orders a holiday . . . working
men go back to work earlier than they should';[19]
or A.H. Gill in the same debate: 'If a farmer gets
money dishonestly by adulterating milk, you do not
blame all farmers . . . working men are the only
people who are blamed because a minority of their
number do wrong'.[20]

To Labour MPs the 'residuum' (a word used only
once in these debates, by Ramsay MacDonald) was
small and largely attributable to conditions of
existence which should be eradicated rather than
pilloried or excluded from public support.[21] The
great mass of the working class, whatever their
occupation or level of skill, were described as
aspiring to respectability and hard work and
prevented from doing so only by circumstances
beyond their own control. Labour members presented
themselves as speaking sympathetically for the
whole of the working classes; often pleading,
indeed, more urgently for state support for the low
paid female and male casual worker outside any
union and outside their own constituency, since
women had no vote and poorer male workers were
least likely to be on any voting register than for
trade unionists and voters. In 1911, 20.5 per cent
of the adult male population of Whitechapel were
registered voters, compared with 75.3 per cent in
Birmingham.[22] Barnes, again, not generally

acknowledged as one of the more radical Labour
members, commented in the pensions debates: 'it was
one of the saddest features, perhaps, of our
present industrial and social system that the
heaviest of life's burdens fell upon the weakest
among them and in that category, of course, must be
placed the women folk. Their wages were smaller
and they therefore had less chance of making any
provision for their old age compared with men and
they were more entitled to more consideration and
help'.[23]

Such pleas were not at all inconsistent with
the defence of trade union independence; the
argument ran, rather, that unionists by reason of
their organization could achieve a degree of
economic and social independence; it was the others
who needed support from the state, in the absence
of anything else. Jowett pointed out in the
National Insurance debates: 'the trade unions do
not merely care for their own members, they care
also for and fight the battles of, other workers
who are not members of their unions'.[24] Later in
the same debate, Charles Duncan, an ex-shipyard
worker, MP for Barrow-in-Furness, told the House:
'I am a skilled worker and I would be prepared to
say, so far as the skilled worker is concerned,
keep him out of it and let him stand his corner;
but there are hundreds of thousands of (labourers)
who cannot afford to be in any union at all'.[25]
Trade unionists were also intensely conscious of
the apparent threat to their own position from the
low paid and desperate, the 'industrial reserve
army'; anything which made the lives of this
reserve more secure was equally to their own
advantage - not to mention the fact that the
reserve might include their wives and children or,
one day, with ill-luck, themselves.

Hence it is difficult to interpret the
language of Edwardian Labour politics as the clear
expression either of sectionalism or of class
unity. It expressed an intense awareness of the
extent to which the experiences of individuals and
members of different occupations within the working
classes differed. But the often passionate,
reiterated defence of the exploited and low paid
from Barnes or MacDonald and many more cannot be
described as a mere expression of the interests of
a working class elite. Labour spoke for a mass of
people whose interests it knew to be varied and
often conflicting.

These themes run through all of the

parliamentary debates, from the election of 1906 to
the outbreak of war. Labour's third success of
1906 was to get through both Houses (interestingly,
the House of Lords let through all legislation of
particular interest to Labour, coming near to
rejecting only the Old Age Pensions Bill 1908, with
which Asquith particularly associated himself) a
bill introduced by one of their members,
W.T. Wilson, and designed to enable local education
committees to provide free or subsidized school
meals. This was a revision of an inadequate scheme
introduced by the Tories in 1905 which provided
free meals for needy children only through the poor
law. Take-up had been low. According to John
Burns, in July 1906 only 151 children in England
and Wales had benefitted, 121 of them in Bradford
where the poor law was controlled by a Labour and
progressive Liberal alliance; the remainder was
spread over only five unions.[26] School meals had
long been an objective of socialist and women's
Labour groups. Some trade unionists were inclined
to regard them with suspicion, as substitutes for
payment of higher wages, but they argued with
little conviction. By 1906 the bill had almost
unanimous support among Labour and the other major
parties and passed easily through the Commons. The
chief opposition came from those fearful for the
fate of the family and for individual
responsibility, notably Harold Cox. Keir Hardie
passionately replied that he

> 'did not think that the honourable gentlemen
> who had spoken so often that afternoon knew
> what it meant to them to sit there and listen
> to their wives being described as slatterns
> and themselves as spendthrifts. Their
> feelings were those of the toad under the
> harrow . . . the insinuation that under this
> Bill there would be an indiscriminate feeding
> of children of drunken and thriftless parents
> was to caricature the Bill and totally to
> misrepresent the ideas of those who supported
> it. They had heard a great deal about home
> life. What proposals had honourable members
> to make who wanted to brighten home life?
> Would they support a Bill for a minimum wage?
> That would be socialism'.[27]

The very self-respect of very poor parents and care
not to pauperize themselves and their children, he
argued, had made them unwilling to apply for poor

relief under the previous measure.

Similar issues arose with the next major piece of social legislation of the Campbell-Bannerman government, the Children Act, 1908. This consolidating act, initiated by the Home Office, aimed to ensure child protection by establishing a separate judicial and penal system for young delinquents, plus a system of protection against child abuse and of punishment of adult offenders against children. Labour members contributed little to the debate on an uncontroversial bill. The normal practice was to avoid uncontroversial debates where Labour had no distinctive interest, in order to conserve the energies of their small number of heavily worked members. They intervened only, again, to defend the working class family. The Labour spokesman, Tom Summerbell, agreed with the need to punish 'neglectful' parents, but insisted that they were few and that it was essential not to confuse wilful neglect with behaviour unavoidably the result of deprivation, such as that of the widow forced by necessity to work whatever her domestic responsibilities: 'If they were to rescue the children for the future service of the state, the House must go a step further and recognize the necessity of putting within the reach of every parent the economic opportunity of looking after his or her children. In the larger towns men who would do better if they had the opportunity were compelled to live amid miserable surroundings and the children had nothing but the pawnshops and public house as their constant companions and the gutter as their playground. These men should have an economic opportunity of doing the best for their children which at present they had not'.[28]

Labour members played a larger part in the more extensive debates on the Old Age Pensions Bill of the same year. Non-contributory pensions of ten shillings a week for all at age sixty five had regularly been the objective of Labour pressure groups since the 1890s and had been supported by L.R.C. conferences and by the TUC since the 1890s. Since the general election Labour members had, through deputations and parliamentary questions, pressed the issue upon the Liberal leaders as had many Liberals. It was expected to be a popular measure.[29] Labour members were divided between those who thought it 'a good beginning' made in good faith by the government, and those who regarded it as 'cynical, vote-catching carrot-dangling'. Most accepted any such scheme as second best: as Barnes put it: 'if a man had work and regular and higher wages he would be able to make some provision which he was not now able to make for old age and would by his own personal effort remove a good many of those questions with which they had to deal'. He recognised however that many of the existing aged and ageing, most of whom were female, had had no opportunity to be effectively self-helping, due to lifetimes of irregular work and low pay. For these only the state could provide, and indeed should for those who worked for its benefit throughout their lives with so little reward.[30] Labour members, however, persistently criticized the many respects in which the measure fell short of the party's proposals. In the interests of cheapness and at the Treasury's insistence, pensions were to be payable only at age seventy, restricted to those with incomes of under ten shillings per week who did not receive poor relief after the Act came into operation and subject to a variety of character tests designed to disqualify the workshy, thriftless, drunken or criminal.[31] Labour amendments converted the means limit to a marginally more generous sliding scale, removed the proposed reduced pension for couples and added a time limit on the poor law disqualification, which was to be reviewed after two years (it was abolished in 1911). Again, while agreeing with the exclusion of criminals and drunkards (though John Hodge protested against the double punishment), a succession of Labour members defended poor people against the accusations of mass malingering which again ran through much of the debate.[32] They also attacked the 'inquisition' which the character clauses would entail - another persistent theme of the parliamentary debates and of extra-parliamentary Labour discussion. Hodge explained that

> trade unionists had unique knowledge of how much working men and their families resented prying officials . . . . Those who took an interest in slum work must realize how difficult it was to get at the truth as to the conditions under which people lived in the poor districts. They were always afraid that something which they did not deserve to become known might become known. As a matter of fact, the honest poor always desired to hide

their poverty and resented anything which savoured of inquisition. The reason for that was that families were often dragged down by sickness, accident or unemployment and did not care to lay bare to officials all the cares, struggles and sorrows of their condition. Their very poverty, it might be, made them extra sensitive and the consequence was they they desired that the inquisitional character of the measure should be got rid of.[33]

Nor, suggested Will Crooks, from his long experience of the poor law in Poplar, could such tests effectively be applied. 'What particular degree of drunkness was to disqualify for a pension? - half stewed, half drunk, steadily drunk, talkatively drunk, quarrelsome drunk, maudlin drunk, dead drunk?' Drunkness, he pointed out, was not unknown in the Houses of Parliament. 'But when it came to idleness', he added, 'that capped the lot . . . no-one would define idleness. It all depended upon the class one belonged to. The ordinary intelligent legislator "cultivated leisure", the poor unfortunate members below the gangway "wasted time" in discussing questions they had not properly devoted attention to'.[34] Other Labour members demanded higher and more redistributive taxation - a land tax and progressive income tax - to finance a more generous pension. They were divided, however, over an unsuccessful Liberal amendment to exclude friendly society and trade union benefits from the means test. David Shackleton argued that, although he was a member of both, 'There were hundreds of thousands of people in this country who had not the opportunity to join them'. In particular

There were thousands of women who never had the opportunity of joining a friendly society or trade union . . . . Two organizations or two methods of investment had become popular especially among women . . . they put their money into a co-operative society and when the small dividend accrued it was left to accumulate to make provision for their age . . another method of investment had been provided by some municipalities, who gave labouring men and women an opportunity of investing in the municipal funds by accepting small weekly sums.[35]

But such forms of thrift were not rewarded by the draft bill. After the passage of the Pensions Act Labour members kept up a flow of criticism of its administration. But a more central and persistent concern of Labour members and of the wider Labour movement was unemployment. The demand for the 'right to work' or full maintenance had been growing for a decade, with its explicit echoes of a conception of a citizen's right to basic security from the state, more familiar in the political language of a century earlier. Demonstrations of the unemployed had forced Balfour's reluctant government to implement the minimum feasible concession, the Unemployed Workmen Act 1905.[36] From the time of the election Labour put the Liberals under pressure to amend or replace it. However, Labour members, with the exception of Keir Hardie, were initially relatively silent on the subject in the House of Commons, since the Liberal leadership gave the impression of being prepared to act; but by 1907 there were no signs of significant action. Indeed, there was positive hostility from John Burns at the Local Government Board to what he called the 'right to shirk' movement. Labour deputations to ministers and public unemployment demonstrations revived and a bill was introduced embodying the right to work proposals.[37] Labour has been accused of having no clear unemployment policy other than a vague conception of the 'right to work'.[38] It is fair to say that few others had remedies to offer at a time when analyses of the causes of unemployment was contentious and undeveloped. Before the publication of William Beveridge's Unemployment. A problem of Industry in 1909 and the unemployment recommendations of the Minority Report of the Royal Commission on the Poor Laws, also in 1909, themselves much influenced by the ideas of Beveridge, plausible remedies for the massive problem were elusive.[39]

The joint Labour Party-TUC proposals were indeed as comprehensive as any others by 1907. Rejecting either tariff reform or free trade as remedies for a problem whose root cause they identified as 'lack of organization of our economic system', their fundamental remedy was for state regulation of the national economy, locally based remedies for the weaknesses of an increasingly integrated national economy, on the lines of the 1905 Act, appearing quite inadequate. Labour argued that modern industry demanded and deliberately retained a surplus labour force. Measures were needed which, by stabilizing the market, would diminish this requirement, whilst expanding demand to provide more permanent employment, together with support for those who remained unemployed. How such reorganization of the economy 'on the basis of production for use rather than for profit' was to be achieved, and the precise desirable relationship between private and public enterprise in the outcome remained vague, partly because these were contentious issues within the labour movement and more so outside it, and because, realistically, Labour leaders recognized that any degree of regulation 'was not going to be done in a day nor in a year'. Meanwhile, however, Labour argued that unemployment could be diminished and growth of the economy and hence of job opportunities encouraged, were national and local authorities to plan public works for periods of unemployment and to invest in new schemes of afforestation, land reclamation, road-building, the creation of co-operative small-holdings on unused land and the training of men to take advantage of such schemes. Such measures were not in themselves expected to absorb all of the unemployed, but to increase home consumption, to help to even out fluctuations in the domestic market and to stabilize and expand the home economy, for 'the purchasing power of the community has a great deal to do with the state of the labour market'. The jobs created, Labour insisted, should not be mere 'relief works', unplanned emergency alternatives to poor relief, but necessary work at standard rates of pay positively directed towards economy regeneration. It was also recognized that such employment would provide work chiefly for the unskilled, whereas there were known to be high rates of unemployment in skilled . trades. Unemployment among skilled men however, was believed generally to be only temporary due to seasonal and market fluctuations, hence the suggested solution to this problem was state maintenance. Shorter hours and an end to systematic overtime would help further to spread the available work; indeed some trade unionists, narrowly concerned with the problems of their own trades, considered this a sufficient solution to the problem of unemployment.[40] There was a certain tension between Labour politicians and trade unionists over the degree of priority to be given to trade union members and policies (as regards, for example, rates of pay) in unemployment policy proposals. David Shackleton admitted that the Right to Work Bill was really designed to help the great mass of non-unionized casual labourers, whose problems were the most acute: 'to bring about regulation by trade union methods alone is a costly, wearying and almost a wasteful process, and we do not want to adopt that policy. We prefer to put before the House Bills to deal with these things'. He hoped thus to deal more speedily with the problems of those for whom the prospects for effective unionization were slight.[41]

The proposals embodied in the Right to Work Bill were pilloried by Liberals for merely perpetuating relief works, and by the socialist left for capitulating to short-run palliatives and playing down the demand for nationalization; they were indeed very similar to the recommendations of the Minority Report and to some of the subsequent actions of the Liberals though, as we shall see, with some important differences.[42] The criticisms owed something to the vagueness with which Labour members presented and justified their case in Parliament, in contrast to the clarity of Labour publications on the subject. Because Labour was unsuccessful in the ballot the 1907 Right to Work Bill had to be introduced by a Liberal MP, P.W. Wilson, who played his part with less than total commitment. Much of the vagueness however, stemmed from Labour's awareness of the political dangers of spelling out in full a programme inimical to many Liberals and hence risking loss of support for the short-term measures which it embodied. Vivid descriptions by Labour members of the conditions of the unemployed could not, alone, get the 1907 Bill past a second reading. However, persistent pressure on and off the floor of the Commons, amid the exceptionally heavy unemployment of 1908-9, forced the government, first, in October 1908 to extend subsidies to local authorities under the 1905 Act and to consider, despite John Burns, some new approaches.[43] By this time Asquith had replaced Campbell-Bannerman as Prime Minister and, more important from the point of view of social reform, Lloyd George had become Chancellor and Winston Churchill President of the Board of Trade. Together they were to steal and adapt many of Labour's reforming clothes and hence to exacerbate Labour's splits on attitudes to welfare. By the time the Right to Work Bill was reintroduced in April 1909 it was overshadowed by Lloyd George's

first budget, introduced on the previous day.
Churchill's Labour Exchanges Bill was also well
advanced. Once more, the Labour measure did not
get beyond a second reading and it was defended
with notably less conviction than it was opposed by
the Lib-Lab MPs Fred Maddison and Henry Vivian,
whom the Liberals shrewdly chose as their
spokesmen. Above all they attacked the "socialist"
character of its nationalization proposals and its
vagueness in other respects.[44] MacDonald
conceded that 'we have only produced this Bill for
the purpose of discussion and for the purpose of
detailed consideration'. He congratulated the
government for adopting Labour's conception of
maintenance in the unemployment insurance proposals
known to be under discussion, the moves towards
progressive taxation contained in Asquith's budget
of the previous year and taken further in the
recent budget and the land taxes and promise of
funds for rural development made in the same
budget. He pleaded however for co-ordination of
unemployment and economic policy under a single
government department, as the Right to Work Bill
proposed.[45]

The budget and Labour Exchanges legislation
placed Labour in its customary dilemma of
supporting 'as a beginning' measures which it felt
did not go far enough and of whose motives its left
wing had acute and often justified suspicions,
above all that they were deliberate half measures
designed to undermine Labour. True or not, there
was little Labour could do, since outright
opposition risked the loss of votes in the
country. Opposition to labour exchanges, however,
went wider in the labour movement. In principle,
Labour had no objection to this method of matching
vacancies and jobs; indeed several unions ran
similar schemes for their own members. However,
trade unionists were suspicious that a state system
would serve to supply blackleg labour. Those
concerned about the problems of casual labour
pointed out that exchanges established by local
authorities had been flooded with labourers for
whom no work was or could be forthcoming.
Beveridge, the author of the proposal, had never
regarded labour exchanges as the solution to the
casual labour problem and he opposed their use as
sources of blackleg labour. However, Labour
suspicion of exchanges remained powerful, though
their MPs gave it critical support in Parliament;
the opposition was a little mollified by the

association in 1911 of labour exchanges with the distribution of unemployment insurance benefits.[46]

Similarly, the 1909 budget was criticized, above all by Philip Snowden, for the timidity of the land taxes and the failure to tax the wealthy more severely.[47] Yet Labour was realistic enough to recognize that it could not push the Chancellor further and in general it regarded the budget as a small step in the right direction. Labour's own taxation policy had been made quite clear in a statement from the executive committee in January 1909: opposition to tariff reform, support for a steeply graduated income tax, a super-tax, greatly increased estate duties, a monopoly tax and land tax. For, said the statement: 'Social reform should aim at securing for the common good the use and benefit of all socially created wealth. In the hands of a democratic government finance can be a very potent instrument to that end'. The existing regressive system, whereby the poor contributed as much to government revenue through indirect taxation as the better off in direct taxes, meant that workers themselves would pay a substantial part of the cost of welfare measures such as pensions. Philip Snowden argued to a Labour Party Conference on taxation, held in 1909:

> What was meant by social reform and what they who were socialists meant by socialism, was to secure for the wealth producers the use and the enjoyment of the wealth which they produced. Our purpose therefore should be to see that social reforms were carried out in such a way that the people would receive the use and enjoyment of some part of that wealth which at the present time was unjustly taken from them.

Though some on the left favoured other radical measures, including a one hundred per cent tax on unearned income, there was broad support in the party for Labour's tax proposals.[48] Similarly, they supported, with reservations, the Trade Boards Act (1909) which established minimum wage machinery for certain non-unionized and largely female sweated trades. This followed a long campaign by Labour and Fabian women. It was criticized by Labour in its brief passage through the Commons for the limited number of trades covered, but otherwise it was welcomed for its help to non-unionized workers. As T. Richards of the Boot and Shoe

Operatives Union (a union then much under pressure from mechanization and the growth of sweated 'slop work') put it: 'whilst we in the trade unions can protect ourselves, the Hebrew workers of our industry cannot . . . . They have no organization simply and solely because their wages are so small that they have not sufficient means to contribute to our association.'[49]

After the publication of the Report of the Royal Commission on the Poor Laws in 1909, Labour shifted from the attack on unemployment to the broader front of the "Break-up of the Poor Law", the campaign launched by the Webbs in support of the proposals of the Minority Report. Once more, however, they were undermined by the 'terrible twins of social reform', Lloyd George and Winston Churchill. The long debates in and out of Parliament on Parts One and Two of the National Insurance Bill, in which Labour members were very active, make exceptionally clear Labour's approach to welfare and the divisions within it. The official position was one of qualified support for both parts of the measure. A substantial section of the left however was suspicious of its motives from the beginning and became increasingly hostile as some of its implications became clearer. The political context had also shifted since the previous welfare debates. Liberal losses in the elections of 1910 left the 42 Labour members and 84 Irish Nationalists holding the balance of power. In the background also was the spread of trade unionism and a growing volume of strikes.

Barnes and MacDonald introduced Labour's official position. Barnes welcomed the initiation of the bill and its support for the established insurance practices of the Friendly Societies and trade unions. He saw the state scheme as desirable and complementary to rather than competitive with established practices of working class thrift, for, he said: 'voluntary effort among the very poorest is practically out of the question'. Again, he saw the state measure as desirably providing for those workers whose conditions of life denied them the possibility of participating in the mutual aid institutions of better off workers, without, it initially appeared, interfering with these institutions. The thirty shilling maternity benefit was especially welcome, for:

> women have to bear not only burdens incidental
> to sex but also the heaviest parts of life's

industrial burden as well. Their wages are lower and their hours of work longer and their conditions more onerous then mens', simply because they are more dependent: and although the Bill does not do all we should like it to do to relieve their industrial burden, yet, if carried into effect, it will provide at the most critical period of their lives a little of that skilled attendance and of the necessities of life which they cannot otherwise procure.

Provision for sufferers from T.B. and for access to a doctor for all of the insured was also welcome, provided, Labour members insisted, that the scheme paid well enough to attract the best doctors, so that the outcome was not a stigmatizing system of care, inferior to the normal standards of general practice.[50]

A succession of Labour speakers vigorously attacked the spectre of the malingerer which - predictably - was evoked by members of the other parties. However, the major Labour criticisms were, first, that although the need was greatest among the poorest men and women outside trade unions and friendly societies, they would be least favourably treated under the special arrangements proposed for casual workers to insure through the post office. Their contributions would be relatively higher than for regularly employed workers and they would have access to lower sickness payments and a more limited range of benefits. Indeed poorly paid workers, it was argued, could not afford to pay contributions at all. The bill allowed those earning below fifteen shillings a week to pay lower contributions, but Barnes argued that those earning so little should pay nothing at all, and the hardly less miserably paid just above them should pay lower than standard contributions, on a sliding scale.[51] Lansbury moved an unsuccessful amendment at the committee stage to exempt low earners from contributions and raised the issue again at the third reading.[52] Among other things he feared that the compulsory employer contribution for casual workers would bring about enforced decasualisation which, in the existing system, could only increase unemployment. This was because under Part One of the scheme casual workers and their employers were obliged to pay a full weekly contribution even if they did not work a full week, as dock labourers, for example, regularly did not. Indeed Beveridge and Llewellyn Smith at the Board of Trade, who were anxious to promote decasualization, hoped that the contributory scheme would have precisely this effect, and sought after 1911 to promote it.[53] Labour was not hostile in principle to decasualization but feared its effects in a labour market which appeared to offer few alternative employment opportunities. Edmund Harvey moved a similar amendment to Lansbury's but was also unsuccessful.[54] Secondly, Labour strongly objected to the clause that prevented any organization from becoming an approved society which 'used its funds other than for friendly benefits': i.e. which aimed to force the unions to separate their benefit and strike funds. This, the unions interpreted as a renewed attempt to achieve what the employers had unsuccessfully sought from the Trade Disputes Bill: the permanent limitation of union strike funds. Barnes insisted that: 'the first principle of trade union organization is the industrial betterment and economic advantage of their members and therefore we claim that, although we pay sick benefit and many other benefits, our first consideration is that we should be in a position if we think proper to spend at any particular time every halfpenny in our coffers'.[55] In addition his major criticism of Part Two of the Act, the unemployment insurance measure, was that contributors could be disqualified from benefit for refusal to take a job at below the 'current rate'. This was a major intrusion upon a principal aim of the trade unions, to establish and sustain higher rates of pay. He commented: 'We say that as workmen we are just as much entitled to a standard rate of wages as Cabinet ministers'.[56]

Part Two also initially prohibited from benefit workers unemployed due to disputes in which they were not directly involved. A succession of Labour members, led by Clynes, pointed out that this was a major cause of unemployment, especially among labourers whose work disappeared when unionized skilled men alongside whom they worked were in dispute.[57] The government conceded, under Labour pressure in and out of Parliament, that payment should be allowed in certain cases but insisted upon excluding all workers in any factory stopped by a dispute, whether or not they were directly involved. The state was prepared to do nothing to subsidize 'industrial warfare'.[58]

MacDonald repeated both these points, adding that Labour would carefully scrutinize the likely effect of the scheme on wages: 'The prime consideration of everyone who is concerned with raising the status of the working class is the amount of wages the working class get. You cannot get out of that . . . we are here to raise wages not to make it easy for low paid labour to subsist at all'. He emphasized that the measure was in no sense socialist, since it was hardly at all redistributive and did nothing to remove or to minimize the causes of social and economic inequality and might indeed reinforce them.[59] Barnes, MacDonald and the majority of Labour members supported the insurance principle as a desirable encouragement of working class self-respect, whilst insisting that, however desirable in principle, it could not yet, practically or humanely, be applied to the lowest paid.

Lansbury, however, asserted that he had been asked by 'the biggest unskilled union in the country . . . specifically to oppose a contributory scheme' because low paid workers could not afford contributions.[60] This was an opposition which he was to develop more fully as editor of the _Daily Herald_ from 1912 after he resigned his seat on the women's suffrage issue and failed to regain it in a by-election fought on the issue.[61] Jowett of Bradford and Stephen Walsh, supported him, as did Will Thorne, speaking for 'the casual workers on the docks, in gasworks and shipbuilding, whose work was intermittent and seasonal'.[62] Snowden 'opposed altogether' the insurance principle and claimed some trades council backing. He pointed out that the high rate of lapse from Friendly Society membership demonstrated how few could afford regular contributions. Nor should employers be made to contribute: 'We have got past the phase where an employer was expected to take a fatherly interest in his workers'.[63] The obligation, he believed, should lie on the community. Keir Hardie supported him. Snowden also objected strongly to the clause prohibiting women from becoming voluntary contributors, apparently on the assumption that a stronger female propensity to malinger would unduly burden the scheme. He argued that 'the husband in the case of the working classes at any rate does not support his wife. The wife supports herself and is contributing by her labour to the economic upkeep of the home', and

hence her speedy recovery from illness was as vital
to the economy as that of the male in paid work.
Crooks also protested at the exclusion of aliens
from the scheme.[64]

The battle between supporters of contributory
and non-contributory benefits was fought out in the
Commons, at conferences and in the Labour press
throughout 1911 and beyond, both MacDonald and
Snowden claiming their contradictory positions to
be 'consistent socialism', as, given the variety of
strategies available for the achievement of
'socialism', they were.[65] MacDonald by July 1911
was arguing for only minimal contributions for
all. His support for the contributory principle,
as distinct from other aspects of the bill, derived
partly from conviction, partly from the belief that
it was popular and hence that Labour had little to
gain electorally from opposing it. It also owed
something to his unwillingness, despite the urging
of the left, including Jowett and Hardie in the
parliamentary party, to use Labour's pivotal
position to bring down the government. This was
partly because the constitutional issue was still
unresolved; partly because Labour, burdened by the
Osborne Judgement could not afford another election
so soon; and partly because he felt that Labour had
little to gain from letting the Tories back in. He
had, after all, secretly agreed with the Liberal
leadership to let national insurance through, to
keep them in office, receiving in return a promise
of legislation for payment of MPs (implemented in
1912). Barnes was in constant negotiation with the
government over the bill throughout the summer of
1911. It should be added that MacDonald faced
simultaneous pressures to bring the government down
over national insurance, the right to work <u>and</u>
women's suffrage. He reasonably pointed out that
it could not be done on all of them, and that
Labour was unlikely to win on any, especially since
the Conservatives also showed little enthusiasm for
another election.[66]

The majority of Labour members broadly
accepted most other aspects of the National
Insurance Bill. Barnes claimed, significantly: 'We
are very glad the Bill has been introduced. We
think it marks a great step forward because it
brings many millions of workmen into direct contact
with the state and is therefore going to be of
immense educational value. We believe people have
been too much inclined to look upon the state
simply as a big policeman and this Bill will enable

a great many of them to realize that the state after all is what they like to make it '.[67]

This benign view of the state as a neutral institution, capable of acting in the interests of all, was one of the central issues upon which left and right in the party divided. Certainly Snowden, Hardie, Lansbury and a handful of others argued and believed that the National Insurance Bill not only gave minimal help to those in greatest need, but contained within it 'policing' measures potentially far more detrimental to working class institutions and traditions than Barnes recognized.[68] This line of argument Lansbury was to develop strongly in the Herald, into the 'servile state' notions which gained currency on the left in these years.[69] Almost certainly they suspected the Liberals of seeking more far-reaching control over Labour institutions and the working class than was the case. The Board of Trade's approach to industrial relations in this period implied government support of trade unionism, provided that it was moderate and controlled.[70] Aspects of welfare legislation do however suggest that social measures were used by the Liberals further to promote controls over unions to bring about the type of relationship in industry which they desired, in particular the attempts to separate union strike and benefit funds and the reluctance to allow unemployment benefit to those unemployed due to industrial disputes even when they were not directly involved.[71] Individual Labour members criticized the bill also on other grounds. Snowden spoke on the Financial Resolution associated with the National Insurance Bill 'from the point of view of a socialist' and quoting J.S Mill's definition of the causes of poverty: 'the subjection of labour to monopoly and the enormous share which the owners of the instruments of production are able to take from labour'. He insisted that: 'any reform must strike at the root of that monopoly. It must in its result transfer to the working people a larger share than they have at the present time in the wealth which is produced'. Speaking 'not in any sense as representing the views of my own party' but, convinced that some at least agreed with him, he believed that the bill 'will organize assistance for times of distress and will give a greater national security' but did not think the advantages such that he could accept them 'without a very vigorous protest'.[72]

Lansbury complained that Part One (health

insurance) did not move far enough towards a
desirable comprehensive health service, above all
because it gave no medical care, apart from
maternity benefit, to the wives and children of
insured men. With encouragement from the Womens'
Labour League and the Womens' Co-operative Guild,
he moved an unsuccessful amendment at the committee
stage to include them. He argued; 'It seems to me
that a wife is just as much a wage-earner as the
husband. She takes charge of his home. She works
just as hard as he and she is just as much a
wage-earner as he is. If the employer shifts the
3d onto the consumer or the workmen, if you take 2d
from the income tax and put it on the consumer or
workers, it is the wife in the home who will feel
the burden'.[73] Thorne and Jowett supported him,
the latter adding the warning that if 'this House
doesn't do something to improve the comparative
position of the working class . . . it will be done
by other action outside'. Unless, Jowett argued,
the current unrest was alleviated, 'we shall throw
them back on more violent action'.[74]

Most Labour members joined the fight to
improve the bill at the Committee stage. Hardie
tried unsuccessfully, with the help of MacDonald
and Lansbury, to include unmarried mothers in the
maternity benefit provision.[75] They were
supported by the navvy's leader, the Lib-Lab John
Ward, who argued that 'navvies are not so very
particular about the marriage lines . . . I could
prove that they are living lives as decent as any
who will come under the Bill'.[76] Hardie claimed
that: 'nine times out of ten the woman is a victim
and is penalized sufficiently for her indiscretion
in the fact of having a child'. Stephen Walsh
unsuccessfully sought a reduced contribution when a
full week was not worked, pointing out that in the
mines men rarely averaged more than four days work
per week over the year.[77] Snowden led an
unsuccessful battle, on which Labour members
appeared united, with much Liberal support, on the
clause requiring workers to pay contributions,
including the employers' contribution, in periods
of unemployment. Those in seasonal trades, casual
workers and those unemployed due to strike in
adjacent trades would, they argued, be in permanent
arrears of payment. The bill, member after member
insisted, assumed general stability of employment
and showed remarkably little understanding of the
actual instability of many occupations, including
even skilled trades in the shipyards and in

engineering. The clause was promoted, once more, as a necessary defence against malingering; in reality, as Hardie pointed out, it punished the unemployed twice over.[78]

Labour members also came to suspect that the bill contained an attempt to pull back some of the concessions made to Labour in the Workmen's Compensation Act. In particular the clause disallowing simultaneous drawing of workmen's compensation and national insurance sickness benefit was seen as an attempt to make workmen's compensation partially contributory. Labour's failure to defeat this clause, despite keeping the thinly attended House awake all night debating it, further suggested that Labour's potential power to bring down the government was considerably less than its left-wing critics believed.[79]

Labour similarly failed to prevent commercial insurance companies from being designated approved societies for the administration of sickness benefits, a clause which threatened to undermine some of the potential gains to working class non-profit making institutions, the trade unions and friendly societies. Through aggressive and expensive promotion the commercial companies were likely to absorb many of the beneficiaries of the scheme who had not previously been members of mutual aid institutions.

One Labour success was to obtain a government promise that the measure would be reviewed after two years. In particular MacDonald emphasized that it was quite unclear how casual workers would fare and their position would require review once the scheme was operative. The temptation for such workers and their employers to collude to avoid payment of contributions from meagre wages was likely to be strong; hence those in greatest need would not benefit from the legislation. It was also, MacDonald pointed out, unknown whether outworkers, mainly female, were covered.[80] It was clear by 1913 that his worries were justified; there was also some evidence that certain employers were reducing wages by the amount of their own compulsory contributions or were refusing employment to those who did not pay the employers' as well as their own stamp.[81] Labour similarly correctly identified many of the weaknesses of the unemployment legislation. It was confined to five major occupations, but the government appeared, among other errors, seriously to have underestimated the problems of defining membership of a specific occupation. For example, Clynes pointed out that shipbuilding was covered but he wanted to know if that coverage extended to the many workers engaged in processes essential to the complex business of building ships, but actually employed outside the shipyard? An engineer would be insured while he worked in a shipyard but what happened if he moved to a similar job in mining, which was not included?[82] These and other Labour assertions made it clear that the bill had been drafted in considerable ignorance of actual working conditions. The resulting anomalies led to extensive confusion, dispute and need for complex adjudication, especially under Part Two.[83] But in 1911 Labour was able to achieve no substantial amendment of unemployment insurance.

When the legislation came up for amendment in 1913 Labour members were able to point out the degree to which their warnings had been correct, but again without a significant success (despite considerable Liberal and Tory support) especially in respect of the failure of Part One in practice substantially to assist casual workers and women. However, a scheme was proposed by Beveridge that employers of casual labour who refused to give regular employment should be compelled to bear the workers' contributions as well as their own, the cost to be pooled among all who employed an individual worker in the course of a week. It was included in the National Health Insurance Amendment Act of 1913, but on a voluntary basis 'subject to consent from local employers'. Its effects, before war came, were few. Labour accepted the clause as the best and most flexible available solution within a contributory scheme, whose inability adequately to assist the casual labourer they now believed proven.[84]

The other major issue which arose in the 1913 debates was the complicated and misunderstood issue of a Liberal amendment for the payment of maternity benefit to the mother rather than, as under the original arrangements, to the insured man. The reason for the amendment was a widespread belief that some men were not giving the thirty shillings benefit to their wives. This was strongly supported by the Women's Co-operative Guild. Labour MPs have been much criticized for opposing it at various stages of its passage through the House. The truth is more complicated. Labour members were, as on other occasions, affronted by the implication that working men were less reliable

or loving husbands and fathers than other men. The
amendment was seen as another attack on the working
class family. G.H. Roberts, 'speaking entirely for
himself', believed that 'abusers do exist. I
think, however, their number is greatly
exaggerated' and he asserted that friendly
societies with long experience of administering
similar benefits had found them to be rare. He
pointed out that women were no more proof than men
against the mis-spending of benefit to which they
might be tempted by poverty. 'I do not think we
ought to legislate against sex'. The amendment
might simply cause conflict between man and wife if
men feel that they were not trusted to handle a
benefit for which they had contributed. Other
Labour members, less vehemently, agreed. Led by
MacDonald, they supported instead an unsuccessful
amendment, proposed by the Womens' Labour League,
to allow mothers to choose whether the benefit
should be paid to the husband, to herself or to
another nominated person. As the League pointed
out: 'we realize that when it is paid directly to
the mother, there will be just the same likelihood
of its going to pay rent or life insurance etc. as
there is now when it is technically paid to the
husband . . . . Family needs are often just as
important to the recovery of the mother as her own
individual needs.'[85] The Liberal amendment
succeeded in the Commons.

This has not been an attempt at a
comprehensive survey of the Labour Party's
pronouncements and policies on social issues in its
first years. This would have required analysis of
party publications, conferences, newspapers etc.,
and of the activities of local as well as of
central government, too extensive for a short
essay.[86] I have, however, tried to show
something of the range of Labour policies on major
social issues. In important respects their
approach was different from that of the Liberals -
above all in regarding welfare as second best to
secure, fairly paid employment, and, where welfare
was unavoidable, desiring that it be more
redistributive and more sensitive in its
administration to the variety of realities of
working class life. The party's approach, however,
was constrained by the fact that it was continually
forced to react to Liberal measures which, even if
it disliked them as being inadequate or actively
inimical to the interests of working people it
could not readily oppose since they brought some

benefits to some in need and Labour was not yet in a position to put anything in their place. For electoral reasons the party could not afford to oppose popular measures. In these years Labour was not yet a credible party of government capable of offering alternative proposals which it had any hope of soon implementing. Rather, its leaders were engaged in the construction of an appeal to a varied electorate and an alliance of groups and individuals within the working classes, some of whom had little in common and whose interests might conflict over welfare as over other issues; hence some of the shifts, divisions and compromises on social questions.

The resulting debates are revealing concerning attitudes in the party on a range of important questions: the relationship of the state to the individual and to the economy, to income and wealth distribution and ownership, to the variety of social political purposes which welfare measures could service, and the attitude of the party itself to the various groups within the working classes. I have tried to demonstrate that Labour attitudes towards welfare cannot usefully be separated from its approach to industrial relations, to the organization and management of the economy and to working people themselves. Despite considerable debate and disagreement within the party on all of these issues Labour cannot be seen, as by some, as merely offering 'passive support for government initiated reforms'.[87] The party held distinctive though divided views.[88] Nor was it just an expression of trade union interests, neglectful of those of the remainder of the working class. Nor were its leaders unaware of the potential of some aspects of the Liberal reforms to undermine, indeed directly to attack working class organizations and institutions. They were realistic about the limitations upon their capacity to resist such assaults.[89] Since 1945 Labour has been so closely identified with the very conception of the welfare state that it is too easy to assume that it has always been so identified. In its first years Labour supported a 'welfare state' as at most, a second best solution to deprivations; and the extent, nature and content of its commitment even to this remained undecided.

NOTES

1. H. Pelling, 'The Working Class and the

Welfare State', in his <u>Popular Politics and Society in Late Victorian Britain</u> (Macmillan, London, 1968). Pat Thane, 'The Working Class and State "Welfare" in Britain, 1880-1914', <u>Historical Journal</u>, vol. 27 (1984). J. Saville, 'The Welfare State: An Historical Approach', <u>New Reasoner</u>, vol. 1, no. 3 (1957). D. Thompson, 'Reply to John Saville', <u>New Reasoner</u>, vol. 1, no. 4 (1957).

2. For a survey of this background see Pat Thane, <u>The Foundations of the Welfare State</u> (Longman, London, 1982).

3. See, for example, J. Harris, <u>Unemployment and Politics. A Study in English Social Policy, 1886-1914</u> (Oxford, University Press, 1972), pp.186 ff.

4. All information on election programmes is taken from A.K. Russell, <u>Liberal Landslide. The General Election of 1906</u> (David and Charles, Newton Abbot, 1973).

5. For example, TUC, <u>Annual Report</u>, 1896, pp.29-31. Ibid., 1902, p.36. N. Whiteside, 'Wages and Welfare - Trade Union Benefits and Industrial Bargaining before the First World War'. Paper presented to the Social Science Research Council Conference, 'Roots of Welfare'. University of Lancaster, Dec. 1983. See also Thane, 'The Working Class and State "Welfare"'.

6. <u>Hansard</u>, 5th Series, vol. XXVI, cols. 726-28. 29 May 1911.

7. Whiteside, 'Wages and Welfare'.

8. Ibid.

9. W. Kendall, <u>The Labour Movement in Europe</u> (Allen Lane, London, 1975), p.344.

10. <u>Hansard</u>, 4th Series, vol. CLII, cols. 886-928. 26 Mar. 1906: vol. CLV, cols. 523-1203. 4 Apr. 1906: vol. CLXVI, cols. 335-1243. 29 Nov. 1906.

11. Ibid., vol. CLX, col. 1421. 16 July 1906.

12. <u>Labour Leader</u>, 1 May 1907.

13. For example, J. Hinton, <u>Labour and Socialism. A History of the British Labour Movement, 1867-1974</u> (Wheatsheaf, Brighton, 1983), pp.75-6.

14. <u>Hansard</u>, 4th Series, vol. CLIV, col. 905. 26 Mar. 1906: vol. CLV, cols. 550 ff. and 1203 ff. 4 Apr. 1906.

15. Ibid., vol. CLIV, col. 905. 26 Mar. 1906.

16. Ibid., vol. CXC, col. 810. 15 June 1908.

17. Ibid., vol. CLXXXV, col. 49. 13 Mar. 1908.

18. Ibid., 5th Series, vol. XXVII, col. 1420. 6 July 1911.

19. Ibid., vol. XXVIII, col. 1223. 19 July 1911.

20. Ibid., cols. 1161-62.

21. Ibid., vol. IV, col. 687. 30 Apr. 1909.

22. P. Thompson, Socialists, Liberals and Labour. The Struggle for London, 1885-1914 (Routledge and Kegan Paul, London, 1967), p. 131.

23. Hansard, 4th Series, vol. CXC, col. 807. 15 June 1908.

24. Ibid., 5th Series, vol. XXVIII, col. 1239. 19 June 1911.

25. Ibid., vol. XXXII, col. 879. 1 Dec. 1911.

26. Ibid., 4th Series, vol. CLXVI, col. 1284. 6 Dec. 1906.

27. Ibid., cols. 1385-86.

28. Ibid., vol. CLXXXVI, cols. 580-81. 26 Mar. 1908.

29. Pat Thane, 'Contributory versus Non-Contributory Old Age Pensions, 1878-1908', in P. Thane (ed.), The Origins of British Social Policy (Croom Helm, London, 1978).

30. Hansard, 4th Series, vol. CXC, col. 805. 15 June 1908.

31. Thane, 'Contributory versus Non-Contributory'.

32. J. O'Grady in Hansard, 4th Series, vol. CXC, col. 621. 15 June 1908: For Taylor see ibid., col. 655: for Burt, ibid., col. 782: for Hodge, ibid., col. 759.

33. Ibid., col. 758.

34. Ibid., col. 1557.

35. Ibid., col. 645.

36. See Kenneth D. Brown, Labour and Unemployment, 1900-1914 (David and Charles, Newton Abbot, 1971): Harris, Unemployment and Politics.

37. Kenneth D. Brown, John Burns (Royal Historical Society, London, 1977), pp. 135-36.

38. Ibid.

39. Harris, Unemployment and Politics.

40. Labour Party, Annual Report, 1909, pp.91 ff.

41. Hansard, 5th Series, vol. IV, col. 669. 30 Apr. 1909.

42. Brown, Burns, pp. 141-44.

43. Ibid., pp.146-47.

44. Hansard, 5th Series, vol I, cols. 334 ff. 19 Feb. 1909.

45. Ibid., cols. 683 ff.

46. Harris, Unemployment and Politics, pp. 373 ff: Thane, 'The Working Class and State "Welfare"'.

47. Hansard, 5th Series, vol. IV, cols. 1072

ff. 3 May 1909.

48. Labour Party, Annual Report, 1909, pp. 102 ff. Appendix II. Report of Conference on the Incidence of Taxation.

49. Hansard, 5th Series, vol. IV, cols. 393-94. 28 Apr. 1909.

50. Ibid., vol. XXVI, cols. 304 ff. 24 May 1911.

51. Ibid., col. 305.

52. Ibid., vol. XXVIII, col. 103. 10 July 1911: ibid., vol. 32, cols. 1485 ff. 6 Dec. 1911.

53. J. Harris, William Beveridge (Clarendon Press, Oxford, 1977), pp. 177 ff.

54. Hansard, 5th Series, vol. XXVIII, col. 209. 11 July 1911.

55. Ibid., vol. XXVI, col. 309. 24 May 1911.

56. Ibid., col. 313.

57. For Thorne see ibid., vol. XXXII, col. 807. 30 Nov. 1911: for Clynes, ibid., cols. 807 ff: for Wilkie, ibid., col. 811: for Barnes, ibid., col. 813; for Duncan, ibid., col. 818.

58. Harris, Beveridge, p. 183.

59. Hansard, 5th Series, vol. XXVII, cols. 1442 ff. 2 May 1911; ibid., vol. XXXII, cols. 1435 ff. 6 Dec. 1911.

60. Ibid., vol. XXVII, col. 1426. 6 July 1911.

61. Thane, 'The Working Class and State "Welfare"'.

62. Hansard, 5th Series, vol. XXVII, cols. 1554 ff. 7 July 1911: ibid., vol. XXVIII, cols. 107 ff. and 131 ff. 10 July 1911.

63. Ibid., vol. XXVII, cols. 1434 ff. 7 July 1911.

64. Ibid., cols. 721 ff. and cols. 749 ff: ibid., vol. XXX, cols. 1063 ff. and 1114-5. 2 Nov. 1911.

65. Thane, 'The Working Class and State "Welfare"': Brown, Labour and Unemployment, pp.145 ff: Labour Party, Annual Report, 1909: Report of Special Conference on Unemployment, p.94: Ibid., 1912, pp..29 ff: Daily Herald, 20 Apr. 1912. Labour Party support for the National Insurance Bill was one of the issues over which forty or so ILP branches broke with the party in 1911 to join the British Socialist Party.

66. Master of Elibank to D. Lloyd George, 5 Oct. 1911. Quoted in Brown, Labour and Unemployment, p.156. 'I need not reassure you that the statement I made to you about the attitude of the Party on the Insurance Bill before we separated in the summer holds good. The Party came to its

decision and its decision will be carried out by the officers loyally and faithfully in spite of what two, or at the outside, three, members may do to the contrary.' Elibank added in his covering note that 'The understanding - after the passage of payment of members - was that he and his friends should give general support to the Insurance Bill.' See also the debates recorded in Labour Party, Annual Report, 1913, pp.17 ff: Brown, Burns, pp.133-45; Harris, William Beveridge, pp.178 ff.

67. Hansard, 5th Series, vol. XXVI, col. 312. 24 May 1911.

68. For Snowden see ibid., vol. XXVIII, cols. 1102 ff. 19 July 1911; for Hardie, ibid., cols. 1117 ff: for Jowett, ibid., col. 1239.

69. Ibid., vol. XXX, col. 456. 27 Oct. 1911. Daily Herald, 8, 11 May, 13 Aug. 1912: Thane, 'The Working Class and State "Welfare"'.

70. R. Davidson, 'The Board of Trade and Industrial Relations, 1896-1914', Historical Journal, vol. 21 (1978).

71. Whiteside, 'Wages and Welfare'.

72. Hansard, 5th Series, vol. XXVII, cols. 1391 ff. 6 July 1911.

73. Ibid., vol. XXVIII, col. 323. 11 July 1911.

74. Ibid., vol. XXVII, col. 1556. 6 July 1911.

75. Ibid., vol. XXVIII, cols. 806 ff. 17 July 1911.

76. Ibid., col. 811.

77. Ibid., col. 941.

78. Ibid., cols. 1078 ff.

79. Ibid., cols. 1234 ff.

80. Ibid., vol. XXX, cols. 885, 908, 1076. 1 Nov. 1911.

81. Ibid., vol. LVI, cols. 3018 ff. 24 July 1913.

82. Ibid., vol. XXXII, cols. 807 ff. 1 Dec. 1911.

83. Whiteside, 'Wages and Welfare'.

84. Harris, Beveridge, p.190. Hansard, 5th Series, vol. LVI, cols. 3015 ff. 24 July 1913.

85. Hansard, 5th Series, vol. LVI, cols. 3146 ff. 24 July 1911.

86. Some of this can be found elsewhere. For instance, Thane, 'The Working Class and State "Welfare"'; Brown, Labour and Unemployment, passim: Harris, Unemployment and Politics, passim: J. Melling, Rent Strikes (Polygon Books, Edinburgh, 1983); R. Barker, Education and Politics, 1900-1951. A Study of the Labour Party (Oxford,

Clarendon Press, 1972).

    87. Hinton, Labour and Socialism, p.76.

    88. For differences between Labour and Liberals at local level in these years see G.L. Bernstein, 'Liberalism and the Progressive Alliance in the Constituencies, 1900-1914: Three Case Studies', Historical Journal, vol. 26 (1983).

    89. This criticism of the early Labour Party is made by G. Stedman Jones, The Language of Class. Studies in English Working Class History, 1832-1982 (Cambridge, University Press, 1983), p.238.

Chapter Nine

LABOUR AND THE CONSTITUTIONAL CRISIS

On 29 April 1909, David Lloyd George, Chancellor of the Exchequer, introduced his celebrated budget, thereby inaugurating the great constitutional crisis which was to dominate politics for nearly two and a half years. In the first phase of the crisis, the over-whelmingly Unionist House of Lords gradually plucked up courage to reject the finance bill, an action which the Liberal majority in the House of Commons immediately castigated as 'unconstitutional'. There followed a dissolution of Parliament, and the general election of January 1910. The Liberals lost a good deal of ground, but with the aid of Labour and the Irish there was still an adequate majority to carry the controversial budget through the new House of Commons, and this time the Lords let it through. The government, appalled at the challenge of the previous year, resolved to cut down the power of the House of Lords permanently. After considerable delay, the proposals to that effect which had passed the Commons were rejected by the Lords, whereupon the second 1910 election ensued, with results almost exactly as before. Again the government proposals passed the Commons. When they were ready for submission to the Lords, the opposition leaders were told that the King was prepared, if necessary, to create sufficient ministerial peers to swamp the Unionist majority in the Lords. At this point the principal Unionists decided that discretion was the better part of valour, and recommended their followers in the Lords to abstain from voting, thus enabling the government bill to pass. Suddenly, a body of diehard Unionist peers indicated that they had no intention of following that advice, but proposed to vote against the bill. As the diehards were more numerous than the Liberals in the Upper House, it looked as if the King's promise would be activated. Eventually, however, great pressure was exerted on peers who normally did not vote on party-political matters, and even on some of the Unionists, to support the bill and avert the mass-creation of new peerages. In August 1911 the diehard revolt was narrowly defeated, the bill received royal assent, and the constitutional crisis was over. There is something to be said for the view that the turmoil engendered by that great national debate did more to challenge and upset current social assumptions in Britain than any other chain of events in the twentieth century, not excepting the first or second world war.

The role of the Labour Party in that debate throws some interesting sidelights on how Labour viewed its own position at the time, and on its attitude to a number of issues other than the one immediately involved. For several years before the constitutional crisis broke, the Labour Party had seemed to be making great organizational and electoral progress. The success of 1906 was followed by a number of by-election victories and the affiliation of the Miners' Federation of Great Britain. In July 1909, the National Agent was able to report that in the previous twelve months the number of agents had more than doubled, and currently stood at about forty.[1] Yet, in a deeper sense, Labour's progress was more apparent than real. A large proportion of the existing Labour MPs, and an even larger proportion of the miners' MPs who proposed to transfer to Labour after the next general election, relied on tactical arrangements with the Liberals for preservation of their seats, and in some cases the local Liberal machine continued to be used in support of a candidate who had transferred to Labour. There was no ideological divide between Labour and the Liberals. Leading Labour personalities like Ramsay MacDonald and Arthur Henderson had been paid workers for Liberal MPs, and there was no evidence that their views had undergone a dramatic change since then. Few, if any, of the current Labour MPs held opinions which could not be matched by those of some of the MPs sitting on Liberal benches. The reason for creating the Labour Party in the first place had not been to give voice to opinions fundamentally irreconcilable with those of the older parties, but rather to set up a pressure group which could influence the government of the day, be it Liberal or Conservative, to pass measures corresponding with the interests of the organised working class. At this stage Labour appears to have had no serious aspiration towards ever becoming the government itself. Its model, if any, was the Irish Party, which had contrived to elicit legislation from both of the great parties in advancement of Irish interests. Labour at this time was a very loose federation indeed. 'Mr Keir Hardie is not my leader; he is my Chairman', declared a Labour MP in 1906. '. . . What he says on the public platform we, as members of the Labour Representation Committee group, have nothing to do with'.[2]

Perhaps the fact that a large proportion of the parliamentary Labour Party had recent Liberal antecedents explains the somewhat muted nature of the criticism which Labour offered, even when it was dissatisfied with the Liberal government. A Labour leaflet of 1907 expressed rather well the spirit in which that criticism was conducted. Mr Asquith's budget of that year, declared the leaflet, 'should not be accepted by workmen with gratitude'. The Labour Party, it continued, wanted Old Age Pensions 'first of all', and regretted the fact that they had got no more than 'a conditional promise that something may be done next year'.[3] Here, as elsewhere, Labour was acting as a rather gentle pressure group, urging the Liberal government to follow radical policies, in terms of which a good many Liberal MPs heartily approved.

Labour often seemed to anticipate what was to be the Liberal government's next move and in the matter of Lloyd George's 1909 budget they were particularly skilful. In January of that year, the Labour Party's conference at Portsmouth called for

> a drastic reform of the system of national taxation so as to secure that it is derived from those best able to pay for it and who received the most protection and benefit from the State.

It further demanded

> the following reforms in the next Budget, namely:
> a super-tax on large incomes
> special taxation of state-conferred monopolies
> increased estate and legacy duties
> and a really substantial beginning with the

taxation of land values.

Lloyd George could hardly have been more obliging three months later. When he rose to introduce his budget, the Chancellor began by telling the House that it was necessary to raise something like fifteen and three-quarter million pounds in extra taxation - a vast sum by the standards of the time - almost exclusively in order to meet the cost of old age pensions and naval rearmament. Forestalling criticism of the expenditure which had occasioned this requirement, he reminded them that 'the attitude of the Government towards these two branches of increased expenditure has not been one of rushing a reluctant House of Commons into expense which it disliked, but rather of resisting persistent appeals from all quarters of the House for still further increases under both heads'.[4] The Chancellor was right. Only a very few Conservatives, like Sir Frederick Banbury, and one maverick Liberal, Harold Cox, had opposed old age pensions and only a tiny minority of backbench pacifists had cavilled at naval rearmament. The great majority of all four parties had backed the government, or pressed it to go further.

To meet these needs, Lloyd George proposed a super-tax - precursor of the modern surtax - of 6d ($2\frac{1}{2}$p) in the pound on incomes over £5,000 per annum; increased taxation on liquor licences - which were in the nature of State conferred monopolies, as understood at the Labour Party conference; a rise in estate duties from eleven to fifteen per cent; and a small tax on developed land, which represented at least a step towards the taxation of land values. Potentially of far greater significance was the proposal to value land, as a necessary preliminary to a more general system of land value taxation.

The first parliamentary statement of considered Labour opinions on the budget was made four days later by G.N. Barnes. On the matter of increased expenditure which had occasioned the proposed new taxation, he welcomed what the government had already done, but in two respects considered that it should have gone further. The disqualification of paupers from receiving old age pensions should be removed, and the new defence expenditure should be supplemented by 'an interchange of international courtesies, of holding international conferences with a view to the perfection of international law and in setting up that sense of self-interest in national defence on the part of the great mass of the people of this country which . . . would be the best guarantee of peace and . . . against invasion'.[5] As for the Chancellor's proposals for new taxation, Barnes's main objection was to the increase in tobacco duty, particularly for cheaper brands, while he expressed more tentative regret that the new super-tax was not lighter at the bottom and heavier at the top. Such criticisms were really peripheral, and the general view which Barnes expressed on behalf of his party was unambiguous: 'We of the Labour Party will give a steady and consistent support to the Government in all the steps necessary to carry this Budget into effect'.[6]

What Barnes and subsequent Labour speakers in the debate particularly welcomed was the proposal to introduce a measure of land taxation. Most of the pre-1914 Labour MPs, like a very large section of contemporary Liberals, were probably more deeply stirred by the land question than by any other. Subsequent public discussion about the budget was increasingly concentrated on the land taxation and valuation clauses, so there was no discernible difference between the line adopted by the Labour Party and that taken by the bulk of the Liberals, particularly back-bench radicals. The Labour Party resolved to participate actively in the pro-budget campaign. At an emergency meeting of the National Executive Committee on 18 June 1909, the party decided to support a great demonstration planned for Hyde Park, and to appoint two leading members to the committee organising that function. They further decided to issue a manifesto 'in favour of the general principles of the Budget and explaining its principal proposals' which would 'be circulated to the Press and affiliated Societies'.[7] The party's _Quarterly Circular_ of July declared that 'the Budget, taken as a whole, but particularly the clauses imposing additional taxes on high unearned incomes and on land and monopoly values, has been heartily welcomed by the Labour Party' - adding:

> That the destruction of the Finance Bill by the House of Lords is a breach of the Constitution, and a usurpation of the rights of the House of Commons; that it creates a menace to the liberties of the people and that those liberties can only be secured by the total abolition of the House of Lords.[8]

This extreme view about the Upper House was by no means confined to the Labour Party. 'The time has come for the total abolition of the House of Lords', wrote Winston Churchill to Asquith not long afterwards.[9]

What was by no means self-evident was how Labour would seek to promote such causes at the forthcoming election, or what its relations would be with others who shared its view on such matters. Labour plainly proposed to run a good many more candidates than the LRC had fielded in 1906. What, if anything, would be done to ensure that such candidates did not foul the prospects of Liberals who entertained similar views on the great questions of the moment? In the great majority of cases, good care was taken to ensure that the spirit of the Gladstone-MacDonald Pact of 1903 was continued, and most of the seventy-eight Labour candidates stood in places where there was no serious danger that the Unionists might win a seat through split voting. Seven seats which the LRC had fought in 1906 were not contested by the Labour Party in January 1910, and in three of these cases inspection of the figures suggests that this withdrawal enabled the Liberal to win, or to hold, a seat which would have gone to the Unionists in a triangular contest.[10] Only three of the new Labour interventions in January 1910 appear to have resulted in the Liberals losing seats to the Unionists.[11] Liberals showed still greater forbearance, even resisting the temptation to counter-attack in most of the seats which they had lost to Labour at by-elections. Colne Valley (where the successful candidate had stood in 1907 as an Independent Socialist, but later joined the Labour Party), and Jarrow (where there had been a four-cornered contest, with all candidates polling strongly), were the only exceptions and in both of these cases the Liberal was successful. At Manchester East, which the Liberals had captured in 1906 from no less a foe than Arthur Balfour, the Liberal withdrew at a late stage of proceedings, and allowed Labour to take it in a straight fight.

Liberal withdrawal at Deptford probably saved a vulnerable seat for Labour. In thirteen two-member seats, Labour and Liberal ran in double harness, and in ten of those cases they were both successful. The miners' seats provide even more striking examples of co-operation. Three of the miners' MPs refused to switch allegiance from Liberal to Labour; none of them had Labour opposition.[12] Thirteen of the miners who had turned to Labour had no Liberal opposition, and in a considerable number of these cases they appear to have had active help from the local Liberal machine as well. The only miner who went Labour and who did encounter Liberal opposition was John Johnson of Gateshead. In this case special factors were evidently at work, for there was a mass-demonstration of local miners on polling day in favour of the Liberal who won the seat, thereby pushing Johnson to a poor third place. In the upshot, forty Labour MPs were returned, not one of whom had had Liberal opposition, and there was only a tiny handful of cases where either Liberal or Labour could complain that the other had refused an act of self-abnegation which might conceivably have affected the result. No doubt in many cases the acts of apparent unselfishness were in truth the product of clandestine arrangements, or tacit understandings of a nod-and-wink variety between the two parties, but the fact that they were disposed to make such deals suggests that both were convinced that they were fishing in the same pond and that a considerable measure of mutual goodwill existed.

The general election gave the Liberal and Unionist Parties almost identical representation in the House of Commons. Most, though not all, of the Irish decided that it was better in such circumstances to support a budget they disliked than to throw out the Liberals and put in the Opposition. As for the Labour Party, its attitude on the great issues of public interest had been almost identical with that of the government, and was likely to remain so. Labour agreed with the Liberals on the budget; it agreed with the Liberals in opposing Tariff Reform, and it agreed with the Liberals that the power of the House of Lords must be curtailed forthwith. In the much tighter parliamentary situation resulting from the election, the Labour Party could hardly afford the luxury even of those occasional anti-government demonstrations in which it had indulged during the previous Parliament. So closely were the two parties bound together that Liberal Magazine began to use the convenient term 'Ministerialists' as a generic word to cover Liberals and Labour.

A simple counting of noses left nobody in doubt that the contentious budget would pass the new House of Commons, and this time the Unionist majority in the Lords decided to let it through

223

without further trouble. So the major parties retired to their respective positions to meditate action on the next great issue which was bound to arise, the relationship between the House of Commons and the House of Lords.

The Labour Party, however, had another great interest, which had come to a head while the election campaign was actually in progress. On the face of it, this matter seemed completely separate from the constitutional and economic issues which had been central to the election, but in practice they could not be kept in watertight compartments, and attitudes taken by the parties on the more general issues were related to that one as well. The celebrated Osborne case, which first went to the courts in 1907, cast doubt on the legality of trade union contributions to Labour Party funds. The matter went to the Court of Appeal in the following year, and in 1909 was remitted to the House of Lords. On 21 December of that year, when the general election campaign was already in full swing, but polling had not yet commenced, their lordships gave unanimous judgment against the legality of such contributions. This had little effect on Labour finances during the current campaign, but it was obvious that eventually the major source of funds would be cut off if the law was not changed. When the matter was considered by Labour's National Executive on 30 December, the members agreed - with only Arthur Henderson dissenting - that payment of MPs would not meet the situation.[13]

The Liberal government had no wish to antagonise its auxiliary troops, and in April 1910, when a Labour MP, J.W. Taylor, proposed legislation which would reverse the Osborne decision, the natural reaction would probably have been to support the proposal. Unfortunately, there were thorny questions involved which did not permit such a simple solution, and in the end Taylor's motion was talked out. The Osborne case had arisen because a Liberal railwayman and the trade union branch of which he was an official had objected on moral grounds to the central organisation of their union using funds which ultimately derived from members' subscriptions in support of a political party of which many of those members did not approve. Simple reversal of the Osborne decision would merely restore the original cause of grievance. In fact the evidence suggests that feeling on the matter was much stronger among

Liberal working men than among party leaders, whose general disposition was to appease Labour when the opportunity arose. Asquith's papers contain a report - probably from the Master of Elibank, Chief Liberal Whip - on the Scottish Liberal Association Conference held at Dunfermline in 1910:

> A discussion of about an hour and a half took place with regard to the Osborne Judgment. Miners from West Fife moved and seconded that this be not reversed or revised. They were backed up by the other two of their colleagues, and all four spoke very strongly as Liberal Trade Unionists against the Socialist domination to which they had been subjected. They were loyal trade unionists in trade matters but considered it a great hardship that they were forced to pay a shilling a year for the spread of Socialist doctrines of which they altogether disapproved.

In the end a compromise resolution was carried, expressing the hope 'that the Government will uphold the law as defined in the Osborne Judgment, so as to safeguard the political liberties of trade unionists'. The author of the report concluded that 'there were a large number of Scottish Members of Parliament present, and they were greatly impressed with the decision, especially with the speeches of the miners'.[14] We may reflect today - pace those staunchly Liberal Fifeshire miners - that very few of the contemporary Labour MPs could properly be called 'socialist' in any ordinary sense of the term, while a few of the Liberal MPs could be so described; but that was hardly the point. Some Liberals were flatly opposed to any change in the law, while others were very anxious that the Osborne decision should be reversed forthwith. Whether an acceptable compromise could be achieved was by no means clear.

The Labour Party's problems were even more acute. Members of trade unions which had been contributing to the Labour Party sought, and obtained, injunctions against the central organs of those unions continuing to do so.[15] A body called the Trade Union Defence League proceeded to send letters to other Unions, indicating that they were aware of members of those unions who were willing to act as plaintiffs against them, if necessary, in a similar cause.[16] Quite early in 1910 the Labour Party's National Agent,

Arthur Peters, reported that lapses in trade union contributions attributable to the Osborne decision amounted to £138,639 and it was plain that other lapses were likely in the near future.[17]

A combination of financial stringency, organisational weakness, knowledge that the Liberals were the only people likely to effect any helpful change in trade union law, and real sympathy with what the government was attempting to do in the constitutional crisis, appears to have operated in determining Labour's policy towards by-elections which arose in the course of 1910. Twenty-one seats fell vacant, seventeen of them in Great Britain. None of the vacancies arose in Labour-held constituencies, and Labour fought in only one place - Mid-Glamorganshire, where in no imaginable circumstances could Labour's intervention have resulted in a Unionist gain. Govan and Crewe, both of which had been fought by Labour in January, and which were a good deal more vulnerable Liberal seats, were ignored.

In the course of 1910, the major parties gradually came to adopt their definitive positions on the future of the House of Lords. The Unionists, who had plenty of evidence that the Lords were unpopular, and who doubtless felt considerable embarrassment at some of the wilder statements from members of the Upper House, had to decide how far they should jettison the hereditary principle.[18] In March, the overwhelming Unionist majority in the Lords went so far as to accept unanimously Lord Rosebery's resolution 'that the possession of a Peerage should no longer of itself give the right to sit and vote in the House of Lords' - a concession which would have been almost unthinkable a year or so earlier. The Liberal cabinet, in whose hands initiative necessarily resided, was deeply divided as to what solution would be inherently desirable, and in any event had to adjust its policy to many different forces pulling in different directions.[19] Eventually the government reached agreement, and its proposals for curtailing the power of the Lords were approved by the House of Commons. Yet they still had hopes of a compromise with the Opposition, and for a large part of 1910 a Constitutional Conference, with members from both parties, attempted to hammer out agreement. In the end, however, such efforts collapsed, and the Lords rejected the govenment's proposals. Parliament was dissolved in preparation for the second general election within twelve months.

The likelihood of a second 1910 election had long been accepted in political circles, and as far back as February the Labour Party had given serious thought to its strategy in that event. There were some areas where it was clear to the National Agent that they had spread their organisation too thinly on the ground in January. Peters reported that in the Glasgow area 'we have been fighting Camlachie and Govan, together with the three adjoining constituencies in the county of Lanark . . . . The wiser policy seems to me to be to stick to Camlachie and let Govan go in the meantime . . .'. There were similar problems in Yorkshire, where 'the blunder of fighting Holmfirth, before circum-stances became favourable to us, was great'.

Quite apart from such special problems there was a general need to restrict Labour's front:

> The alternative before us is, a much shorter list of candidates than we had last January, with a much bigger proportion of wins; or a slightly shorter list of candidates (I do not believe that if an election came this year we could possibly put so many candidates in the field as we did in January) with a proportion of failures pretty much as we had then. In considering these alternatives . . . I would strongly urge . . . necessity of (a) . . . considering the financial situation, (b) the equally great necessity of increasing our present representation in the House of Commons.

No less striking is his assessment of the impor-tance of Liberal behaviour on Labour votes:

> . . . We ought to keep a very watchful eye upon the trend of events so as to discover whether the Liberal Party is coming· out in disgrace, or whether it will work with the same enthusiasm as it did in the last election by convincing the democratic electorate that it means business. In the first event, we might do slightly better in three-cornered fights than last January; in the latter event we will probably do worse than we did last January because our weakness was then revealed and the relative position of Parties is now perfectly well known.[20]

'Tactical voting', which has attracted so much

attention in recent years, was familiar to experienced political organisers in 1910.

At an early stage in the second 1910 campaign, Asquith made a pronouncement which was probably tolerable to most people in his own party, and - while not wholly satisfactory to Labour - went a good way towards meeting its most acute anxieties. The government, if returned, would 'propose legislation empowering Trade Unions to include in their objects and organisation the provision of a fund for parliamentary and municipal action and representation and kindred objects'.[21] From this promise would eventually spring the Trade Union Act of 1913, which would do incalculable good to the Labour Party and incalculable damage to the Liberals. From the short-term point of view, however, it was yet further evidence for Labour as to which of the major parties was more likely to serve its own interests.

Only fifty-eight Labour candidates took the field in December 1910. Thirteen stood in harness with a Liberal in double-member constituencies. The ten such constituencies which the two parties had held in January were all succesfully defended, and in Sunderland the two allies each captured a seat from the Opposition. In single-member constituencies, Labour made four gains and suffered three losses - all of them in straight fights. In the London seat of Woolwich, which Labour recaptured, and three Lancashire seats of Newton, St. Helen's and Wigan which they lost, there had been straight fights against Unionists in January as well as December, and the change in representation is evidently due to no more than small local swings one way or the other. At Whitehaven and at Bow and Bromley, however, the Labour gain seems attributable to the withdrawal of a Liberal who stood in January. In the second of these, Lloyd George actively encouraged Liberals to rally behind the Labour candidate, George Lansbury.[22] One Labour gain - West Fife - took place in freak conditions, and was the only seat which the party contrived either to win or to hold against Liberal opposition. In January, there had been a triangular contest, and the Liberal was returned. In December the Unionist withdrew, and Labour captured the seat in a straight fight against the Liberal. Examination of the figures suggests that most of the local Unionists, in the absence of a candidate of their own, preferred Labour to Liberal.

The Liberal gains at Cockermouth and

Manchester South-West seem attributable to
withdrawal of a Labour candidate who had stood in
January. There are a few places like Gateshead
where Labour withdrawal made an otherwise very
vulnerable Liberal seat fairly safe. By contrast,
at Glasgow Camlachie the Labour man, who had polled
badly in January, remained in the field, and this
may be responsible for the very narrow Liberal
failure to capture the seat. The Liberals were at
one point thinking of running a candidate against
Labour's George Barnes in the nearby Glasgow seat
of Blackfriars, but eventually they decided to the
contrary. As Reynold's News put it, from a radical
Liberal standpoint, '. . . two blacks do not make
a white. We have nothing to gain by losing
Mr Barnes' vote against the Lords.'[23]
  Labour's failure to accommodate the Liberals
at Camlachie, and the remarkable result at West
Fife, appear to be manifestations of a phenomenon
of which both earlier and later examples exist.
Reporting on the Scottish Labour Conference in
August 1911, Peters observed that 'the strength of
Liberalism in Scotland had had the effect of making
the active man in the Labour movement there even
more (violently) anti-Liberal than pro-Socialist or
pro-Labour'.[24] The National Agent did not
analyse the matter closely, but it does seem
possible that Labour's rise in central Scotland -
and, indeed, in some parts of Lancashire and a few
other places - follows an aberrant pattern as an
indirect consequence of late nineteenth century
Irish immigration. Where this took place on a
large scale, the political cooperation between
Irish and Liberals induced many local working men
to support the Conservatives. In most of the
country, the Labour Party drew overwhelmingly on
erstwhile Liberals; but where working-class
Conservatives were exceptionally numerous, Labour
drew quite heavily on them. In most of the country
the erstwhile Liberals could readily revert to
their old party if no Labour man stood; while in
these special places voters could more readily
transfer between Labour and Conservative than
between Labour and Liberal. Thus the Unionists of
West Fife could transfer more readily to Labour
than to Liberal; the Liberal miners of West Fife
felt exceptional antagonism to the idea that trade
unions should give financial backing to the Labour
Party; while the Labour supporters in Camlachie
were unwilling to pull down their candidate in the
hope of putting out a Unionist; and it is quite

possible that the Liberal would not have benefited if they had done.

Taking the December 1910 results as a whole, there was practically no change on those recorded earlier in the year. A couple of dozen marginal seats changed hands in one direction, a couple of dozen in the other. The Liberals and Unionists still almost exactly balanced, but with Labour help the Liberals were well ahead, and on this occasion the Irish did not have the reason for hesitation about supporting the government which they had felt in January. The possibility of taking a few Labour members into the government was bruited, but Labour refused to cooperate. Close as the Liberal and Labour Parties might be on current issues, the original raison d'être of the Labour Party had been the perceived requirement of total independence and any action which might be seen as qualifying that independence would have caused a great furore among some of the party's members.

In the concluding phases of the constitutional crisis, co-operation between Liberal and Labour was close. The final form of the government's proposals was that the Lords would lose the right to block a money bill, while on nearly all other matters they would henceforth be able to block measures for no more than two sessions of a particular Parliament. Halsbury's diehard revolt added considerable spice and excitement to the controversy, but in the end wise counsels prevailed even among the Conservative peers. On 18 August 1911, the Parliament Bill at last received royal assent.

During the earlier part of 1911, down to the passage of the Parliament Act, Labour followed the same policy of general abstinence from by-elections as it had pursued in the previous year. The one exception was N.E. Lanarkshire, which it had contested in January 1910 but not in December. This seems to be a further example of truculence among Scottish Labour supporters, for they had no realistic hope of winning the seat.

Once the constitutional crisis was over, the mariage de convenance between Liberal and Labour rapidly broke up. During the autumn of 1911, the main issue of parliamentary controversy was the National Insurance Bill, which received royal assent in December. In our own day there is little doubt that this measure represented one of the principal milestones towards the welfare state, yet Labour showed little gratitude. The support given by MacDonald in the bill's concluding stages was distinctly lukewarm; while five Labour MPs went so far as to vote against the third reading.[25] Labour began to contest by-elections again with considerable eagerness. In the closing months of 1911, and in 1912, it fought not only in places where it had stood before, but also in many new ones. In three by-elections of the period, it appears likely that Labour intervention was responsible for the Unionist winning a Liberal seat on a minority vote.[26] At Hanley it was the Liberal who intervened in a Labour seat, and actually captured it in his own party's interest. By June 1914, the Liberal Magazine was complaining that of fifteen Unionist by-election gains, seven had occurred on a minority of the total poll in triangular contests where there had been a straight fight in December 1910.[27]

The history of the Labour Party down to 1914 divides into three periods. Down to a date just a little after the constitutional crisis began, Labour was winning considerable support, and was also serving as a goad, urging the Liberals in a radical direction. During the period of the constitutional crisis, Labour sought to minimise the damage it was doing by quid pro quo electoral arrangements. In the third period, which commenced immediately the constitutional crisis was over, Labour reverted to its old tactics of fighting the Liberals, but with profoundly different results. If Labour had sought before 1909 to make the Liberals more radical, this effect persisted. Nowhere was this brought out more sharply than at Hanley in July 1912, where the Liberal - an extreme land-taxer - was visibly most radical of the three candidates. In this period, Labour was neither stimulating the Liberals nor benefitting itself through its renewed truculence. The sole beneficiary was the Unionist Party.

NOTES

The author acknowledges with thanks facilities offered at the Bodleian Library, Oxford, to consult the Asquith papers, and facilities offered by the Labour Party to consult the National Executive Committee Minutes.

1. Labour Party, NEC Minutes, 7 July 1909.
2. John Jenkins on 27 Oct. The Times, 29 Oct. 1906

3. Leaflet No.26. This and other printed leaflets, etc., from the Labour Party cited in this article are in the British Library.

4. _Hansard_, 5th Series, vol IV, col. 473 _et seq_. 29 Apr. 1901.

5. Ibid., col 794 _et seq_. 3 May 1909.

6. Ibid.

7. Labour Party, NEC Minutes, 18 June 1901.

8. Ibid., 2 Dec. 1909.

9. Churchill memorandum, 14 Feb. 1910. Bodleian Library. Asquith Papers, 23, f.70.

10. Grimsby; Stoke-on-Trent; York.

11. Bow & Bromley; Cockermouth; Whitehaven.

12. Thomas Burt (Morpeth); Charles Fenwick (Wansbeck); John Wilson (Mid-Durham).

13. Labour Party, Special NEC meeting, 30 Dec. 1909.

14. 'The Osborne Judgment'. n.d., not signed. Bodleian Library. Asquith Papers, 23, f.298.

15. See list in Labour Party, NEC Minutes, 30 June 1910.

16. Labour Party, _Quarterly Circular_, 26 (July 1910).

17. Labour Party, NEC Minutes, appendix, 24 Feb. 1910.

18. Like the Duke of Beaufort, who declared at Cirencester on 7 Aug. 1909 that he would like 'to see Winston Churchill and Lloyd George in the middle of twenty couple of dog hounds'.

19. See, for example, J. Morley to H.H. Asquith, 14 Apr. 1910; L. Harcourt to H.H. Asquith, 14 May 1910. Bodleian Library. Asquith papers, 23, f.94, 96.

20. Labour Party, NEC Minutes, 24 Feb. 1910, and appended National Agent's Report.

21. _The Times_, 23 Nov. 1910.

22. _Reynold's News_, 27 Nov. 1910.

23. Ibid.

24. Report of Scottish Conference, 5 Aug. 1911.

25. For MacDonald's speech see _Hansard_, 5th Series, vol. XXXII, col. 1433 _et seq_. 6 Dec. 1911; for analysis of voting see _Liberal Magazine_ (1911), p.768.

26. Oldham; Crewe; Midlothian.

27. _Liberal Magazine_ (1914), p.323.

Chapter Ten

LABOUR AND WOMEN'S SUFFRAGE

The relationship between the labour movement and the women's movement in the early twentieth century might well have been a straightforward story of harmonious alliance by two natural allies; indeed such an assumption does inform some recent writing on the subject.[1] No doubt there are some grounds for this. As early as February 1901 the new Labour Representation Committee committed itself to adult suffrage for men and women. Labour was neither encumbered by the Conservatives' instinctive fear of a mass electorate, nor, since it did not hold office, unduly taxed by the dilemmas of legislating on the subject as were the Liberals. Yet British labour in 1900 was very far from feminist. Its female contingents were mostly small and peripheral. Among the constituent elements in the LRC women remained negligible in the trade unions, the Fabians and the SDF. Only in the ILP were they and their interests regarded sympathetically. Nor, until 1918, was there any provision for women's representation on the National Executive of the party itself. Moreover, as the women's question grew more acute Labour's approach to it repeated that of the older parties. One sees a similar display of male prejudice, a similar reluctance to divide the party by giving priority to the women, similar calculations of party advantage, and a similar fragmentation of the suffragist forces themselves. Women's enfranchisement presents the classic dilemma of a political party with a wide range of interests confronted by a pressure group urging priority for its own cause. Only a handful of Labour politicians were prepared to elevate women's suffrage above all else, even temporarily. Many, while supporting the idea, really wanted to wait for adult suffrage; and some actually preferred adult male suffrage. Even if the vote had been accepted as an urgent matter, what, in any case, could Labour do about it? With few MP's the balance of power was never in its grasp and the party felt bound fairly closely to the post-1906 Liberal governments both by policies and by electoral necessity.

On the other hand it should be stressed that Labour showed itself less acutely divided and more generally favourable to women's suffrage than its rivals, at least if measured in terms of voting in parliamentary divisions.[2] Had the party, however, been enthusiastically and inherently feminist it would scarcely have become embroiled in bitter controversies over the suffrage and, more importantly, it would have been quicker to seize the opportunity to outflank the other parties on the issue. Not until the eve of the first world war can it plausibly be argued that Labour was on the verge of accomplishing this. In order to account for the timing of these developments we must see the Edwardian phase in a longer-term context.

Towards the end of the eighteenth century the potential of women for radical politics in Britain appeared promising. Among the reform clubs and societies of the revolutionary era women were active participants; before 1832 they contributed to the campaign for parliamentary reform, suffered at Peterloo, and sometimes formed their own Female Reform Societies. After this time, however, things began to grow complicated. The Great Reform Act pronounced male persons as alone eligible as voters while the Chartists' sweeping constitutional demands noticeably ignored female enfranchisement. Though women assisted in the Anti-Corn Law League they did so largely as providers of teas and decorators of meeting places. Whereas around the turn of the century women's claims had been viewed in fairly abstract terms as a matter of individual rights, fifty years later their demands conjured up more concrete fears and expectations. In the 1860s the very specific causes of the women's pressure groups capitalised on the last years of Victorian optimism but during the 1870s they were overtaken by the sense of shrinking opportunities and economic decline which cast both middle and working-class women as competitors in the eyes of many men. Nor could the political 'radicals' any longer be relied upon to march with the women, partly because they had achieved their objectives. When Mill advocated women's enfranchisement in the 1860s it was not solely on grounds of justice but as a matter of expediency. By the 1880s when trade unions and socialist societies had begun to make some inroads on parliamentary politics women no longer seemed natural or necessary allies. The only party to succeed in harnessing women in hundreds of thousands was the Conservatives in the shape of the Primrose League after 1883. Radicals of all kinds pondered the meaning of the League's success. Did it mean that women were naturally conservative? Many thought them more religious and thus susceptible to Anglican influence. Some felt that they were captivated by the romantic appeal of monarchy and the manly cause of empire and patriotism while others simply put it all down to skilful manipulation of snobbery and deference.

Of course, radical campaigns by small numbers of women were not lacking in this period. Unfortunately, however, pressure for improved women's education, entry into the professions, reform of the marriage, property and divorce laws, birth control and the abolition of the Contagious Diseases Acts profoundly disturbed politicians of all kinds. For the emerging labour movement in particular this appeared to be largely an argument among the middle classes, which is why late Victorian socialists often spoke disparagingly of 'Bourgeois Women's Righters'. The Fabian Society, for example, though interested in the conditions of life of women, displayed little sympathy for their political-legal status. Beatrice Webb had actually signed the petition of women anti-suffragists in 1889, though she later retracted. But it was not until 1906 that Fabian women managed to organise a revolt sufficient to force the inclusion of equal citizenship among the official objects of the society. Socialists often argued that the women who were clamouring for the vote and professional careers would promptly relapse into political inertia once their limited demands had been satisfied. Inspired by mere individualism they lacked any appreciation of the greater needs of working-class women, or of the collectivist solutions their condition required. Such thinking is reflected in key figures among labour women like Margaret Bondfield. Reduced to fundamentals by Robert Blatchford it amounted to a warning that it was not yet safe to give women votes because they would undoubtedly use them against socialism.[3]

Socialist anti-suffragists were inclined to rationalise their view by arguing that it would scarcely be worth the trouble of tinkering with the franchise for the benefit of a minority of women, for only after the accomplishment of socialism would women find emancipation through the eradication of industrial sweating, slum landlords and sexual exploitation.

Of course these attitudes reflect a mixture of ideology with personality and temperament. One senses the blend of emotions in John Bruce Glasier's supreme irritation with the Pankhursts:

> A weary ordeal of chatter about women's suffrage from 10 pm to 1.30 am - Mrs and Christabel Pankhurst belabouring me as chairman of the party for its neglect of the question. At last get roused and speak with something like scorn of their miserable individualist sexism . . . . Really the pair are not seeking democratic freedom, but self-importance . . . . Christabel paints her eyebrows grossly and looks selfish, lazy and wilful. They want to be ladies not workers, and lack the humility of real heroism.[4]

Undoubtedly it was the prickly, self-doubting personalities like Glasier and MacDonald who reacted most strongly towards the dominant middle-class women so often encountered in the campaign. Like many parliamentarians Ramsay MacDonald's original suffragism tended to evaporate swiftly when he came under pressure to give precise pledges of support. Apart from a certain lack of sympathy with the dilemmas of middle-class women he also displayed an Asquithian sensitivity to extra-parliamentary agitation and thus was quickly alienated by militancy. Further, MacDonald reflected typical male fears as to the implications of enfranchisement for both sexes. Echoing Sir Almroth Wright he warned that there was 'much physiology at the root of the suffragette movement'.[5] Similarly when he encountered a Women's Labour League proposal for a liberalisation of the divorce laws, he promptly condemned the idea as 'revolution' and 'a very great menace'.[6]

Nonetheless, it must be remembered that MacDonald agreed with the keener Labour suffragists as to the ultimate necessity for women's enfranchisement. They differed over the degree of urgency each was prepared to give it. Advocates of

the women's cause pointed out that adult suffrage
remained a fairly distant prospect, while the grant
of a vote even to a few women would at least bring
the wider reform somewhat nearer. As to the
argument that women would hinder socialism,
suffragists took advantage of the growing tendency
among the women themselves to argue their case from
expediency. For example, Mrs Fawcett of the
National Union of Women's Suffrage Societies was
prepared to accept the anti-feminist view of women
as different to men - at least in so far as most of
them were unavoidably absorbed by child-birth,
family and household management - but she contended
that so far from being a disqualification for
politics this experience enabled women to add a
valuable extra dimension to it. Indeed social
reform seemed to many contemporaries the natural
rallying point for Labour and women. This approach
was developed much further by some left-wing women
like Isabella Ford and Charlotte Despard of the ILP
who argued that as a result of the reponsibilities
and sacrifices forced upon them women as a class
were morally superior to men. Their entry into
politics, therefore, could be expected to have an
improving, even purifying effect upon the system.
Among male socialists Keir Hardie and George
Lansbury notably subscribed to such sentiments.
For them a socialist society had less to do with
the efficient state of Fabian aspiration than with
the creation of a compassionate, humanitarian
society which would be greatly facilitated by what
Hardie called 'the coming of the mother element
into politics'.[7] Again, this was as much a
reflection of personality as of ideology on their
part. Far from feeling threatened by middle-class
ladies they responded warmly to them and felt
prompted to make sacrifices on their behalf.
Hardie, who exhibited an uncomplicated passion for
women in general, retained a close affection for
the Pankhursts in particular which had begun in the
1890s with the ILP and survived the WSPU's break
with Labour in the Edwardian period. Contemporaries ascribed what they saw as Hardie's
obsession with women's suffrage to his fondness for
Mrs Pankhurst - 'the Delilah who had cut our
Sampson's locks', as Glasier archly remarked - but
the evidence now suggests a much closer
relationship with Sylvia.

    With Hardie and Philip Snowden among its
leaders the ILP emerged as the most suffragist
section of the labour movement in the sense that it

advocated even a very limited enfranchisement for
women as a first instalment rather than holding out
for universal enfranchisement of both sexes.
However, even the ILP's reputation is easily
exaggerated. Although its membership was open to
women we do not know how many women actually
joined. A recent exhaustive study of the party and
its support largely ignores women.[8] Indeed, the
well-known ILP husband-and wife teams - Glasiers,
Snowdens, Pethwick-Lawrences and MacDonalds -
probably convey a misleading impression, for the
rank and file do not seem to have welcomed the idea
of women joining them actively in politics. As
late as 1908 a labour organiser in the north-east
complained:

> Some of the men - old Socialists - confessed
> to many years of work outside but had yet
> failed to win over their own wives . . . .
> (I) found some of the old trade unionists
> afraid we should spoil their homes by taking
> women out to meetings!!![9]

Whatever the views of the ILP it remained only
one element in the LRC which tended to move at the
pace of its slowest and weightiest section - the
trade unions. The TUC's position fluctuated
somewhat on the women's question. In 1884, when
adult suffrage was not a serious prospect, it
supported the municipal vote for women ratepayers.
But it then forgot the subject and by 1901 adopted
adult suffrage and subsequently condemned any
limited vote for women. By 1913, in line with the
party itself the TUC pronounced the inclusion of
women to be an essential part of any government
reform bill. Before this conclusion was reached,
however, the union leaders had been greatly
inhibited in their approach to women's emancipation
by pride and fear. This was the pride of men for
whom the franchise was one element in their
improved status which they would not easily
share.[10] Their fear was the fear of the skilled
for women as unskilled workers who would hold down
wages and inhibit union agreements in an
overstocked labour market. This attitude was
expressed in terms of the 'Living Wage', the idea
of raising wage levels to the point where a single
(male) wage-earner would be able to support an
entire family. As trade unionists attained the
vote and some direct representation in Parliament
they used their influence on industrial legislation

to exclude women from occupations on the grounds
that heavy, dirty and dangerous work was
inappropriate. Meanwhile, with the exception of
cotton textiles, women were practically excluded
from British trade unions.[11] It was to remedy
this state of affairs that the Women's Protective
and Provident League had been founded in 1874,
subsequently changing its name to the Women's Trade
Union League. Barely tolerated at TUC conferences
the WTUL's leaders in the Edwardian era, Mary
MacArthur and Margaret Bondfield, did their best to
play down suffragism in general and militancy in
particular. This was partly tactical. Male unions
were apt to refuse them funds because they believed
the WTUL to be a suffragist organisation.[12] But
it was also a genuine sign of working-class women's
dislike of the Pankhursts.[13] One labour woman
summed it up in 1908: 'how very theatrical they
are!!!'[14]

A far more independent women's section of the
labour movement was the Women's Co-operative Guild,
established in 1883, which attained a membership of
30,000 under its secretary, Margaret Llewelyn
Davies, in the Edwardian period. Even more than
the WTUL the WCG aroused suspicion for teaching
working women to organise and assert their rights
vis à vis their husbands.[15] Moreover it
consistently asserted the need for women's rather
than adult suffrage, although by 1909 antagonism
towards the WSPU had weakened the WCG's resolve and
led to the adoption of an adultist policy - clear
evidence of the damaging effect of the Pankhursts
within the women's organisations.

Perhaps because of the existence of these
suffragist groups it was not until 1906 that the
Labour Party itself risked setting up a women's
section in the shape of the Women's Labour League.
This was overdue if only as a means of remedying
the party's chronic deficiency in electoral
organisation by tapping the energy of those who
were unlikely to join through the usual routes. In
the early days the WLL made considerable use of
Margaret MacDonald whose visits to local groups
were designed partly to 'break down the prejudice
which prevails even in our own ranks'.[16] By 1913
the WLL had established branches in 122 places,
though some had lapsed, and claimed a small
membership of 4,000.[17] In view of its dependence
on the party for an annual grant the WLL was not
strongly placed to influence it over the women's
question. Moreover, with orthodox party figures

like Bondfield, MacArthur, Kathleen Bruce Glasier and Margaret MacDonald among its leadership the WLL never seemed likely to allow women's suffrage to take priority over party loyalty. As a result the WLL, along with the WCG and the WTUL adopted adult suffrage and aligned itself under the People's Suffrage Federation from 1909.

This acceptance of the adultist line, along with their working-class character, set these three groups somewhat apart from the more feminist organisations for whom the suffrage was the over-riding objective. Inevitably it took the Labour Party some time to establish a working relationship with any of the suffragist groups not only because of their social character and neglect of adult suffrage, but because of their tactics. The largest was the National Union of Women's Suffrage Societies which since 1897 had been a loose federation of the constitutional societies in London and the provinces, some of which had existed since the 1860s. Though remarkably small before 1900 the NUWSS grew rapidly after 1905, stimulated by militancy, reaching 54,000 members by 1914. A natural home for Liberals and Liberal Unionists, it also included Conservative and socialist women thus making good its claim to non-party status. Above all the NUWSS remained sedately middle class in its fondness for drawing room meetings and earnest lectures. The only significant exception to this concerns the Lancashire textile workers, many of whom actively sought the franchise and preferred the constitutional to the militant approach, though even they were only temporarily within the NUWSS.[18] However, the real stumbling block to co-operation with Labour lay in Mrs Fawcett's flat opposition to adult suffrage as tactically mistaken and undesirable in itself, which of course was inextricably bound up with the insistence on a non-party strategy. Not until 1912 did the NUWSS infringe its non-party stance and Labour modify its adultist views.

Despite its extravagant claims the Women's Social and Political Union was even less in touch with working-class women, though the Pankhursts' personal connection with the ILP did persist into the early 1900s. Nonetheless it seemed important to lay claim to wide support. A late as 1905 Mrs Pankhurst had the impertinence to attack the adultist Harry Quelch at the LRC conference in the following terms:

> Mr Quelch was probably able to speak for the women of property because he mixed with those of the highest aristocratic circles. She and those associated with her spoke for those working women who would benefit under the Bill.[19]

This, of course, was pure fantasy. After their move to London in 1906 the Pankhursts abandoned any attempt to mobilise the Lancashire cotton textile girls. However, they took care to retain one, Annie Kenny, whose function was to prove that working women wanted the vote. The anti-suffragists also produced tame workers to prove that they did not. Meanwhile the Pankhursts threw their energies into cultivating the Conservative leaders and tapping the funds and support of metropolitan society.[20] For Labour the turning-point came in 1906 when the WSPU intervened in a by-election at Cockermouth to secure the defeat of the Liberal but refused to urge support for the suffragist Labour candidate rather than the Conservative. However, the break was of no great significance to Labour except insofar as it complicated the position of Keir Hardie, for the WSPU had but a small and diminishing following. Co-operation would only have brought discredit upon the party.

On the other hand the repeated splits within the ranks of the militants did serve to detach left-wing women more congenial to Labour. Sylvia Pankhurst herself, who retained her father's radical-socialist faith, was eventually evicted from the WSPU for attempting to mobilise working women in her East London Federation. However, even in the East End her support remained very small, while Sylvia herself was so incapable of co-operating with others that she remained peripheral to the labour movement. A major breakaway occurred in 1907 which led to the setting up of the Women's Freedom League under Charlotte Despard, Anne Cobden Sanderson, Marion Coates Hanson and Teresa Billington Greig. Though committed to militant methods they were ILP supporters who could no longer stomach the Pankhursts' autocratic control of the WSPU or their increasingly Conservative sympathies. In addition 1912 saw the painful extrusion of Frederick and Emmeline Pethwick-Lawrence from the WSPU, which led to another new body, the United Suffragists. In the long run this continual division of suffragism along political lines was greatly to Labour's advantage, though in the immediate situation it seemed only to complicate an already confused picture.

For the first few years of its life the LRC regarded women's suffrage as peripheral to its main concerns. After 1903, however, it became increasingly difficult to do so. For as enfranchisement appeared to grow imminent the party could not easily avoid saying what sort of franchise it would accept, and what pressure it would exert in Parliament on behalf of the women. At this stage all the suffragist organisations were willing to accept enfranchisement for women on the same terms as men, which was often referred to as 'equal suffrage'. In practice this would have meant that the great majority of married women would be excluded because their husbands were the householders, and thus restricted the franchise to women who possessed a household qualification in their own right or a ten pound occupation qualification. An 'equal suffrage' measure along these lines was variously estimated to create one to one and a half million women voters against the existing 7.5 to 8.0 million men. Both male and female supporters of this strategy simply contended that the vital thing was to establish the principle of parliamentary votes for women regardless of the numbers initially involved and, although it would mean enfranchising a few women before several million men, there was no general demand for the wider measure yet. Therefore to insist on adult suffrage or nothing was merely prevarication.

Outside the ranks of the ILP, however, adult suffrage remained the usual preference in the labour movement. It was felt that the system was already too heavily biassed in favour of propertied people, and Labour candidates in local government contests sometimes blamed their defeats on opposition by the women on the municipal registers who were the ones likely to qualify for a parliamentary vote.[21] Efforts were made to counter this damaging criticism through surveys of women municipal electors in 1904, 1905 and 1911 which showed that, far from comprising merely wealthy widows and spinsters, the electorate was at least four-fifths working class.[22] Although industrial areas were chosen for these canvasses the working-class proportion seems suspiciously high, and the fact that they were conducted by two interested parties, the ILP and the WCG, deprived the findings of authority.

Despite their reservations Labour MPs invariably voted for 'equal suffrage' bills in the knowledge that they would not progress beyond a second reading stage. However, they preferred the kind of measure proposed by the Liberal, Willoughby Dickinson, in 1907 and 1913 which included the provision that a married woman living in a dwelling house or lodging for which her husband was entitled to register should not be disqualified merely on account of being married. This was the idea most favoured by leading suffragist ministers like Lloyd George, but it fell between two stools. It could not be introduced as a government bill while the Liberals remained divided, especially in the cabinet. Nor was it likely to succeed as a back-bench bill because it alienated many Conservative suffragists who were only prepared to go as far as an 'equal terms' measure. Thus most of the parliamentary initiatives took the form of futile attempts to legislate for equal franchise by an all-party Conciliation Committee. David Shackleton, the Labour MP for Clitheroe, whose union included many women, promoted the first of the Conciliation Bills in 1910.

This hopeless Conciliation strategy arose out of the original miscalculation of Victorian women suffragists in refusing to commit themselves to a political party in the hope of uniting suffragists of all shades. As a result they were as slow to appreciate the significance and potential of the new LRC as it was to seek co-operation with them. At the 1904 LRC Conference a resolution backed by Isabella Ford and the ILP, for enfranchisement of women on the same basis as in municipal elections, slipped through with little discussion. In the same year a bill on similar lines, drawn up by Hardie, was introduced in the Commons by Will Crooks. These moves, plus the growing attention attracted by the militant campaign, provoked the opponents of limited reform. Consequently the 1905 conference resolution from the Amalgamated Society of Engineers which supported adult suffrage but also endorsed Crooks' bill, was amended on a proposal from the London Trades Council. This had the effect of committing Labour to adult suffrage and accepting nothing less. Moreover, five subsequent conferences between 1906 and 1910 reaffirmed this line. As a result Labour and women's suffragism drew apart during these years. An indication of future trouble came in 1907 when

243

conference threw out an 'equal suffrage' resolution
by 605,000 votes to 268,000. As the conference
drew to a close Keir Hardie stunned the delegates
by threatening that if the decision on 'equal
suffrage' were to restrict MPs voting in Commons'
divisions he would have to reconsider his membership of the party. Although it was accepted that
the MPs were free to vote as they wished on bills
that fell short of adult suffrage, Hardie got into
a similar row only three months later at the ILP
conference. To his dismayed colleagues it seemed
that Hardie was getting the whole issue out of
proportion.

The argument between adultists and 'equal
suffragists' rumbled on until 1912 when it reached
a climax as a result of the Bow and Bromley
by-election. After 1910 when the Liberals lost
their overall majority Labour's 42 members were
expected to be able to exert real pressure on
them. In fact this was not easy, if only because
the Irish, with twice as many members, had the
power to keep the government in office. Even so,
the Pankhursts insisted that Labour should prove
its good faith by opposing the government on every
question until women's suffrage had been enacted.
For reasons already suggested there was never any
question of Labour contemplating such a step,
especially on this issue. Hardie, however, did
much to improve the party's reputation by his
vociferous attacks on successive Home Secretaries,
Herbert Gladstone, Churchill and McKenna. In the
end Asquith's obstructionism pushed him beyond
this. In 1911 the pressure on Asquith from within
the Liberal Party led the Prime Minister
reluctantly to promise parliamentary time for the
Conciliation Bill. Once given, this offer was
quickly regretted and at the instigation of Lloyd
George the government next announced its own
Franchise and Registration Bill which, although not
including women, would be capable of amendment so
as to enfranchise them if the House wished it.
Although this was the first real chance of success
the women had had in forty years of campaigning
their leaders reacted with uniform hostility on the
grounds that it was just another ploy to scuttle
the Conciliation Bill and advance to full male
suffrage. For the critics this interpretation was
proved subsequently when the third Conciliation
Bill was defeated by fourteen votes and the
government's own bill was abandoned following the
Speaker's ruling in January 1913 that it could not

be amended by a women's clause.

Hardie and Lansbury, outraged by what they considered Labour's feeble response to Asquith's chicanery and forcible feeding of suffragettes, now demanded tougher sanctions by the party. Lansbury, who had not endeared himself to his colleagues by getting expelled from the House for insulting Asquith in the summer, next circulated all the local parties urging them to insist that the MPs voted against the government's bill unless women were included. The NEC, having consulted the parliamentary party, agreed to urge the inclusion of women, but ruled that Lansbury's proposal was out of line with the decisions of party con-ference.[23] A memorandum drawn up privately by the NUWSS at this time suggested that as many as eleven Labour members, mostly from the ILP, would opppose the Liberals on the third reading.[24] This, however, was probably optimistic. The only test arose over the government's bill to abolish plural voting in 1913 when only Hardie, Snowden and James O'Grady rebelled.

Lansbury felt so disgusted with his colleagues that he took the fool-hardy step of resigning his seat with a view to obtaining a specific mandate for his suffrage views from his electors. Bow and Bromley, though a working-class constituency in the East End, had never been an easy one for radicals. Liberal and Labour frequently fought against each other, and the Conservatives had won the seat as recently as January 1910. Lansbury was rather lucky that in the December election the Liberals withdrew and he received public support from Lloyd George. Not surprisingly he enjoyed no financial and little moral backing from the Labour Party or the ILP in the by-election of November. Hardie resigned from the NEC in order to be free to speak for him, but Will Thorne and James O'Grady were the only other MPs to take part in his campaign. Both money and organisation had to be improvised by the local LRC, the NUWSS and the WSPU.[25] Unfortunately each group seemed to run its own campaign from separate committee rooms. The result, for the electors, was a confusing debate over militancy within the other debate on the merits of women's suffrage. Though the Pankhursts prided themselves on their powers of persuasion the fact is that WSPU meetings in the area had been attracting a good deal of hostility for some time[26]. Their descent upon the working-class voters simply stirred up male resentment,

particularly as they went out of their way to
emphasise their opposition to Lansbury's
socialism. Lansbury himself only compounded the
problem by ignoring the Labour Party except to draw
attention to his disagreements with it and to
emphasise his record or rebellion against Liberal
legislation. This inept display could hardly have
been better calculated to alienate his former
supporters. Lansbury's share of the poll fell from
55 per cent to just under 45 per cent, allowing his
Conservative anti-suffragist opponent a comfortable
victory.

Nor was this loss the end of this particular
chapter. For 1913 brought a new measure, the
Prisoners (Ill Health) Temporary Discharge Bill
(later known as the 'Cat and Mouse' Act) which
enabled the authorities to release suffragettes in
serious ill-health and re-arrest them later. While
Hardie was outraged by this MacDonald, Chairman of
the parliamentary party since 1911, considered that
the women had deliberately invited severe treatment
and should not expect martyrdom to be anything but
painful. Lansbury completed his own martyrdom by
earning a three month prison sentence during 1913
when he too went on hunger strike. More serious
was the estrangement of Hardie from the party
throughout 1912-14. Indeed, despite a rapprochement with the ILP when it celebrated its
twenty-first year in 1914, he never returned to the
centre of the movement again.

The fiasco of Bow and Bromley seems to mark
the nadir of Labour's relations with the women's
movement. This, however, is scarcely a complete
view of the situation. Much earlier in 1912 an
alternative strategy had emerged which in the long
run was to prove infinitely more important than the
increasingly peripheral antics of the Pankhursts
and Lansbury. At the party conference at
Birmingham in January the usual debate took a new
turn when Arthur Henderson incorporated into an
adult suffrage resolution a warning that 'no bill
can be acceptable to the Labour and Socialist
movement which does not include women'. Though
less than a promise to vote against a government
bill it marked the first step in that direction.
Henderson, a consistent if phlegmatic suffragist,
was ideally placed to bring the two sides together
and from 1912 to 1917, when women's suffrage was
finally written into a government bill, he played
the key role on the Labour side.

Henderson's resolution was well-timed to draw

a response from the moderate women suffragists, for by 1912 many of the NUWSS leaders were ready to accept that their strategy had been mistaken. In particular the Conciliation Bill looked both futile and slightly dishonest in that it involved harnessing the support of politicians of quite inconsistent views. If the non-party tactic was doomed the obvious alternative was to identify the party most likely to pledge itself as a party to the cause. Clearly Labour was the best candidate. When the third Conciliation Bill went down to defeat by fourteen votes in March 1912 it was noted that no Labour MPs had voted against it whereas many Liberal supporters had done so.

Initial approaches were made by the NUWSS through Henry Noel Brailsford, a journalist, who had resigned his post with the Daily News in 1909 on account of his disagreement with the paper's views on forcible feeding. After talks with Henderson in April the NUWSS called a meeting of representatives of 370 affiliated societies in May who approved the new policy by a large majority.[27] Essentially they were offering to raise a special fund (the Election Fighting Fund) and designate election organisers to assist Labour MPs and candidates in seats held by anti-suffragist Liberals. At this stage they denied that this amounted to an alliance with Labour on the grounds that they would not work against 'tried friends' in other parties and would extend the policy to any party willing to give support as a party to the cause. The EFF work was kept separate from the rest of the NUWSS activity and directed by Margaret Robertson, Catherine Marshall and Kathleen Courtney. Other EFF activists included Helena Swanwick, Maud Royden, Isabella Ford, Margaret Ashton, Ada Nield Chew, Selina Cooper and Annot Robinson, all of whom had experience in trade union or socialist politics. Some, like Ada Nield Chew had dropped out of labour affairs, alienated by the uncompromising adultist line, to concentrate on the women's cause. Now a rapprochement began to occur under EFF auspices.

All the evidence suggests that the initiative came from the women's side. Indeed, Labour, as Brailsford complained, responded but hesitantly and suspiciously, fearing, to some extent rightly, that the NUWSS was trying to use the party for its own purposes. This was a time when, owing to the Osborne Judgement, the party felt hindered by lack of ready funds, but perhaps as a result of that was inhibited by pride from taking the NUWSS money. MacDonald for one expressed the fear that the party was being, or might be thought to be, bought by the women's organisation. Partly for this reason Labour wanted its co-operation to be unacknowledged. Yet this was unacceptable to the women, for the immediate advantage of the scheme lay in frightening the Liberals with an imminent collapse of their electoral strategy. In addition the NUWSS was taking considerable risks in helping Labour at all. Many Liberal loyalists resigned during 1912-14, while Conservative and Liberal Unionist members were much embarrassed by the new policy.[28] Nonetheless, although the party formally discussed the matter with the NUWSS through a sub-committee of the NEC, it never gave pledges as to its actions in Parliament, nor did it interpret the EFF as applying to the party.[29] Rather it was for the assistance of individual Labour candidates, which if true in the letter was increasingly inconsistent with the spirit of the scheme.

MacDonald's hesitation over the EFF was justified by the serious immediate and long-term electoral implications it carried. After only a decade of life Labour had attained a parliamentary strength of forty-two, mainly as a result of the electoral pact with the Liberals and the affiliation of the Miners Federation. Yet this no longer impressed or satisfied local activists especially in the ILP, who constantly agitated for extra candidates to be sanctioned by the NEC and disparaged the MPs for tamely supporting the government. But since few Labour members expected to hold their seats in a three-cornered fight MacDonald was far from convinced, in 1912-13, that the time had come to declare complete independence of the Liberals. Indeed, in May 1912 there were only six constituencies other than those held by Labour where the NEC had approved a candidate.[30] On the other hand the NUWSS had no wish to confine its work to defending the sitting members. To shift the log-jam it must squeeze the Liberals where they were most vulnerable by fomenting revolt among their working-class voters. In short any Labour co-operation with the EFF was inconsistent with its existing arrangements with the Liberals. Fortunately the 1903 pact itself had never been formally acknowledged. In 1912 it was not strictly in existence, though the expectation was that it would be resuscitated for the next general election.

Although the initiatives of the NUWSS in no sense caused the breakdown in electoral co-operation between the Liberal and Labour parties, which took place from 1912 onwards, it certainly made it more feasible and electorally effective for Labour. For the EFF strategy worked with the grain of local Labour activism. It brought the satisfaction of four seats lost by the government in the first eight by-elections in which its workers were involved.[31] Labour gained no seats but achieved some high polls which were freely attributed to EFF organisation. A number of the NUWSS women had experience in tasks such as registration in which Labour was notably deficient, and its practice of using women in full sympathy with Labour's priorities to address cottage meetings throughout the working-class communities was much better calculated to win sympathy for suffragism than the shriller exhortations of the militants.

From Labour's side there was a sufficiently positive response to justify the new strategy. In January 1913 conference advanced a little beyond the 1912 decision by calling on the parliamentary party to oppose any franchise bill from which women were excluded. Whereas the margin had been three to two in 1912 it was now two to one, largely as a result of the miners' vote which had been hostile in 1912, neutral in 1913 and was to be suffragist thereafter. Not that MacDonald had any intention of leading a revolt in the Commons. Even at this early stage the sovereignty of conference was largely theoretical. But the possibility of a Labour rebellion served the NUWSS purpose tolerably well, for it complemented the efforts it was making simultaneously to build up expectations of an imminent Conservative commitment to an 'equal terms' bill. In this context the EFF does appear as a purely tactical device. Undoubtedly for Mrs Fawcett and others it never represented more than a temporary expedient to be abandoned as soon as the desired legislation was safely on the statute book. However, a strategy of this kind gathers a momentum of its own, especially if it coincides with the mood of the rank and file on each side. By 1913 fundamental cracks were opening up in the Liberal Party over the suffrage question. During the last two years of peace the Women's Liberal Federation was losing thousands of members as a result of the impasse, and Liberal women workers were adopting a non-co-operation policy towards unsatisfactory Liberal candidates.[32] The NUWSS adhered to its promise to avoid opposing tried friends in only one case, that of Stanley Buckmaster, the Liberal candidate at Keighley. It opposed Liberal suffragists at both Houghton-le-Spring and North West Durham. By April 1913 plans were being laid with the Labour chief agent, Arthur Peters, for a joint general election campaign involving initial registration work under the EFF followed by the adoption of new candidates.[33] Agreements had been concluded to assist twenty-five sitting members most in need, and many prime targets had been identified among Liberal anti-suffragists, notably McKenna (North Monmouth), Hobhouse (East Bristol), Harcourt (Rossendale) and Pease (Rotherham). As a result joint Labour-suffragist committees sprang up in these constituencies regardless of the apprehensions of those at party headquarters.[34] As Catherine Marshall recognised, these developments could not easily be halted even if a sudden change in the Prime Minister's position occurred. If the EFF was crystallising into a wider alliance with Labour than originally contemplated this was probably unavoidable, for 'there is nothing to hope for from the Liberal Party, even when Home Rule and Welsh Disestablishment are out of the way'.[35]

During the last two years of peace all the indicators suggest a steady convergence of the Labour and moderate suffragist forces. In 1913 the TUC rallied behind the party's line on franchise legislation. The NUWSS built on the sympathy engendered by its electoral work by enrolling some 46,000 working-class men and women as Friends of Women's Suffrage by August 1914. At the same time the predictions made by Brailsford in 1912 about the middle-class movement were beginning to come true:

The Liberal women are in the midst of a split, and all the more active of them are preparing to back our plan. Indeed, I am sure that the whole suffrage movement, excluding the inner ring of the WSPU, would have come into it, if the Labour Party had cared to take it . . . . I believe that in the course of a fighting alliance most of them would end by becoming decided and permanent adherents of the Labour Party.[36]

The significant thing is that although the first world war diminished interest in the vote for a time, it pushed the process outlined by Brailsford further and faster ahead. In undermining the faith of many radical Liberals in their party it exacerbated the existing divisions within Edwardian Liberalism. Even the NUWSS rapidly split three ways over the war. The most anti-war faction led by Helena Swanwick, Isabella Ford and the former Liberal, Ethel Williams, quit and joined the Union of Democratic Control, while a more moderate group including Marshall and Margaret Ashton recoiled from Mrs Fawcett's pro-war stance and subsequently became involved in the No Conscription Fellowship. By such routes many of the women activists who had drifted away from Liberal loyalties over the years gravitated to Labour after 1918 in the belief that it had become the better vehicle for the radical tradition in British politics.

NOTES

1. L. Middleton (ed.), Women in the Labour Movement (Croom Helm, London, 1977).
2. See B. Harrison, Separate Spheres: the Opposition to Women's Suffrage in Britain (Croom Helm, London, 1978), pp.28-9.
3. R. Blatchford, Some Words to Socialist Women (Social Democratic Federation, London, n.d.), p.3.
4. L.Thompson, The Enthusiasts: a Biography of John and Katherine Bruce Glasier (Gollancz, London, 1971), p.136.
5. J.Ramsay MacDonald to Kathleen Bruce Glasier (copy), 4 Apr. 1914. MacDonald Papers. PRO/30/69/5.
6. Ibid.
7. Quoted in Sandra Holton, 'Feminism and Democracy: the Women's Suffrage Movement in Britain with particular reference to the NUWSS 1897-1918', p.25, unpublished Stirling Ph.D. thesis, 1980.
8. D. Howell, British Workers and the Independent Labour Party 1888-1906 (Manchester, University Press, 1983).
9. Mrs Simm reporting on Gateshead for the Women's Labour League, WLL/1/93. Labour Party Archives.
10. P. Snowden, An Autobiography (2 vols., Nicholson and Watson, London, 1934), vol.I p.279.
11. See N.C. Soldon, Women in British Trade

Unions 1874-1976 (Gill and Macmillan, Dublin, 1978), p.49. By 1904 there were 126,000 women trade unionists of whom 111,000 were in textiles.

12. Ibid, pp.74-5.

13. J.Liddington and J.Norris, One Hand Tied Behind Us: the Rise of the Women's Suffrage Movement (Virago, London, 1979), pp.193, 205, 219.

14. WLL/1/89.

15. M. L. Davies (ed.), Life As We Have Known It By Co-operative Working Women (1931; Virago Reprint, London, 1977), p.48.

16. WLL/1/46, Report on Barrow, 1907.

17. WLL/2/164.

18. Liddington, One Hand Tied Behind Us, pp.211-30.

19. Labour Party, Annual Report, 26 Jan. 1905.

20. See Balfour's correspondence with Christabel Pankhurst, 6 Oct. 1907; 23 Oct. 1907; 28 Oct. 1907; 16 Dec. 1907; 1 Jan. 1910; 14 June 1910. Balfour Papers. BL. Add. MSS 49793.

21. Labour Party, Annual Report, 26 Jan. 1905.

22. Discussed in C. Rover, Women's Suffrage and Party Politics in Britain 1866-1914 (Routledge, Kegan Paul, London, 1967), pp.182-4.

23. NEC Minutes, 15 Oct. 1912. Labour Party Archives.

24. Catherine Marshall Papers, D/MAR/3/33; see also D/MAR/7/8. Cumbria Record Office.

25. Catherine Marshall Papers, Bow and Bromley folder, D/MAR/3/53.

26. Andrew Rosen, Rise Up Women! the Militant Campaign of the Women's Social and Political Union 1903-14 (Routledge, Kegan Paul, London, 1974), p.180.

27. Kathleen Courtney to Henderson, 23 Apr. 1912. Labour Party Archives, Labour Party WOM/12/4. Report of the NUWSS Special Council, 16 May 1912; Marshall to Henderson (copy), 14 Oct. 1912. For a full account see Leslie Parker Hume, The National Union of Women's Suffrage Societies 1897-1914 (Garland, New York, 1982), pp.143-191.

28. Miss A.M. Dowson to Miss Crookenden, 13 June 1913; Alice Percy to Miss Crookenden, 23 May, 1914, Marshall Papers.

29. NEC Minutes, 2 July 1912.

30. Assistant Secretary to Miss Palliser, 22 May 1912. Labour Party Archives, Labour Party WOM/12.

31. Hanley; Crewe (lost); Holmfirth; Midlothian (lost); Houghton; South Lanark (lost); NW Durham; Leith Burghs (lost).

32. Membership - 133,000 in 1912; 121,000 in 1913; 106,000 in 1915. Eleanor Rathbone to Catherine Marshall, 23 May 1912, Marshall Papers. Cumbria Records Office.

33. Catherine Marshall to Eleanor Acland (copy), 25 Apr. 1913; EFF Council Meeting Report 1914. Ibid.

34. EFF Council Meeting Report, 12 July 1912.

35. Catherine Marshall to Eleanor Acland (draft), 4 Nov. 1913.

36. H.N. Brailsford to Arthur Henderson, 4 May 1912. Labour Party Archives, Labour Party WOM/12/14.

Chapter Eleven

LABOUR AND IRELAND

Ever since the 'Hawarden Kite' of December
1885 the Liberal Party had been viewed as the
friend of Ireland. The Irish National League and
the United Irish League were the means of rallying
nationalist support in Ireland and Britain, and in
the latter country the emigrant vote was directed,
without fail, to the Liberals. The arrival of
working class candidates, or candidates poaching
specifically for the labouring vote, upset the
earlier neat arrangement. Some of these new
candidates were Irish, or of Irish descent; many of
the Irish voters worked in poor surroundings and
could identify with the new programme. At the same
time Irish Catholics often found the socialism of
these candidates distasteful, or believed that
voting for a worker would only give the seat to the
Tories. Torn between the claims of class
solidarity and the national question the leaders of
the Irish community supported the Liberals.[1] Up
until the establishment of the ILP in 1893 the
battle for the Irish vote was not keen. Labour's
early hopes were often dashed. Hardie angrily
asked the Irish electors of West Ham South in 1895,
'So you say that it is a case of Home Rule first?
I can understand an Irishman in Connememara saying
that but here in West Ham it is Labour first'.[2]
Despite having James Sexton, Tom McCarthy and Pete
Curran, who began their political careers in the
Nationalist movement, as candidates, the ILP failed
to get the Irish vote. One Irishman explained the
situation thus: 'We had not one word to say against
the Labour party . . . but the Labour party was
still young and all it could do at the moment was
to transfer seats to the Tories'.[3]
By the turn of the century however the
situation had changed somewhat. The Liberals under

Rosebery were becoming increasingly imperialistic, while the formation of the LRC in 1900 meant that Labour was able to fight more effectively. Labour candidates got Irish support in a number of by-elections and in 1906 Hardie was hopeful of Irish support in Leeds where 'the Irish vote will be cast solidly for LRC candidates as Redmond is bent on a war of extermination against Roseberyian candidates'.[4] Irish speakers in Britain, after stressing that to be effective the Irish vote must be united, seemed to be veering towards Labour. J.G. Swift MacNeill said in Stockport that 'when the choice lies between a Labour and Liberal member, and the Labour member has a chance of election, the Irish vote should be recorded for him'.[5] Redmond uttered the same sentiments in Glasgow. 'Wherever it is possible, the Irish electors ought to give preference to the Labour candidate'. He hoped Labour would greatly increase its representation in the new Parliament.[6] The UIL manifesto had good news for Labour also. It believed that 'a great opportunity now seems to offer itself to increase the representation of British Labour in the House of Commons'. It urged the Irish voters in all cases 'where a Labour candidate who is sound on Home Rule is in the field, to give their vote to that candidate'. Since all Labour men were Home Rulers it appeared they had obtained the Irish vote, but two conditions were attached. Where Labour was 'standing against an old and tried friend of the Irish cause', or where the support of the Labour candidate would ensure the return of the Unionist candidate, the vote was not to be given to Labour. These two qualifications meant that a Labour man in a three-cornered contest would not receive the Irish mandate unless the Liberal was a Roseberyite.[7] The Labour Leader claimed the Irish had 'made the claims of the Labour candidate subordinate to the interests of Liberals', and were 'only supporting the Labour man because he was punishing some anti-Home Rule Liberal of a par- ticularly obnoxious type'.[8] In the event the destination of the Irish vote in the 1906 election was of only slight importance as the Liberals were returned with a massive majority and Home Rule failed to materialise as a major election issue. Labour's performance was probably most disap- pointing in Scotland where twelve candidates polled almost 34,000 votes, but only two were elected. The 1903 Gladstone-MacDonald pact did not apply to

Scotland which was a factor in this. So also was the prevalence of sectarianism which saw workers attacking each other 'so that the true religion (and the contractor) might flourish'.[9] The Irish were often the victims in these clashes, and in their ghettos tended to be directed to a large extent by the priest, who despite reservations about their educational policies, preferred the Liberals to the strident socialism of the Labour men. Labour's two Scottish wins were Blackfriars (Glasgow) where Barnes triumphed, and Dundee where Wilkie was elected. The Irish vote had helped Barnes to his 310 vote victory over Bonar Law, but Wilkie was elected 'without conspicuous help from the Irish'.[10] The Irish vote in Camlachie, Govan and Lanark North East was given to Burgess, Murray and Sullivan, the Labour candidates. Here the Unionists made three gains, but it was not suggested that the Irish switch from the Liberals was solely responsible for the change. Because of the electoral pact there were few triangular contests in England and Wales, and Labour won only four seats against Liberal opposition. In South West Ham the substantial Irish vote went to Will Thorne, while in Newcastle upon Tyne the Irish voters agreed to split the vote between the Liberal and Labour candidates, with two candidates for two seats. Labour's F. Rose (Stockton), F. Jowett (Bradford West) and J. O'Grady (Leeds East) got the Irish vote, and while the two latter were elected, Stockton passed to the Tories from the Liberals. Irishmen J.R. Clynes and Stephen Walsh got the Irish vote and were elected, but the Liberal rather than Pete Curran got the Irish support in Jarrow. Hyndman was opposed at Burnley, but at Deptford where Bowerman was one of Labour's triangular winners and where it appeared the local Irish were not too enthusiastic, T.P. O'Connor wired his support, 'You have the full support of the Irish party and organisation'.[11] Irish leaders helped anti-Tory candidates, with Davitt addressing nineteen Labour meetings, finishing in Leeds, and T.P. O'Connor addressing up to five meetings nightly in favour of Liberal and Labour candidates. In the 1906 general election, therefore, Irish voters supported the Home Ruler most likely to win. Unfortunately for Labour, the Liberal candidate was often a better bet. The <u>Freeman</u> accepted that 'Labour has a good deal to complain of in the way it has been treated in the allotment of seats', but found it hard to understand 'on what principles the ILP proceeds in the choice of seats to be contested'.[12] Despite the frequently admitted justification of Labour's demands, it is clear that the Irish, placing Home Rule in the primary position, wanted the return of a strong Liberal ministry.

When the extent of the Liberal victory made them independent of the Irish votes, the Irish party organisation was less inclined to give full support to Liberal candidates in early by-elections. At the same time, Labour could not be trusted either on the education question, the most pressing Irish issue after Home Rule. Not surprisingly therefore, no official advice was given to the Irish voters in the Cockermouth and Huddersfield by-elections late in 1906. It was believed that in both cases the Irish vote assisted the Unionist candidates. In the remaining by-elections before 1910 Irish involvment was slight. The one notable exception was the Jarrow by-election in July 1907. At the general election the Liberals had defeated Irishman and socialist, Pete Curran. Now the Unionists intervened, as did the Irish, running J. O'Hanlon of Wallsend. The Labour Leader reported that 'the relationship between the Irish Nationalist and the Labour party has hitherto been difficult enough in British constituencies, the new policy will make it harder than ever'.[13] Curran won and O'Hanlon finished last behind the Liberal. O'Hanlon's vote of 2,122 was about the estimated Irish vote, but Irish leaders would not accept that any missing votes had gone to Curran. The Freeman chose to emphasise the fact that a majority of the voters were for Home Rule.[14] Jarrow was a severe demonstration of the tension among Irish voters between the demands of a Liberal ministry engaged in other social reforms and a Labour Party sound on Home Rule but unable to deliver. The dilemma would reappear in 1910.

The 1906 general election returned a strong Irish Party, a vast Liberal majority and a small Labour presence, all in varying degrees favourable to Home Rule. The Irish issue was not dealt with during the first year of the new Parliament, as it became clear that among the Liberals, the old Gladstonian enthusiasm for Home Rule was no more. When the Irish Council Bill was introduced in 1907, Shackleton reminded the House that Labour members were 'certainly strong Home Rulers before we were ever constituted as a separate party', and as such they 'should have been better pleased this

afternoon if we had been listening to a Home Rule
speech'. He regretted that the Liberals had lost
their old democratic spirit, argued that 'self-
government for Ireland will have to come some day',
and believed that 'the longer it is delayed the
more will have to be paid'. He accepted the
measure as a step in the right direction and
pledged the Labour Party's support for any efforts
the Irish would make 'to extend the measure in the
direction of giving greater power to Irishmen to
administer the affairs of their own country'.[15]
The government withdrew the measure in face of
Irish opposition. When the Irish Party moved an
amendment to the address in 1908, raising Irish
self-government, Labour tendered 'their wholehearted sympathy and support'. Barnes stated that
'British rule had proved itself to be alien to the
spirit of the Irish people, and contrary to their
wishes, and that was sufficient to condemn it'. In
his summary he declared that he was in favour of
Home Rule because the Irish were entitled to it,
British rule was not working, and he had long been
in favour of general devolution.[16] For the
remainder of that Parliament Home Rule faded into
the background.

By 1909 it became clear that a general
election could not be long delayed and the Liberals
and Labour resumed their canvass of the Irish
voters. As the 1910 election approached, the
Freeman and probably the Irish and Liberal parliamentarians hoped that triangular contests would be
at a minimum. The Freeman rejoiced to see
'evidence of Liberal and Labour agreements', but
its joy was premature.[17] Hardie was resolute.
'As regards three cornered fights, so far as we are
concerned, they are all to go on'.[18] Asquith
had made a powerful bid for the Irish vote in
Britain and more importantly for Irish support in
the next Parliament in his Albert Hall speech on
10 December 1909, when he pledged himself to grant
Home Rule to Ireland. The National Directory of
the Irish Party shortly afterwards announced its
support for the anti-Tory candidate most likely to
win. After the election the Freeman reported that
ninety nine per cent of the Irish had followed this
advice, though it did admit that 'in Scotland there
was at first some disappointment that the Standing
Committee did not see their way to supporting the
Labour candidate in some of the constituencies'.
It argued however that the large Liberal majority
over Labour 'proved that votes given to the Labour

men would have been thrown away and would have
resulted in the seats being handed over to the
Tories'.[19] The Liberals were even more
acceptable than in 1906 since the party was now
pledged to Home Rule. At the same time however,
where a Labour man was the only anti-Tory candidate
or the outgoing member he could expect Irish
support. In Denbeigh Burghs where Edwards (Labour)
failed by only eight votes to get elected, a United
Irish League delegation from outside the constituency had come to canvass for him. Blewett has
shown that the Labour Party was more vocal on Home
Rule than the Liberals, seventy per cent of its
candidates treating of it in their addresses as
against thirty-nine per cent of Liberals.[20]
Indeed one quarter of Liberal addresses mentioned
it only to oppose it, to support some measure of
devolution unlikely to be acceptable to the Irish,
or to promise complicated and distant plans for
Home Rule all round. On the other hand Labour's
enthusiasm 'was not solely the result of principle. It arose partly because the majority of
Labour candidates stood in constituencies with a
significant Irish vote'.[21] As the election
approached Redmond advised the Irish to back the
anti-Tory candidate most likely to win. He was
impartial between Liberal and Labour claims, 'but
there was one type of Labour candidate which they
always refused to adopt, and that was the hopeless
and the wrecking one'.[22] In every triangular
contest in Scotland the Irish vote was ordered
behind the Liberals.[23] In England the Irish vote
was instructed for Labour in only two triangular
contests - at Gateshead where a sitting Labour
man was being opposed by a Liberal, and at
Middlesbrough where the Labour candidate, Patrick
Walls, was a Catholic and a strong defender of the
Catholic schools. At Camlachie, the Irish vote
went to the Liberal contender, an ex-Unionist MP,
even though the Labour candidate was strong on Home
Rule. Labour was dismayed at such behaviour. At
the 1910 party conference Hardie complained that
the Irish vote was being directed 'by rule of thumb
and without regard being taken to the actual facts
or circumstances of the local situation'. He felt
that the Irish leaders were 'using their power to
bludgeon down Labour candidates', but he was
convinced that the Irish working-class would soon
ignore its leaders' directives.[24] Of the
twenty-one by-elections between January and
December 1910, only ten were contested and no

change occurred in the party representation. The manifesto of the UIL to the Irish voters for the December general election stated the 'issue at this election is between a party which works for the self-government and the reconciliation of Ireland and a party which has nothing but a message of hate and despair for Ireland'.[25] In the aftermath of Asquith's speech at the Albert Hall and Lloyd George's declaration at Mile End, both in favour of Home Rule, it seemed to the Irish leadership that the fight was between two parties. The Labour Party, by implication at least, was treated as a section of the Liberal Party. As in January, the Liberals were the chief recipients of the Irish vote. Although opinions about the impact of the Irish vote varied, it appears that until after the war 'the Irish vote was almost invariably thrown behind the Liberal party'.[26] An Irish National League leaflet, in a series of questions and answers, dealt with this problem of Liberals and Labour contending for the Irish vote. 'In the Liberal party Irishmen recognised the party of progress . . . . A Labour candidate who is not also a Liberal, weakens the Liberal party and gives the advantage to the Tories'. Accepting Labour's right to organise it urged that the party 'should take care that the result of their efforts should not be to strengthen the Tories, and so delay the march of progress'.[27] In practice, if not in theory, the Labour Party was seen as the radical wing of the Liberal Party.

Middlemas has noted a 'steady swing of the Irish vote from Liberal to Labour after 1910', but the absence of a general election meant that any switch took place at local elections, as evidenced by Wheatley's election to the Glasgow City Council in 1912.[28] Local rather than national issues may have been predominant in any such change of allegiance. Only the 1918 general election would give a reliable guide to Irish voting patterns. By then of course the politics of both Britain and Ireland would have undergone a profound change.

The period 1910-14 saw much discussion of the government's Home Rule proposals in Parliament and Labour members contributed extensively. They claimed that they were Home Rulers of long standing and that their manifestos had always dealt with this question in detail. Walsh reminded members that 'in 1906, although I have not a large Irish electorate at all, I placed Home Rule for Ireland in the very centre of my programme, I did the same in January 1910 and I took a similar course in December last'.[29] Parker, Sutton and Barnes spoke in similar terms. Hudson, Clynes and Goldstone denied Tory claims that the 1910 elections did not give a mandate for Home Rule. Members also supported Home Rule because they believed that the alternative, continued British rule, would be a costly failure. Barnes related how he had visited Ireland to acquaint himself with the situation and 'the conclusion I have arrived at was that the Irish people could govern themselves a great deal cheaper than we misgovern them'.[30] Home Rule was supported because it would prove beneficial to Britain. Firstly, there would be more parliamentary time available once the Irish question was out of the way. Parker noted that 'Irish questions do take up a very large proportion of the time of this House'.[31] Sutton agreed, arguing that 'so long as Home Rule is being discussed here year after year, questions of social reform affecting the interests of the workers are constantly being neglected'.[32] MacDonald supported the bill for a different reason, because 'the whole of our Empire is based upon self-government'.[33] James Parker added that 'you will not have real unity worthy of the name until you give each nation inside the United Kingdom the power to govern itself according to the wishes of its people'.[34] O'Grady denied that Home Rule would lead to separation, and Parker believed that 'all this talk about separation is very largely a bogey'.[35] Rather than Home Rule spelling the end of the empire, he argued, 'the British empire is based upon a foundation of self-governing states, and it cannot exist without that basis'.[36] MacDonald had a third reason, relating exclusively to domestic British politics, for supporting Home Rule. Once it was granted, the Irish in Britain would be free to vote along class lines. 'I want to see the Irish labourer released, knowing that his country is safe so far as his nationality is concerned, to use his political influence in order to improve his social condition here'.[37] MacDonald also supported Home Rule because, as an example of Britain's justice to Ireland, it would improve the international status of the former. Up until that point 'when we try to influence other nations in the world responsible for the government of subject races, over and over again our conduct to Ireland has been thrown in our faces and numbed and paralysed our moral enthusiasm'.[38] Many

Labour members argued that the granting of Home
Rule to Ireland would end existing religious,
economic and political differences and lead to new
national unity. Thus Parker voted for Home Rule
because 'traditional divisions will end when the
Irish parliament is set up'.[39] Barnes took a
similar line, expressing his conviction that
self-government 'will heal a long, open and
weakening sore in the body politic'.[40] Haslam
believed 'the religious hatred and bigotry will
soon be a relic of the past'.[41] Hudson felt that
'the whole face of Irish politics will undergo a
change'.[42] Gill assumed that the change would be
'the representatives of industrial Ireland dividing
themselves into parties as in this house'.[43]
Although they believed that Home Rule would heal
many of the divisions in Ireland, Labour members
had to face the reality of Ulster's unwillingness
to become part of an independent Ireland. While
admitting to the problem, they did not accept
Ulster's claim to special treatment. Unionists did
not represent a majority. They only represented
the 'ascendancy interest'. The Unionist cause had
no basis in reality. They 'were living largely in
the memory of the past', and appealing to people's
fears. Labour denied Unionists' claims to be loyal
to the British constitution. Their loyalty was
conditional, constitutionalism was no longer their
doctrine. Labour members attempted to show that
Ulster fears were groundless. Belfast's economy
would not suffer under Home Rule. The workers' lot
would improve. A Dublin Parliament would not be
anti-protestant.[44] A neat summary of Labour's
attitude to Home Rule is provided by Goldstone:

> The Labour members will support this bill
> first, because they believe in the principle
> of Home Rule. They will support it because
> they are voicing, in some instances - and I am
> one - the wishes of as many Irishmen in their
> constituencies as are spoken for by some of
> the honorary members on the Irish benches, and
> we shall support it too, not only from
> conviction, not only because we have a mandate
> from a large number of Irishmen who believe in
> it in our own constituencies, but because it
> will serve to clear the way and make possible
> some of those further reforms on which we have
> set our hearts.[45]

Labour members were outraged when opposition to

Liberal plans for Ireland surfaced among British army officers in the so-called Curragh 'mutiny' of March 1914. Clynes accused the Unionists of joining 'the Syndicalists to the British army'.[46] J.H. Thomas argued that freedom had been interfered with.[47] MacDonald said that the officers would not coerce Ulster 'but they are perfectly willing to coerce this government,' and he warned the Tories that disobedience in Ulster would have effects elsewhere - 'you cannot say one thing regarding Ulster, and a different thing regarding Lancashire'.[48] Labour members also questioned the government about Ulster's preparations to oppose Home Rule and when violence in the shipyards was at its height, met a delegation from Belfast, representing the expelled workers and obtained for them a meeting with Birrell.[49] Late in July 1914 the King held a conference of Irish, Liberal, Tory and Ulster leaders to attempt to break the impasse. This afforded the Labour Party its last opportunity to speak on Home Rule before the outbreak of war in August. The move was viewed as 'an undue interference on the part of the crown and calculated to defeat the purpose of the parliament act'.[50] Three days after its start, the conference collapsed. A week later the first world war broke out, effectively removing the future nature of Anglo-Irish relations and the problem of Ulster from the forefront of the British political scene.

Addressing the 1905 ILP conference Philip Snowden had promised Labour's support for Home Rule, affirming that 'the Irish party will receive the wholehearted support of the Labour party in their efforts to compel the concessions of a full and complete parliament'.[51] The exhaustive parliamentary debates gave Labour many opportunities to repeat this commitment. In two respects however, the party displayed differences of opinions - was the Home Rule bill the beginning or end of Irish demands?; and what was to be done in face of Ulster's intransigence? There were those who thought that Home Rule would strengthen the empire, but others argued that 'the more we separate Ireland from England the better for both'.[52] Barnes believed that Britain would retain control in imperial affairs but Parker argued that 'this bill is not final. If it worked well, the Commons will probably give extra powers later'.[53] This difference in emphasis, relatively minor in importance in 1914, would appear more pronounced at the turn of the decade, as Home Rule, Gladstonian-style, became irrelevant to the Irish situation. As regards Ulster, Labour argued that Unionist fears were unfounded but the party was forced to accept the situation and unenthusiastically agreed to amendments. Labour failed, however, to take any decisive action over the incidents of sectarianism, and in the entire situation chose to blame the Tories, wealthy capitalists duping sweated workers by means of out-dated slogans. But if Belfast sectarianism had such a facile explanation, it is amazing that Labour did not take practical steps to woo the Belfast workers, to realise the oft-promised, much-desired, new political alignment along class lines. Labour's hopes that Home Rule would lead to a new political game in Ireland, with modern, civilised, British-style rules were completely unrealistic. Like the Liberals, Labour was powerless in the face of Ulster's threats, and the party's approach to the 1912-14 Ulster problem foreshadowed its handling of the post-war situation, arguing on the one hand that Ulster fears were groundless but promising on the other that there would be no coercion. Indeed in 1905 and 1907 the Labour Party contested elections in Belfast and compromised on its Home Rule stance.[54] MacDonald assured the voters that the candidate, William Walker, would be free to vote as he pleased on the issue of Home Rule.[55] Hardie claimed that on questions 'outside labour such as Disestablishment, Home Rule and other kindred topics' each Labour member was free to vote as he pleased.[56] Tyson Wilson denied that the Labour Party was committed to Home Rule and Barnes went so far as to say that the people of England and Scotland believed Home Rule was unattainable.[57] Henderson spoke of preserving 'one unbroken imperial family' and restricting Home Rule to local matters.[58] British Labour not only faced Unionist opposition in Ireland to Home Rule, but also had a less than harmonious relationship with the Irish Labour Party and ICTU. The parliamentary committee of the latter body was often unhappy with its British counterparts' efforts to ensure proper labour representation under Home Rule, to oppose Ulster's exclusion, and to fight for proper drawing of constituencies. It also opposed Labour's close agreement with the Irish Party on individual details of the Act and reminded British Labour that 'we have fought them at the polls'.[59]

Labour and Ireland

From the earliest days of the British Labour
Party there had been cross-fertilization with
Ireland. Keir Hardie influenced and was influenced
by Michael Davitt; early Labour attempts at
separate political organization and action owed
something to Parnell's success; Glasier and the
Fabians visited Ireland, hoping to provide
solutions to Ireland's social problems; exiles like
James Connolly, Pete Curran and John Wheatley
engaged in pioneering socialist and Labour activity
in Britain, while retaining hopes for, and interest
in, the political and social well-being of their
homeland. The Irish Question re-emerged early in
the twentieth century in the wake of a Liberal
revival and a re-united Irish Party, the latter
facing the future with hope, much of the post-
Parnellite bitterness eradicated and the Land
Question settled.

The parliamentary Labour Party spoke
eloquently on the political and industrial
questions affecting Ireland at this time,
advocating Home Rule and industrial fair-play.
Many Irishmen, however, saw Labour only as the
radical tail of the Liberal Party. Labour
candidates often failed to get the exiles' vote
because of their desire to return a strong
reforming Liberal ministry. In Parliament, Labour
supported reform measures but was rarely in advance
of Liberal thinking. The Irish Party's close ties
with the Liberals and Labour's lack of members
would have doomed any advanced proposals. It was
not until after the wartime coalition, the coupon
election and the Anglo-Irish war, that Labour
appeared as the new friend of Ireland. It was not
until 1918 that Irish support was overwhelmingly
Labour's. By then an ill-defined but attractive
policy of 'self-determination' marked Labour as the
new party of reform.

NOTES

1. E.P.M. Wollaston, 'The Irish Nationalist
Movement in Great Britain 1886-1908', unpublished
MA thesis, University of London, 1958. H. Pelling,
Social Geography of British Elections (Macmillan,
London, 1967). M. Kinnear, The British Voter, An
Atlas and Survey since 1885 (Batsford, London,
1968).

2. K.O. Morgan, Keir Hardie (University
Press, Oxford, 1975), p.80.

3. Manchester Guardian, 11 July 1895.

265

4. Morgan, <u>Hardie</u> p.149.

5. <u>Freeman's Journal</u>, 10 Nov. 1905.

6. E.D. Steele, 'The Irish Presence in the North of England, 1850-1914', <u>Northern History</u>, vol. XII (1976), pp. 220-41.

7. Wollaston, 'The Irish Nationalist Movement', p.120.

8. <u>Labour Leader</u>, 5 Jan. 1906.

9. T. Johnston, <u>The History of the Working Classes in Scotland</u> (E.P. Publishing, Wakefield, 1974), p.336.

10. W.M. Walker, 'Irish Immigrants in Scotland, Their Priests, Politics and Parochial Life', <u>Historical Journal</u>, vol. XV, no. 4 (1972), p.663.

11. Wollaston, 'The Irish Nationalist Movement' p.193.

12. <u>Freeman's Journal</u>, 19 Jan. 1906.

13. <u>Labour Leader</u>, 14 June 1907.

14. <u>Freeman's Journal</u>, 6 July 1907.

15. <u>Hansard</u>, 4th Series. vol. CLXXIV, col. 128. 7 May 1907.

16. Ibid., vol. CLXXXVII, cols. 187-194. 30 Mar. 1908.

17. <u>Freeman's Journal</u>, 10 Dec. 1909.

18. Ibid., 18 Dec. 1909.

19. Ibid., 27 Jan. 1910.

20. N. Blewett, <u>The Peers, The Parties and The People - The British General Elections of 1910</u> (Macmillan, London, 1972), p.317.

21. Ibid., p.324.

22. <u>Manchester Guardian</u>, 24 Jan. 1910.

23. <u>Scotsman</u>, 13 Jan. 1910.

24. Labour Party, <u>Annual Report</u>, 1910, p.55.

25. <u>Freeman's Journal</u>, 23 Nov. 1910.

26. Wollaston, 'The Irish Nationalist Movement' p.120.

27. N.L.I., 300 p.12 (Item 58).

28. K. Middlemas, <u>The Clydesiders</u>, (Hutchinson, London, 1956) pp.39 and 46.

29. <u>Hansard</u>, 5th Series, vol. XXI, col. 1819. 21 Feb. 1911.

30. Ibid., vol. XXXIV, col. 356. 19 Feb. 1912.

31. Ibid., vol. XXXVII, col. 1789. 30 Apr. 1912.

32. Ibid., vol. LX, col. 1084. 31 Mar. 1914.

33. Ibid., vol. XXXVI, col. 1455. 11 Apr. 191.

34. Ibid., vol. XXXIV, col. 484. 19 Feb. 1912.

35. Ibid., vol. XXXVII, col. 1789. 30 Apr. 1912.

36. Ibid., vol. LIII, col. 1497. 10 June 1913.

37. Ibid., vol. XXXVI, col. 1457. 11 Apr. 1912.

38. Ibid., vol. XXXVIII, col. 639. 9 May 1912.

39. Ibid., vol. XXXVII, col. 1792. 30 Apr. 1912

40. Ibid., vol. XXXVIII, col. 129. 6 May 1912.

41. Ibid., vol. XXXXIV, col. 900. 25 Nov. 1912.

42. Ibid., vol. LV, col. 122. 7 June 1913.

43. Ibid., vol. XXXXII, col. 1866. 21 Oct. 1912.

44. Ibid., for treatment of Ulster see vols. XXXVII, XXXVIII, XXXXI, XXXXVI, LIII, LX.

45. Ibid., vol. LX, col. 1713. 6 Apr. 1914.

46. Ibid.

47. Ibid.

48. Ibid., col. 278. 25 Mar. 1914.

49. Freeman's Journal, 31 July 1912.

50. Labour Party, Annual Report, 1917, p.49.

51. ILP, Annual Report, 1905.

52. Hansard, 5th Series. vol. XXXXII, col. 1124. 15 Oct. 1912.

53. Ibid., vol. XXXXVI, col. 2195. 15 Jan. 1913.

54. J.W. Boyle, 'The rise of the Irish Labour movement, 1888-1907', unpublished PhD thesis, T.C.D. 1961, pp. 340-373.

55. Northern Whig, 7 Sept. 1905.

56. Ibid., 23 Mar. 1907.

57. Ibid., 6 Apr. 1907.

58. Ibid., 16 Apr. 1907.

59. Irish Labour Party and TUC, Annual Report, 1917, p.33.

Chapter Twelve

LABOUR AND FOREIGN AFFAIRS: A SEARCH FOR IDENTITY
AND POLICY

Bernard Shaw insisted that he had no time to
concern himself with foreign policy before 1914
because he was too much preoccupied with the Fabian
Society, working out a practical programme for
English socialists and establishing a parliamentary
Labour Party. For once, his attitudes and
priorities were typical. In the years before the
Great War, very few socialists took any interest in
foreign affairs. In a lecture to the Fabian
Society in 1913, the young Australian historian,
Marion Phillips,. noted that despite the growing
menace of the international scene, rank and file
Labour members seemed not a bit concerned. They
behaved as though it were enough to confine their
exertions to passing peace resolutions. Did they
not understand that constantly to reaffirm the
pious, pacific platitudes of others was no longer
sufficient? If international peace was to be
maintained and secured then socialists would have
to play a more positive part. They ought to
promote their own policies. The problem with this
advice was promptly pointed out by another Fabian
lecturer, R.C.K. Ensor. He doubted 'whether any
view of foreign policy could be so far deduced from
the principles of Socialism that only Socialists
could hold it.'[1]
    Although dignified by the name party, in the
pre-1914 Parliaments, Labour amounted to little
more than an outsize, provincial, pressure group.
It exerted little influence on the conduct of
foreign affairs. Nor was this surprising. The
stamina of Labour members at Westminster was
all but exhausted by two consuming interests:
the substantive problems of domestic policy and
the no less complex or intriguing procedural
riddles posed by parliamentary custom and etiquette.

Temperamentally unsympathetic towards the traditional objects of British foreign policy, with little time and even less energy or inclination to think originally and constructively, quite unable to agree upon any coherent, alternative policy of their own, when it came to foreign affairs most Labour MPs were obliged 'to borrow and to share the views traditional in Radical circles.'[2] In the circumstances, a crisis of identity was almost inevitable - a condition made more difficult to resolve because the Labour Party was an uneasy coalition of various groups that in almost every enterprise were more often competing than co-operative partners.

The largest, most important of the fractions that made up the Labour whole was the Independent Labour Party. Its views on international issues may most conveniently be garnered from the pages of Keir Hardie's weekly newspaper, the Labour Leader. Months often passed without any significant report or comment in its columns upon imperial or foreign concerns in its columns. When these subjects were considered, the commentators deployed a blend of moral and practical arguments. A pacifist idealism illumined a practical critique of the way in which Sir Edward Grey, the Liberal Foreign Secretary, was conducting the nation's overseas affairs. If one ignores the Marxist verbal trappings which constantly imply a canny, working class distrust and awareness of capitalist and royal intrigue, what is left of the Labour Leader's criticism differs not at all from that expressed more frequently and elegantly in radical Liberal journals or by radical MPs from the government's own back benches.[3] The radical weekly, Nation, under H.W. Massingham's sensitive editorship, never sought needlessly to damage Labour's amour propre, yet it could not discern any essential difference between the radical and Labour critiques of Grey. Perhaps more significantly, nor could the super-patriotic editors and writers of the Tory, yellow press. When defending Grey they altogether ignored Labour, concentrating their abuse instead upon Sir Edward's critics among the 'Potsdam pacifists' and the 'cheese-paring Cobdenite Radicals' of his own party. Regular, substantive criticism of the parliamentary Labour Party's views on foreign policy before 1914 was largely confined to the columns of the small socialist press. Among the best informed, entertaining and most perceptive was New Age, a literary and political weekly edited by

A.R. Orage.[4]   In the autumn of 1909, it published three successive articles bewailing Labour's 'disgraceful neglect' of foreign policy issues. The author considered that Labour MP's would 'remain ignorant and apathetic' because reliable information on foreign affairs was difficult to secure, they knew nothing about the Diplomatic Service and, given that the principles of the subject were admittedly obscure, their study would be too tedious and difficult for men who were so untouched by their baleful ignorance that they complacently abdicated their responsibilities to a few, self-designated, 'experts'.[5]

On foreign and imperial affairs Orage's weekly had no good opinion of the ILP and looked more kindly upon the interest displayed in those subjects by members of the Social Democratic Federation.   Even at the Federation's founding, Frederick Engels had noted that the strange, hybrid mixture of 'Comtists, Tories, middle class Radicals, MPs . . . and ancient Chartists combining internationalist phraseology with jingo aspirations', was likely to become a belligerent group.[6]   Frequently engaged in iternecine strife occasioned by a seemingly endless series of problems of secession and revision, in 1912 there emerged from this self-inflicted carnage, the British Socialist Party led by the still unbowed vieux terrible of British socialism, Henry Hyndman.   The party, like its predecessor, remained loyal in theory to the ideal of maintaining international peace.   But for professed internationalists, members demonstrated strangely parochial attitudes.   Hyndman was every bit as exuberantly patriotic as his friend, the ultra Tory, jingo editor and owner of the National Review, Leo Maxse.

Since the turn of the century, Hyndman, like another socialist warrior, Robert Blatchford (of the Clarion - sometimes the Daily Mail), had been plagued by thoughts of the possibly disastrous consequences for Britain of Wilhelmine Germany's pursuit of Weltmachtpolitik.[7]   Both men supposed that Kaiser Wilhelm's Neue Kurs would best be frustrated by building British Dreadnought battleships to excess - a thought they shared with the Tory Party and most senior Liberal ministers. Because they were constantly expecting the Kaiser's armed hordes to descend upon Britain's vulnerable shores, Hyndman and Blatchford demanded not only more battleships but also conscription for home defence, pitching their claims as loudly, frequently and consistently as Lord Roberts, Rudyard Kipling and other assorted extremists of the bellicose patriotic right. In the pages of innumerable magazines - and not least his own monthly journal, _Justice_ - Hyndman censured ILP criticism of his schemes as the 'ignorant, blind, emotional, pacifism' of those happy to share with 'Cobdenite Radicals the belief that the only proper object of diplomacy is trade'. In its turn, and encouraged by the Radical and pacifist press, Keir Hardie's _Labour Leader_ censured Hyndman and Blatchford for their 'disgraceful, dangerous, emotional junketing.'[8]

If the views of the BSP and the ILP are taken to represent the range of opinion on issues of naval, military, imperial and foreign policy held by Labour MPs before August 1914, it has to be remembered that the differences between individuals were usually much more complex than can be implied from the major policy objectives of organisation. Invariably there were considerable differences of opinion and emphasis between individual members of the same group. So also, quite different expectations were raised by opposition to or support for what, to the uninitiated, might seem the self-same measure. When a De Leonite Marxist member of the Socialist Labour Party talked about the general strike as an anti-war measure he did not mean at all the same thing as a member of the ILP. The opinions of leaders frequently differed from those of their followers. When meeting comrades from other countries at international conventions, British Labour leaders were inclined to over-emphasise their internationalist sympathies. Public statements - at home and abroad - usually owed more to the desire to satisfy the expectations of audiences than any undue straining after a consistent adherence to an earlier agreed policy. For a parliamentarian, the simple facts of political survival could impinge upon the most delicate conscience and convert the member for a constituency that contained a munitions factory from a supporter of armament retrenchment into an ardent advocate of increased and prodigal expenditure upon the army and navy.[9] For the party leader what was perceived as a 'national' interest sometimes had to take precedence over narrow, sectarian arguments. Opposition in the British parliamentary system implies its 'responsible' exercise. During the

1911 Agadir crisis, Ramsay MacDonald was criticised by some for adopting a stance contrary to agreed party policy when, in a speech to the Commons he indirectly warned the Germans that they should not assume that party divisions would weaken the spirit of national unity. What MacDonald's critics chose to ignore was that in the same crisis it was enough for a Liberal Chancellor of the Exchequer to mention the <u>possibility</u> of war with Germany for the railway workers to abandon their strike. As in 1914, so in 1911, an appeal to patriotism and national interest struck a more ready and sympathetic chord with trade unionists than any claim of class loyalty or international solidarity.[10]

Since the Boer War, when Radical Little Englanders had shared platforms, sentiment and rhetoric with Labour speakers, MPs from both groups were inclined to intone in unison, 'The peoples of the earth want peace. It is the governments of the earth that organise war'. <u>New Age</u> swiftly dismissed any such claim as 'sentimental drivel'. It was asbsurd for responsible politicians to suppose that the man in the street was other than 'all for bloody war, if only for the sake of sensation. The working classes are being misrepresented by their soi-disant leaders . . . . Quaker natured individuals, almost invariably of the upper middle class'. If anyone asked why the Labour Party in Parliament, as upon other public platforms, 'too often denied the evidence of its intellect and senses', the answer, <u>New Age</u> suggested, was 'because MPs are always glad to be petted and taken notice of'.[11]

It was frequently asserted by Labour supporters that, once elected to Westminster, their members allowed themselves to be 'taken in', to be neutered as effective advocates of political change by the blandishments of a cunning Establishment. In part such criticism was inspired by jealousy, envy and an over-fondness for conspiracy theories. But it also rested upon an understandable yet hopelessly unrealistic estimate of the influence that Labour possessed in the House. This last was the result of the euphoria generated by the sensational general election result of January 1906 which took a long time a-dying. One commentator, for example, seriously proposed that because the new Labour MPs had 'no selfish mercantile or capitalistic aims to hide under the sounding title of "patriotism"', and as they were as yet 'unspoiled by aristocratic patronage, society intrigue or the tyranny of capitalist pressure', they would inevitably exercise a considerable and benign influence upon the conduct of international affairs. When, instead, Labour MPs made no discernible impression, it was assumed that they had fallen victim to those same evil pressures and influences from which they had so recently been pronounced immune.[12] The disappointed as much as the outraged asked themselves what exactly was the strange Westminster alchemy that worked upon Labour MPs. What was it about the Commons that (with the exception of Victor Grayson) turned every visionary, every eloquent street-corner agitator, every voluble Marxist dialectician of the Socialist International into just another parliamentary sheep who when not dumb was seemingly content to bleat the well-worn Radical/Liberal litany? 'Why', asked one frustrated socialist supporter of his fellow-traveller Wilfed Scawen Blunt, 'do Labour members when they get into the House at once get bitten with the absurd idea that they are statesmen and then try and behave as such? I would rather that they came to the House in a body, drunk and tumbling about the floor'. Another, younger and less poetic critic, Edgar Jepson, supposed it no less than a mortal sin for Labour members to be intent upon cultivating 'gentlemanliness . . . . You do not behave nicely when you upset people; so the Labour Party no longer prods the fat-fed swine which snore on the front benches; it has grown far too gentlemanly to act in such an ill behaved manner'.[13] Simple-minded, rude and facile, such easy explanations convenienty ignored one extremely important reason why Labour exercised no influence. On foreign affairs it had no specific of its own to offer, no unique socialist anodyne to soothe away the fears, hatreds, passions, and hurts induced and suffered by a frightened world.

Because he had long and early recognised just how debilitating this was, Ramsay MacDonald frequently insisted that it was 'the Labour Party and the Labour Party alone that can make Europe sheathe the sword'.[14] How it was to do this he did not tell his audience for he could not without revealing his claim as a sham. Yet, it was to provide the answer to just this question that in January 1911, before its annual conference, the Labour Party held a special meeting on the problems of disarmament and international relations.

With virtually no dissent, this special meeting soon proposed and agreed two resolutions.

The first expressed the party's conviction that ever increasing armaments were a cause of war. The second urged the settlement of all international disputes by reason and arbitration. Neither resolution could claim to be a distinctive Labour nostrum. Both were long-familiar, well-advertised, Radical and pacifist remedies. It was Keir Hardie who proposed the adoption of a third resolution that encompassed the recommendation made the previous year by the International Socialist Congress at Copenhagen, but amended so as to support 'the investigation of the possibilities of a general strike as an anti-war weapon'.[15] Here was a different resolution from its two predecessors but it promoted nothing but uproar among the delegates. Mild, 'Uncle' Arthur Henderson, Secretary of the British Section of the International, whose socialist beliefs owed nothing to Karl Marx, little to the ILP and most to Methodism, led the opposition to Hardie's resolution. The general strike, so Henderson averred, was quite unacceptable as a weapon to be deployed by British Labour against war, for 'it would divert attention from parliamentary action'. This was the argument that eventually won the day. It particularly angered those critics who for long had complained that the parliamentary system was designed to make Labour an impotent Opposition force. Parliamentary debate was a waste of time, it was no more than a game 'innocuous as bridge for love at which all that can be lost is honour or temper - things that do not matter'. Such was the frustration Henderson induced by his arguments that in an editorial even a journal as mild and pacific as <u>Concord</u>, sounded an unusually impatient note and even the faintest hint of revolution: 'Rank and file workmen are getting tired of the ineffec-tiveness of the "elected person" on this subject, and will soon be ready to take the matter into their own hands'.[16]

In 1912, an emergency meeting of the International Socialist Congress reminded the Labour Party that as members they were required to state whether they thought it worthwhile and practical to organise a general strike against war. The Labour Party conference instituted its own enquiry. It never reached a conclusion! Despite the claims of critics even within his own party, it was never Hardie's intention to employ the general strike to foment mass revolution and insurrection. The intended limits of the exercise

were clearly demonstrated in a 1911 article by
W.C. Anderson in the Labour Leader. 'A few
sections of industry refusing to aid warlike
preparations' would be enough to check the
government's plans of mobilisation.[17] Whether
this could have been effective is another matter.
The contemporary arguments demonstrated the
ambivalence of attitude towards the role of the
worker held by British socialist leaders that was
to be debilitating both in the immediate August
1914 crisis and subsequently throughout the war.
On narrower grounds, long before 1914, it was
apparent that the strategy of a general strike had
inherent weaknesses, not least the requirement that
socialists in different countries should act in
unison. If war between Germany and Britain was the
most likely and most dreaded possibility, it was
inconvenient, to say the least, that for years
Bebel had made it very clear that there were
circumstances in which German Social Democrats
would not hesitate to fight for Germany. Hardie,
and those in the British labour movement who
thought like him, chose to ignore Bebel's
uncomfortably pugnacious sentiments and confidently
asserted the general strike would succeed in
stopping war, for all workers were pacific and
would reject any call to arms by their government
resting on an appeal to patriotism or national
interest. Worker would never again kill worker.
Such faith was burnished and maintained by its
acolytes insulating themselves from general working
class opinion, by association with like-minded
pacifists and by preaching to the converted. Noble
if not wise, Keir Hardie was cruelly and swiftly
disabused of his illusion in August 1914.[18]

It was because they were all too aware that
their views on foreign policy and related military
and naval issues were remarkably little ·different
from those held by Radical members of the Liberal
Party that Labour's parliamentary spokesmen sought
every opportunity to denigrate those who, on so
many issues, were their natural allies. The
quarrels over the 1909 naval estimates provide many
examples. In an unguarded moment the Lib-Lab MP,
John Ward, exclaimed that the Liberal government
was 'the wisest, the most progressive with which
this country has so far been blessed'. This earned
Ward a dreadful wigging from the Labour Leader.
Did he not realise that 'Liberalism is moribund'?
What sense did his claims make when Liberals were
'prepared to sacrifice old age pensions for extra

unwanted battleships . . . eight monstrous steel obsolescences'? It was in the Commons debate on the naval estimates that Arthur Henderson made one of the two most effective speeches against ministerial policy. Yet he spent much of his time and invective upon those Radical MPs who had been 'frightened out of their wits by the opinions of their own front bench that are based, not upon irrefutable evidence but assumption and suspicion'. The irony was that in the rest of his speech Henderson employed 'not Socialist but Liberal ideas on retrenchment'. New Age cruelly but accurately concluded that, 'On every vital issue the Labour Party with the regularity of the tail follows the Liberal dog in its most extreme peregrinations'.[19] Likewise, in debates on the army, although they more readily than Radicals coupled 'military topics with the evils of financial speculation . . . the blood taxes of evil financiers', for the rest, Labour MPs, when they chose to speak at all, adopted the same senti-mental, simplistic, anti-militarist line. They made no attempt to 'think for themselves about the problems involved . . . . Too many of them write and speak as if the question was not worth considering or use language implying that the country could safely be left without any means of defence'.[20] In debates on foreign affairs, when they censured Grey's entente policy - and particularly the 1907 Anglo-Russian Convention - their opposition was certainly noisier than that of the Radical Liberals, but it was otherwise different only in that Labour MPs were always less ready to forgive Grey. In his private correspondence and by his public manner, the Foreign Secretary was angry yet dismissive of 'Keir Hardie & Co'. They were 'dram drinkers . . . people who do not want to know the truth . . . but to express their own emotions . . . . When you attempt to dilute their emotions with the truth they are as a drunkard whose whisky you dilute with water'.[21] Labour frequently asserted that in Parliament it exercised 'a formidable, independent influence'. The hollowness of that claim con-cerning foreign affairs was conclusively demonstrated in the spring and summer of 1907 when Grey totally ignored its opposition as he brought his Anglo-Russian agreement to the desired conclusion. It is a nice paradox that the diplomat, George Young, who entirely approved of the anti-Russian campaign, should have supposed that he paid Labour members a compliment when he described them as 'voicing the best traditions of Liberal foreign policy'.[22]

The campaign against Grey's Russian policy repays more detailed examination, for it clearly reveals the full range of weaknesses that made Labour MPs so ineffectual as critics. Their views on the subject of Russia, as on much else in foreign affairs, were generally ill-informed and sentimental. They invested the Russian Parliament, the Duma, with a significance in Russian affairs that it did not begin to merit.[23] They were always over-reacting to events, one minute plunged into hopeless pessimism and the next, impossibly optimistic. This was never better demonstrated than in their exaggerated response to Sir Henry Campbell-Bannerman's 'vive la Douma' speech.[24] Their arguments and rhetoric failed to capture the conscience of the British public. Labour MPs claimed otherwise but the public remained indifferent about Russia's internal problems and was, if possible, even less caring that the British government, by seeking an agreement with that country, was 'countenancing despotism' or 'preparing to purchase a diplomatic advantage at the price of the soul of a people'.[25] Possible public sympathy and support that might otherwise have existed was alienated by the emotional imbalance of so much Labour invective, or the violence occasioned by the public demonstrations, such as that organised in Trafalgar Square by the Friends of Russian Freedom on Bastille Day, 14 July 1907.[26]

In the Commons, the ignorance and inexperience of Labour members, when combined with Grey's supreme capacity for vagueness and circumlocution, defeated all attempts to expose, hinder or reform the Foreign Secretary's policies. Even when, in time, Labour MPs grew more skilled at the parliamentary game and learned to employ question time to their advantage, they were usually frustrated by the rulings of the Speaker. And when their sniping campaign was eventually rewarded with a full-scale debate on the Foreign Office vote, Grey routed them. Apparently incapable of sustaining a worthwhile and convincing argument, his Labour critics were reduced to the repetition of tired slogans and catch-phrases. G.H. Perris, although a sympathetic commentator, for he had joined the ILP specifically because it had campaigned more vigorously than had the Radical

Liberals against Grey's Russian policy, noted how very easily the Foreign Secretary defeated his Labour critics. His 'cold, detached, gracefully arrogant manner was exactly calculated to impress weak minds. Labour men were thrown on the defensive when the Foreign Secretary should have been defending his own actions'. In the division lobby less than sixty MPs mustered to vote against Grey - a mixture of Irish and Radical MPs with some, but not every Labour member.[27] It was not until the final crisis of July 1914 that Labour critics concentrated their censures upon the anti-German inspiration behind Grey's Russian policy which, from the beginning had been its true raison d'être.[28]

On the central diplomatic issue of the period, Anglo-German relations, when not borrowing Radical ideas and rhetoric, Labour members were busy insisting that Radicalism was a 'spent force' and that they and not the Radicals were leading the campaign against Sir Edward and his policies. But Keir Hardie rather gave the game away when he censured Grey's policies as 'an offence to the Liberal tradition'.[29] Labour speakers and writers claimed that Radicals had 'ceased to count since the death of Sir Charles Dilke'. They were 'leaderless, timid and ineffective'.[30] Yet it was a theory promulgated by a prominent Radical MP, Arthur Ponsonby, and designed to explain exactly why the conduct of foreign policy had gone so sadly wrong under a Liberal government, that Labour members advertised as their own. They agreed that the 'serious danger' in the conduct of foreign policy is the way in which 'power is concentrated in the hands of one individual'. The solution was therefore both simple and obvious. 'The pacific, progressive, moderating opinion of democracy must be introduced into international affairs and democratic states must find a way of expressing themselves in the Council of the Nations'.[31] There was nothing novel about the idea. It had first been given currency by Henry Richard, a Radical predecessor of Keir Hardie as one of Merthyr's two parliamentary representatives, in a debate in the House in 1886.[32] The one novel twist to an old theme was the suggestion that, in some way, involvement in the conduct of foreign affairs could vitiate an otherwise reasonable politician's rational capacity. How else might Lloyd George's amazing Mansion House speech in the summer of 1911 be explained? 'When he took a hand in the game of Anglo-German snarling, he talked the usual twaddle about national honour and dignity . . . . He remembered only false shibboleths and catchwords . . . . Our real enemies are the diplomatists and foreign ministers'.[33]

The essential, theoretical, socialist view of war and peace had hitherto remained sternly pessimistic - war was the inevitable consequence of the economic structure of capitalism. Socialists, who at first had simply ignored stern logic as too depressing to contemplate, now found some reason for supposing that perhaps war was not inevitable after all! In this context, closer links, earlier abandoned, were now reforged with the pacifist, internationalist element among the Liberal Radicals whose faith in peace was always proof against either reason or evidence. As Felix Moschelles had pronounced their catechism: 'War will go . . . . Anti-militarism and anti-patriotism will triumph . . . Caesarism and national egotism will pass away. . . . You may deplore and disbelieve; I have faith and rejoice'.[34] Not that Labour's new-found optimism was altogether a matter of simple faith - it was afforded some intellectual and theoretical support from a number of disparate sources. For example, Karl Kautsky had argued that war became less likely because of the mounting strength of European Social Democratic parties and the increasing cartelization of capitalist industries. As to Kautsky's first claim, New Age in harmony with the Northcliffe press, declared it to be 'absurd to suppose a few Socialist Deputies are going to change Germany's policies. That', avowed C.H. Norman, 'is not an opinion but a fact'.[35] Kautsky's thinking is clearly apparent in the central idea of H.N. Brailsford's seminal study published in 1914, The War of Steel and Gold. At a less theoretical level we can see the influence of Kautsky's thinking in that sense of bemused disbelief with which W.C. Anderson wrote about the possibility of British involvement in any war at the very end of July 1914. 'I am not certain even now, that the Big Powers in Europe and the financial interests behind them will allow the struggle to be carried very far'.[36] But in Anderson's words we can also clearly discern an influence in addition to that of Kautsky - Norman Angell.[37] Although when he published his enormously popular, successful and influential book, The Great Illusion, Angell was much criticised by left-wing political elements, there remained considerable enthusiasm and attachment to his ideas in the Labour movement so that, for example, the future Communist MP, J.T. Walton Newbold, totally accepted Angell's central argument that City financial interests would never allow the British government to go to war.[38]

Thus as the European storm clouds gathered, most members of the Labour Party both within and outside Westminster, abandoned or significantly modified their former pessimistic thoughts on the international system and instead of forecasting its imminent demise supposed that it might be preserved from destruction. For this reason, in re-found unison with the Radicals, Labour MPs sought to publicise and advocate better technical means to promote universal stability. This amounted to the diplomatic process, the adoption of arbitration as the agreed means of settling disputes between powers, and rapid and significant retrenchment of expenditure upon armaments.[39] All three campaigns proved crushing failures, but this seemed to have little effect upon the new spirit of optimism that filled Labour ranks. The Agadir crisis came and went without war breaking out between the great powers. The Balkan Wars, if anything, appeared to bring London and Berlin closer together than they had been for years. Yet to declare as a consequence that everything would be well in the future was to take a ridiculously optimistic and very superficial view of the international scene. Presumably, the Radical Liberals adopted this pose because they could not face yet another humiliating and resounding defeat at the hands of their own front bench. It was in this context that the normally level-headed Massingham, at last despairing of the Radicals exerting any influence upon the foreign policy of a Liberal government, made the extraordinary claim in Nation that, 'in Britain, Socialism alone now represents the only potent force for peace'.[40]

With an awful suddenness, in one short summer week in 1914, any claim Labour may have had to be worthy of Massingham's accolade was tested and found wanting. The first statement on the European crisis issued by the parliamentary Labour Party on 30 July, announced the unanimous adoption of a resolution that Britain should stay out of any conflict. After this certainty, the vague wording of the resolution's conclusion suggests that although members were persuaded that in the circumstances it was better to be seen doing something rather than nothing, they had no real idea what they should or could do, having rejected the one positive original action the movement had ever suggested - the general strike against mobilisation. Advice that 'All Labour organisations in the country (were) to watch events vigilantly so as to oppose, if need be, in the most effective way, any action which might involve Britain in war', for all its wide scope merely begged the question - what exactly could or should Labour supporters do?[41] There was no sense of immediacy or urgency until it became known that Jean Jaures had been murdered.[42] Then disbelief and helplessness pervaded Labour's ranks.[43]

On 1 August, the British Section of the International issued a manifesto signed by Hardie and Henderson, <u>An Appeal to the British Working Class</u>. This document was replete with fine phrases and sentiments. 'Down with war . . . . The days of plunder and butchery have gone by . . . . Workers stand together for peace . . . compel the governing class to respect the decision of the overwhelming majority of the people'. It did not provide any indication how these noble ends were to be realised. Was it intended that the workers should impose their will upon the nation? In some, more revolutionary, socialist hearts and minds, there remained a vague attachment to the idea that one day the working classes would actually overturn the government - whether painfully and violently or peacefully was not certain - after which would follow a millennium of assured international and domestic social amity, co-operation, harmony and good will. This vision of the future, however, was postponed indefinitely and the workers found themselves recruited instead for something much more familiar and prosaic - attending anti-war demonstrations. This proposal had come from C.P. Scott's <u>Manchester Guardian</u> but was enthusiastically adopted by Labour and Radical supporters alike. The declared hope was that each demonstration 'might serve as a rallying point for public opinion'.[44] Given at last a definite objective rather than empty rhetoric, the rank and file of the Labour movement worked feverishly to organise a series of meetings to be held on Sunday, 2 August, in all the major urban centres throughout the country.

Inevitably, the most important of these meetings was a 'monster rally', organised by the British Section of the International in Trafalgar

Square. Under lowering skies the crowd was
addressed by speakers representing a range of
British socialist opinion.[45] All the speakers
were united in their protestations against Britain
being 'dragged into a war as Tsarist Russia's
ally'.[46] They extolled British neutrality while
denouncing the needless horrors and costs of war.
There were extravagant cheers from the audience
for any mention of international working class
solidarity, and spirited singing of the
'Internationale' and the 'Red Flag'. When a
violent downpour of rain threatened the meeting, a
group of 'feeble-hearted jingo demonstrators . . .
scattered before the storm's fury (but) the
comrades stood gallantly to their umbrellas and
cheered for "war against war"'. It only remained
for the usual resolution to be carried - this time
by acclamation - protesting against 'any step being
taken by this country to support Russia either
directly or in consequence of an undertaking with
France . . . . We have no interest direct or
indirect in the threatened quarrels which may
result from the action of Servia . . . . The
Government of Great Britain should rigidly decline
to engage in war but should confine itself to
efforts to bring about peace as speedily as
possible'.[47]

In her Diary, Beatrice Webb provided a less
heroic account of the Trafalgar Square meeting.
What she recorded was 'an undignified and futile
exhibition,' given by 'Labour, socialist, pacifist,
hooligans, warmongers and merely curious holiday
makers'. After the meeting, most of the speakers
had wandered unhappily over to Ramsay MacDonald's
flat in Lincoln's Inn Fields. The leader of the
parliamentary Labour Party had not attended the
Trafalgar Square demonstration as he had been
summoned to Downing Street to assure Liberal
ministers who thought otherwise, that the war would
be the most popular the country had ever
fought.[48] It remained only for Sir Edward Grey,
speaking to the assembled Commons on the afternoon
of the next day, 'to crush out all hope of peace
and of our being able to keep clear'.[49] Grey's
words of 'national honour' and 'moral duty', were
greeted with delight by the House. In the words
of the Manchester Guardian lobby correspondent
describing the scene, if there still remained
at Westminster any who needed convincing of
the soundness of the government's decision, 'one
thing only was needed - a declaration from

Mr Ramsay MacDonald that the Government was doing wrong. This was given at once'.[50]

MacDonald spoke to the House as Labour's leader. 'So far as we are concerned, whatever may happen, whatever may be said about us, whatever attacks may be made upon us, we will say that this country ought to have remained neutral, because in the deepest part of our hearts we believe that is right, and that alone is consistent with the honour of the country.' When the debate was resumed, few other Labour voices of dissent were raised. Almost all the speeches critical of Edward Grey – subsequently described by the Tory ex-Premier, Arthur Balfour, as 'the dregs and lees of debate', to the obvious approval of most MPs – were made by Radical Liberal MPs.[51] Within two days MacDonald had resigned as his party's leader and had been succeeded by Arthur Henderson. The Labour Party had bowed to the will, not of the government but the nation. Only four Labour MPs chose to stand by their executive's earlier resolution in support of neutrality. For the rest, Labour in Parliament like the nation, embraced the prospect of war with evident enthusiasm. The few who still insisted that the British people actually wanted peace, were scarcely audible above the din of the nation's new-found martial enthusiasm.

The outbreak of war in August 1914 emphasised the ambiguity and helplessness of the parliamentary Labour Party on foreign policy. Keir Hardie admitted as 'the great outstanding fact' that Labour was 'impotent . . . contemptuously passed over . . . without trace or vestige of power to prevent war. Our demonstrations and speeches and resolutions all alike futile. We simply do not count.'[52] Yet such are the paradoxes of political no less than human life, it was at this moment of supreme weakness, of impotence and confusion that was born the movement that was eventually to give the British Labour party in foreign affairs a distinctive policy that could be called its own.

After a meeting on 5 August 1914, with Arthur Ponsonby, Arthur Henderson and Ramsay MacDonald (who was still leader of the Labour party), Charles Trevelyan, a junior Liberal minister who had resigned his post because of Britain's entry into war, wrote to E.D. Morel, inviting him to join 'with a body of Liberal members united in common action on the war question' and who were intent upon forming an organisation 'to establish connection with the Labour party . . . and with outside efforts and groups'.[53] Morel responded eagerly to Trevelyan's invitation. A month later, the Union of Democratic Control was founded.[54] To match the two founding Liberal Radical MPs, Trevelyan and Ponsonby, the ILP provided Fred Jowett and Ramsay MacDonald. All four parliamentarians counted much less than E.D. Morel, the group's secretary. In the words of the Union's historian, 'EDM was the UDC, and the UDC was EDM'. The claim was not an exaggeration. It was Morel who, in providing the UDC with a critique of the pre-war conduct of foreign policy also provided Labour with a policy outline that in time allowed the unification of the minority who had opposed the war with the majority who supported it.

Stealing a political opponent's clothes was not unknown in the history of modern British political parties. Lloyd George, once Radical and pacifist leader, showed a gift for the ploy by stealing Tory clothes to maintain himself in power. Morel, the Radical Liberal who joined the ILP in 1918, anticipating only by months the public recognition of their own transfer of allegiance by Ponsonby and Trevelyan - did not exactly steal, but rather availed himself of the best of the Liberal garb on foreign policy abandoned by Grey and Asquith, and offered it to Labour who eagerly seized it to hide its embarrassing nakedness.[55] Thus the problem of Labour possessing its own distinct policy on foreign affairs was at last, temporarily, solved. The problem of identity was, and remains, rather more difficult, if not impossible, to resolve.

## NOTES

1. See A.M. McBriar, Fabian Socialism and English Politics, 1884-1918 (Cambridge University Press, 1962), pp.134-145. Marion Phillips favoured the General Strike as the most effective anti-war weapon available to the toiling masses - a view shared by some members of the ILP and the Women's Labour League. Ensor, temporarily unemployed during this period because of the amalgamation of the Daily News and the Morning Leader, acted as secretary to the short-lived Lord Courtney Committee on foreign affairs that was obliged to close within a year, 'for lack of members and funds'. See A.J.A. Morris, Radicalism Against War, 1906-14; the Advocacy of Peace and Retrenchment

(Longman, London, 1972), p.269.

2. C. Atlee, The Labour Party in Perspective (Gollancz, London, 1937), p.200.

3. After the two elections of 1910, the restored fortunes of the Tories meant that Labour MPs were obliged to move from the Opposition side of the Commons and take two benches on the government side of the House thus emphasising the problem of separate identity.

4. New Age, despite its small circulation, enjoyed a deserved influence. If not consistently, it regularly reviewed foreign affairs. From 1907 to 1911 its foreign affairs column was generally written by C.H. Norman using the pseudonym, 'Stanhope of Chester'. He was replaced by another editorial writer, J.M. Kennedy, 'Verdad', as a result of pressure upon the editor (who himself frequently contributed notes on foreign policy) by the Foreign Office. The substitution of authors made no discernible change to the content, style or bias of the column. See P. Maret, A.R. Orage: A Memoir (Dent, London, 1936), p.61; W. Martin, The New Age under Orage (Manchester University Press, 1967) p.123.

5. 'Social Democracy and Foreign Policy', New Age, 9, 16 Sept. and 7 Oct. 1909. The 'expert' argument had a special place in debates on military and naval topics where most Radical and Labour MPs took a pride in demonstrating disinterest and ignorance.

6. Engels to Laura Marx (Lafargue), 16 Feb. 1884, quoted in Y. Kapp, Eleanor Marx (Virago, London, 1979), vol. I, p.211.

7. On Blatchford's exchanges with Fred Jowett, see Fenner Brockway, Socialism over Sixty Years (Allen and Unwin, London, 1946), pp.122-25. On Hyndman's friendship with Maxse and other Tory editors, his campaign with Blatchford for conscription and Blatchford's articles in the Daily Mail, see A.J.A. Morris, The Scaremongers, 1896-1914 (Routledge, Kegan Paul, London, 1984), chs. 8, 13, 16 and 18 passim.

8. The invasion argument was part of the case made for conscription. While supporting Hyndman's notion of the 'citizen army', New Age poured scorn on the 'notion of invading England. It has never seriously entered the head of any German statesman in his sober senses . . . . There are at least a thousand reasons against it, every one conclusive; and not one, if we except lunacy, in favour of it.' New Age, 25 Mar. 1909. For the ILP campaign

against conscription before 1914, see Denis Hayes, Conscription Conflict (Sheppard, London, 1949), pp.13-136. Hyndman's comments were quoted in Labour Leader, 14 Aug. 1908.

9. See, for example, P. Snowden in Labour Leader, 11 Dec. 1913. 'It is no sufficient excuse that these members represent dockyard and arsenal towns . . . . Socialist principles must not be abandoned in order to keep seats.' But, of course, they were.

10. On MacDonald and the Agadir Crisis, see Lord Elton, Life of James Ramsay MacDonald (Collins, London, 1939), pp.201-31. On the general problem of the range and variety of opinions within the Socialist movement, see and compare, Howard Weinroth, 'The Dilemma of British Socialists during the Great War', in S. Wank (ed.), Doves and Diplomats: Foreign Office and Peace Movements in Europe and America in the Twentieth Century (Greenwood, New York, 1978), pp.178-201; K. G. Robbins, 'Foreign Secretary, Parliament and Parties', in F. Hinsley (ed.), British Foreign Policy under Sir Edward Grey (Cambridge, University Press, 1977), p.9.

11. New Age, 23 Mar. 1911. This outburst was in response to an editorial in the Star, 15 Mar. 1911.

12. H.S. Perris, in Concord, XXII, Feb. 1906, p.19.

13. W.S. Blunt, My Diaries (Secker, London, 1919-20), vol. II, p.205; 'Occasional Reflections', in New Age, 24 Dec. 1908. See also, Ibid, 1 Aug. 1907; C.T. King, The Asquith Parliament (Hutchinson, London, 1910), p.68 ff; C.F.G. Masterman, Nation, 24 Aug. 1907.

14. See MacDonald's arguments in response to Keir Hardie concerning the importance to Labour of the Liberal landslide victory in January 1906. MacDonald accurately forecast the incubus under which Radical critics of the Liberal government had to operate after 1910. See Labour Record, I, Feb. 1906, p.369. For the sword quotation, see C. Heath (ed.), Peace Year Book (National Peace Council, London, 1911), pp.69-70.

15. This was a compromise verbal formula riddled with dubious assumptions that had first been issued by the International in 1907. 'To use every effort to prevent war by all the means which seem to them most appropriate, having regard to the sharpness of the class war and to the general political situation.' It proved a quite useless

banner behind which the forces of European socialism might organise to wage their war against war.

16. See New Age, 2 Mar. 1911; Concord, XXIV, Feb. 1911, p.17.

17. Labour Leader, 23 June 1911.

18. See I. McLean, Keir Hardie (Allen Lane, London, 1975), p.156.

19. Labour Leader, 19 Mar. 1909: New Age, 25 Mar. 1909.

20. New Age, 2 May 1907.

21. See G.M. Trevelyan, Grey of Fallodon (Longman, London, 1936), pp. 190-91. The reason why Radicals more easily forgave Grey was because they wanted to believe him. A good example of this was the attitude adopted by C.P. Trevelyan towards the Foreign Secretary right up to and including the final crisis of 1914. It also explains why Trevelyan attached so much blame for Britain's involvement in war to Grey personally. See A.J.A. Morris, C P Trevelyan, 1870-1958: Portrait of a Radical (Blackstaff, Belfast, 1977), ch. 6, passim. On the procedural restraints upon the Radicals which made them less effective critics in this context, see M. Swartz, 'A Study in Futility', in A.J.A. Morris (ed.), Edwardian Radicalism, 1900-1914 (Routledge, Kegan Paul, London, 1974), pp.246-59.

22. Quoted in Morris, Portrait of a Radical, p.104.

23. See, inter alia, G. Murray, The Foreign Policy of Sir Edward Grey (Clarendon Press, Oxford, 1915), pp.82-83; Contemporary Review, XCI (1906), p.888 ff.

24. On this incident, see H.W. Nevinson, Fire of Life (Gollancz, London, 1935), pp.204-6; John Wilson, Life of Sir Henry Campbell-Bannerman (Constable, London, 1973), pp.535-37.

25. The examples quoted are taken from Albany Review, Aug. 1907, pp.515-16, New Age, 23 May and 20 June 1907; and, Concord, XXIV, Jan. 1908, p.3.

26. The Friends of Russian Freedom was a long-standing Liberal group that had recently been taken over by extreme Radical and Labour supporters.

27. The Perris criticism is from Concord, XXIV, June 1908, p.64. For the Reval debate, see Hansard, 4th Series, vol. CXC, col. 211 ff. 4 June 1908. For the procedural rules designed to protect the Foreign Secretary from critics in the House, see F. Gosses, The Management of British Foreign Policy (Sijthoff, Amsterdam, 1948), pp.86-89.

28. Fear of Russo-German rapprochement had dominated Foreign Office thinking throughout negotiations for the Convention. In private Grey always emphasised that the ententes were a system to thwart Germany. See, _inter alia_, G. Monger, The End of Isolation (Nelson, London, 1963), passim; B. Williams, 'Great Britain and Russia', in Hinsley (ed.), British Foreign Policy, pp.133-47.

29. Writing in the Manchester Guardian, 4 Dec. 1912.

30. Labour Leader, 15 Nov. 1911. Similar attacks continued in the paper up to the end of 1913. Typical are W.C. Anderson's comments, 27 Nov. 1913: 'They (the Radicals) will murmur and complain but nothing more . . . feeble folk, singularly well meaning and singularly futile and ineffective. They have not among them one strong, forceful and fearless personality. If they develop one, efforts would quickly be made to tame and muzzle him by office.'

31. A. Ponsonby, Democracy and the Control of Foreign Affairs (Methuen, London, 1912), pp.5-7. On the problems in relation to the confusions of the theme of 'secret diplomacy', see Morris, Radicalism Against War, 1906-1914, pp.266-67 and footnotes.

32. Hansard, 3rd Series, vol. CCCIII, col. 1397. 19 Mar. 1886.

33. E.G. Smith, 'A plea for common sense', in Concord, XXVIII, Dec. 1911, p.115.

34. My emphasis. Ibid, pp.112-13.

35. New Age, 25 May 1911. The Radicals, while discounting the value of the British Labour party, placed considerable faith in the German Social Democratic party as a force for peace, Nation in October 1907 going so far as to describe it as 'the best available guarantee of peace in Europe'.

36. Labour Leader, 30 July 1914.

37. See H. Weinroth, 'Norman Angell and The Great Illusion', in Historical Journal, XVII (1974), pp.551-74.

38. See Weinroth, 'The Dilemma of British Socialists', p.181.

39. Of these three Radical themes adopted by Labour, the last, and arguably the most successful, containing genuine Labour innovations, presents certain difficulties. Retrenchment in armament expenditure divided the Radicals in the sense that the Progressives and not the Economists, emphasised that funds saved on armaments would (not could) be deployed to finance social, ameliorative

legislation. As a writer in New Age, 25 Mar. 1909, warned Labour MPs: 'Retrenchment is the cheesemonger's cry . . . . Do not think that the Liberals will give a penny more for social reform if the Naval Vote were abolished tomorrow'. The arguments are conveniently abridged and summarised in chapter XVII of Paul Kennedy's monumental study, The Rise of Anglo-German Antagonism (Allen and Unwin, London, 1980), particularly pp.330-32.

40. Massingham's absurd claim (contrary to everything else he had said previously in that journal since 1907), appeared in Nation, 17 May 1914, and was reprinted in Labour Leader, 30 July 1914. Arthur Ponsonby, probably the most prominent, certainly the best informed of Radical Liberals on foreign policy, and the moving spirit behind the newly formed Radical Foreign Affairs Group (Committee), made a number of extraordinarily confident and complacent statements to the House concerning the peacefulness of the contemporary European scene. Hansard, 5th Series, vol. LIII, col. 374. 29 May 1913. Ibid., vol. LXIV, col. 1397. 10 July 1914. The estimates were surprising because Ponsonby knew that the Balkan Wars, although they brought Germany and Britain closer together, increased antagonism between Vienna and St Petersburg, long feared by experts as the most likely cause of a major European conflagration. See, for example, G.P. Gooch, Under Six Reigns (Longman, London, 1958), p.169.

41. Reported in Manchester Guardian, 31 July 1914.

42. For examples of a lack of urgency and subsequent helplessness among activists, see, inter alia, Kate Courtney's Diary. British Library of Economics and Political Science. Courtney Mss. C.P. Trevelyan's personal statement on the July/ August crisis, 1914. Newcastle University. C.P. Trevelyan Mss. Courtney Mss (British Library of Economics and Political Science); C P Trevelyan's personal statement of the July/August crisis, 1914, C P Trevelyan Mss (Library, University of Newcastle upon Tyne). For attitude of young Socialists, see M. Cole, Growing up in a Revolution (Longman, London, 1949), pp.47-50.

43. Keir Hardie had been with Jaures and other European Socialist leaders at a hastily summoned meeting in Brussels of the Socialist Bureau to consider the effect of Austria's declaration of war on Serbia. Delegates were so little apprehensive of general European war that they merely promoted

the date of the International's meeting and changed
its venue from Vienna to Paris. There are vivid
personal accounts of the impact of Jaures' death in
E.D. Morel, Truth and War (National Labour Press,
London, 1914), pp.44-45; W. Stewart, J Keir Hardie
(Cassell, London, 1921), pp.342-43.

44. Manchester Guardian, 1 Aug. 1914.

45. The meeting even had three chairmen, Keir
Hardie, George Lansbury and Hyndman. The divisions
of opinion at this meeting and among British
Socialists are well represented in F.J. Gould,
Hyndman, Prophet of Socialism (Allen and Unwin,
London, 1928), chapter VI.

46. Norman Angell's Neutrality League - a
group made up essentially of Radical Liberals -
published and distributed a manifesto entitled
'Shall We Fight for a Russian Empire'. See N.
Angell, After All (Hamish Hamilton, London, 1951),
pp.182-88.

47. Labour Leader, 6 Aug. 1914. The paper
also provides several pages of detailed accounts of
similar meetings held throughout the country on
Sunday, 2 Aug. 1914.

48. Elton, Ramsay MacDonald, pp.242-44. For
Mrs Webb's reaction see M. Cole (ed.), Beatrice
Webb's Diaries, 1912-14 (Longman, Green and Co.,
London, 1952), p.25.

49. C. Addison, Politics from Within (Herbert
Jenkins, London, 1924), vol. I, p.32.

50. Manchester Guardian, 4 Aug. 1914.

51. For the debate, see Hansard, 5th Series,
vol. LXV, col. 1809. 3 Aug. 1914.

52. Labour Leader, 6 Aug. 1914.

53. C.P. Trevelyan to E.D. Morel, 5 Aug.
1914. British Library of Economics and Political
Science. Morel Papers, F6, File 1.

54. See M. Swartz, The Union of Democratic
Control in British Politics during the First World
War (Oxford, University Press, 1971). Swartz's
standard account confirms the opinion expressed by
Mrs H.M. Swanwick in her Builders of Peace
(Swarthmore, London, 1924), of E.D. Morel's central
importance to the UDC. See also, C.A. Cline,
E.D. Morel, 1873-1924: the Strategies of Protest
(Blackstaff, Belfast, 1980), and the same author's,
Recruits to Labour (Syracuse, University Press,
1963), for an informed view of the Radical Liberal
contribution to Labour attitudes to foreign policy
during and after the Great War.

55. This view, although not readily admitted
in Labour circles at the time, is well reflected in

C.P. Trevelyan's <u>From Liberalism to Labour</u> (Allen and Unwin, London, 1922).

# CONTRIBUTORS

Kenneth D. Brown. Reader in Economic and Social
   History. The Queen's University of Belfast.

David Martin. Lecturer in Economic and Social
   History. University of Sheffield.

W. Hamish Fraser. Senior Lecturer in History.
   University of Strathclyde.

Peter Stead. Lecturer in History.
   University College of Wales, Swansea.

Michael Cahill. Lecturer in Social Administration.
   Brighton Polytechnic.

Deian Hopkin. Lecturer in History.
   University College of Wales, Aberystwyth.

Chris Wrigley. Reader in Economic History.
   University of Loughborough.

Clive Griggs. Senior Lecturer in the Sociology of
   Education. Brighton Polytechnic.

Pat Thane. Senior Lecturer in Social
   Administration. Goldsmith's College, University
   of London.

Roy Douglas. Reader in History.
   University of Surrey.

Martin Pugh. Senior Lecturer in History.
   University of Newcastle upon Tyne.

Dan McDermott. Sometime research student.
   National University of Ireland, Galway.

A.J.A. Morris. Professor History.
   University of Ulster.